BREAKOUT BRANDS

# BREAKOUT BRANDS

## WHY SOME BRANDS TAKE OFF... AND OTHERS DON'T

JARED SCHRIEBER

BREAKOUT BRANDS
*Why Some Brands Take Off...and Others Don't*

ISBN    978-1-5445-3505-0   *Hardcover*
           978-1-5445-3504-3   *Ebook*

# CONTENTS

Author Bio    vii

Acknowledgments    ix

Introduction    xi

1. A New Kind of Study    1

2. People and Lifestyles    25

3. Usage Occasions and the Job to Be Done    55

4. Purchase Occasions    73

5. Product Attraction and Distribution    101

6. Brand Equity    131

7. Social Validation & Earned Media    149

8. Media and Advertising    173

9. Trade versus Brand Promotion    217

10. Product Experience and Innovation    233

11. The Brand Growth Flywheel    251

12. From Insights to Action    281

13. Conclusion: Hindsight Is More Than 2020    293

APPENDIX. The Science behind Consecutive Repeat Rates and Market Share *by Joel Rubinson and Jared Schrieber*    305

# AUTHOR BIO

Since graduating from MIT's Engineering Systems Division, Jared Schrieber has been rethinking how brands harness consumer data to drive growth. He was the co-founder and CEO of Numerator and the former head of products and services at Retail Solutions, two successful startups that have shaped how brands better understand their consumers and win at retail in the twenty-first century. He co-founded the Pat Tillman Foundation and recently established the Revolution Robotics Foundation to bring the inspirational joy of educational and competitive robotics to all kids globally.

# ACKNOWLEDGMENTS

A quick hat-tip to my co-founder, Jon Brelig, and all the other InfoScouters and Numerati whose innovative work made this book possible. Two deserve special recognition for taking on the heavy load of being my primary collaborators in the research and writing of this book: Jake Grocholski and Paul Stanley. You guys rock!

To my steadfastly supportive wife, Reka Cseresnyes. Without you, Numerator and Breakout Brands would not exist.

# INTRODUCTION

Rao's Homemade launched its premium pasta sauce in 1992 when the proprietors of the famous New York City restaurant by the same name started bottling its sauce in small batches. The sauces were slow-simmered and made from just a few ingredients, including pure Italian olive oil and naturally ripened tomatoes from southern Italy. The restaurant never cut corners by adding water, starch, filler, colors, or added sugar. From time to time, the brand added new products, such as the tomato-basil and sausage-and-mushroom flavors it launched in 2005, but the recipes remained simple and natural.

Availability was limited, and with a price tag of under eight dollars, Rao's was often the most expensive brand in the spaghetti sauce section of the select grocery stores that carried it. But in 2016, new company president Jim Morano set out to change that by convincing retailers across the country to carry the brand.

Morano took a fact-based approach, using data to make his case. Pasta sauce, in general, was "premiumizing," Morano noted, with more and more higher-end products competing against low-price brands like Ragu or Barilla's. More stores were seeing sales growth among five-dollar-and-above sauces, and Rao's would perform best among these upscale products, Morano argued. He also noted that for every eight-dollar jar of Rao's sauce sold, retailers captured $2.22 in profit—nearly six times the profit offered by lower-priced brands. And despite its high price, Morano argued, 60 percent of shoppers who try Rao's will repeat buy—a staggeringly high percentage.

"We don't have consumers," Morano told the supermarkets. "We have fans."[1] In other words: if your customers can't find us on your shelves, they'll leave and look for it elsewhere. Carry our sauce, and your customers will thank you.

## BUCKING THE TREND

Morano's pitch made sense to many retailers, but few could have predicted what would happen next. Over the next few years, Rao's sales grew from $48 million annually to $130 million. While the pasta sauce category grew by about 5 percent during this time, Rao's grew 40 percent yearly, increasing its market share by nearly 3 percent.

What's astonishing, though, is that Rao's enjoyed this remarkable success despite ignoring long-held and widely accepted principles of brand management. Most brand managers believe heavy advertising will grow a brand. They think they have to run promotions ("Buy One, Get One Free!") or compete on price—especially in a commoditized product category. They might think they have to market to a specific demographic segment or try to appeal more to occasional "light" buyers.

Rao's Homemade did none of these things. Instead, Rao's continued doing what it's always done: deliver the best damn product they could so consumers would love it and buy it again and again. Rao's grew its market share by saying, "We're a premium product that captures a premium price, and we deliver a premium margin back to the retailer."

Rao's is a powerful example of what happens when you deliver a product consumers love. They will pay a premium price and repeatedly buy the product. By adding a brand like Rao's to their assortment,

---

1    Elaine Watson, "Rao's Notches Up Double Digit Growth: 'We Don't Have Consumers, We Have Fans,'" FoodNavigator-USA, April 30, 2017, https://www.foodnavigator-usa.com/Article/2017/05/01/Rao-s-Homemade-notches-up-double-digit-growth#.

retailers see an increase in sales and profit for the entire category, which convinces more retailers to carry the brand. That increases the brand's distribution and allows even more consumers easy access to repeatedly buy their products. And the cycle continues.

Rao's surprising rise was one of the highlights that emerged from a pioneering study my team and I conducted of more than twenty-five thousand consumer packaged brands purchased by the more than one million consumers we tracked over a billion shopping trips between 2016 and 2019. Our analysis of these fast-moving consumer goods (packaged foods, beverages, toiletries, candies, cosmetics, over-the-counter drugs, dry goods, and other consumables) revealed that Rao's was one of only fifty-eight brands during this time that increased retail sales in America by $10 million a year while expanding their market share by at least 1.5 percent. Rao's was part of an elite group that included many well-known brands, including Dove, Oral-B, Jimmy Dean, and Reese's. But our fifty-eight winning brands also included some surprising upstarts, like Caulipower frozen pizza and Bang energy drinks.

These 58 winning brands increased their market shares by an average of 470 basis points (e.g., growing market share from 10 percent to 14.7 percent in three years) while their closest competitors—many of them well-known brands like Palmolive, Kraft, DiGiorno, and Gatorade—lost an average of 350 basis points (-3.5 percent). In every case, the winning brands rose while a losing brand selected from the same category sank throughout our study. What had these winning brands done to separate themselves from the pack? Likewise, why had some of their prominent competitors slipped? How did the Energizer Bunny beat up Duracell? How did Hillshire Farm steal share from Kraft Lunchables in the meal-combo category? How had Premier Nutrition outmuscled Muscle Milk among performance shakes?

The answers revealed that many commonly held beliefs about how brands grow are erroneous. The data in our study is far deeper and more detailed than any previous study, revealing fresh insights and spotlighting how much brand management rules must change. Our unique study upends many of the accepted standards and practices of the CPG industry. It reveals why successful brands in the future must rethink their outmoded ideas and adopt a new paradigm. The study posed a clear question: in light of this empirical evidence, should brand managers rethink their timeworn methods?

## THE OLD WAY OF THINKING

Leading brand marketing experts have long held that brands grow by getting more people to buy their product or by getting existing customers to spend even more on the product. In their mind, it's all about acquisition and loyalty. We're told that brands grow by luring in more one-time "light" buyers. Or that brands grow by winning their customers' devotion and unwavering loyalty. We've been sold on so-called "laws of marketing," which lead us to believe that to grow, brands must be "distinctive, not differentiated" and must "continuously reach all buyers of the category," especially via mass media advertising.

The problem is that these hidebound ideas rely on incomplete or one-dimensional data that doesn't paint a full picture of how brands really grow. One study will be based on advertising data and show how advertising affects brand growth. Another will examine pricing and show how price elasticity shapes your brand's sales. Another study will examine how promotions drive immediate sales lift without considering any longer-term side effects. No one has been able to integrate all this data to conduct a long-term study. No one has ever explained how these factors work together to dictate how brands perform. The result is a lot of confusion. There is no clear framework or principles for brand managers to follow. We treat brand marketing like a simple structure built upon the pillars of Product, Price, Place, and Promotion. But our study revealed **brand building is a very complex, nonlinear system full of feedback loops.**

There is no shortage of theories about why brands win. A brand manager might pull from the work of Philip Kotler and David Aaker or contemporary thought leaders like Byron Sharp and Peter Fader—only to find their practical implications in direct conflict. How should a brand manager or marketer know whose recommendations to follow?

Sadly, brand managers and marketers have been led in circles since the very inception of marketing science—a term coined by my predecessors who pioneered the consumer purchase panel industry in the 1960s. For example, there is still an unresolved, sixty-year-old debate about whether past purchases affect future buying—let alone a consumer's next purchase. How can something so fundamental to the science of our field remain so controversial? One study will claim that the only way to grow your brand is to introduce it to more and more new customers, while another study will conclude that building loyalty is crucial to growth. But if past purchases don't affect next purchases, then what is brand loyalty? And if loyalty is a myth and all focus should be on acquiring new customers, what's the point in reminding existing customers how much they love your products? Should marketers focus on sampling and messaging that implores consumers to *try* their products, or is there greater benefit from using loyalty rewards and messaging that reminds consumers how much they already love your products? It's no wonder brand managers and marketers are left scratching their heads, unsure what tactics to employ.

There has to be a way out of this maze, right? As it turns out, there is. Read on.

## A NEW APPROACH

Our study was different. We analyzed over a billion (that's right: *billion*) shopping trips to over nineteen thousand retailers in-store and online. We gathered millions of purchase-triggered survey responses from consumers, who happily answered questions about their purchase decisions as they pushed loaded shopping carts out to their cars. We folded in information on advertising from nearly a million unique ads and over $150 billion in ad spend in an attempt to monitor every single advertising campaign across twenty-two media types. We even analyzed every in-store promotion at over 1,500 retail chains and dove into more than 100 brand equity–related metrics continuously tracked for the brands we studied.

An elite group of brands like Rao's Homemade pasta sauce emerged that significantly outperformed their competitors with strategies that fly in the face of conventional wisdom. How had these winners pulled this off? And why had the losers slipped?

The answer to those two simple questions forms the foundation for this book. As we analyzed our winners and losers, many old rules of brand management emerged as flawed and rickety, and a new, robust set of conclusions took shape and moved to the fore. These new principles showed how wrong we've been over the years and revealed a new paradigm in brand management. Brand management is not about managing price, promotion, place, product, and every other marketing "P" as stand-alone pillars to build upon. Instead, it's about how these and other factors fit together like gears to build momentum for your brand with every turn.

This book is to brand management what Jim Collins's book *Good to Great* was for company management. While Collins and his research team focused on how eleven publicly traded **companies** achieved breakout growth and contrasted them to paired losers from the same industry, my team and I focused on **brands**. And for brand managers struggling to drive sustainable growth, more than a few surprises emerged, including:

- Winning brands grow by attracting and retaining heavy category buyers while losing brands hemorrhage those heavy category buyers. Moreover, heavy buyers attract light buyers, not the other way around, as some experts suggest. Heavy buyers work like a gravitational force pulling in light buyers; heavies influence what light buyers see on the shelves and the ratings and reviews that lighter buyers consult before making a purchase.

- Should you find the demographic groups with high affinities toward your brand and redouble your marketing efforts to keep them engaged? No. Winners focus on closing their affinity gaps so that their consumers look more like the consumers of the category as a whole.

- Winning brands win occasions. What's that mean? It means that a winning brand understands the consumer's usage context and purchase criteria and then steps up and delivers with excellence—over and over again.

These are just a few of our many findings. In the following chapters, we'll take a macro view of brand management, from consumers and their lifestyles to the complex role of media and advertising. We will share insights from our study in each chapter. How did Febreze outduel Glade? What did Nicorette do right to overcome a strong challenge from private label brands? Why did Kellogg's Nutri-Grain bars lose traction while Kind bars excelled? How did Rockstar energy drink fall from glory, and what led to Bang's rise in fame? In answering these questions, we'll unveil a new framework to help managers develop winning brands and increase market share and profits.

We'll also show how we developed our Brand Growth Flywheel, which depicts how such key factors as usage occasions, product experience, brand equity, and product attraction interact to create a powerful repeating purchase loop that can accelerate your brand into a category-leading juggernaut.

I'll also share how my own company, Numerator (originally named InfoScout), exhibited the characteristics we found in many winning brands and provided us with the unmatched data we used to fuel this study and build this new framework.

Before founding Numerator, I had already spent a dozen years working within the retail space, with roles as varied as a simple associate out on the retail sales floor before becoming store manager to my postcollegiate work on the data and analytics side of retail. Shortly after graduating with a master's degree from the Engineering Systems Division of Massachusetts Institute of Technology (MIT), I joined the nascent startup that became Retail Solutions, where I led research, product, and services. The company rapidly grew from a handful of early clients to shape how more than 500 consumer packaged goods (CPG) companies leveraged retailer point-of-sale (POS) data to drive top-line sales growth. Leading clients such as Procter & Gamble, PepsiCo, and Unilever were hungry for a better view of their consumers. When they began asking for my help to answer strategic business questions beyond the realm of retailer POS data, I saw an opportunity to leverage the emergence of smartphones, mobile apps, crowdsourcing, and computer vision to rethink how brands could engage and understand consumers in the twenty-first century.[2]

## SUPERIOR DATA

In 2011, I set off with my former Retail Solutions colleague Jon Brelig to found what is known today as Numerator. The story of Numerator is itself quite indicative of how great brands grow. Our core idea was

---

2    Many of the research techniques I have applied to derive the insights revealed in this book were the fruit of my studies of complex systems at MIT.

to create mobile apps that would incentivize hoards of consumers to consistently take pictures of their everyday shopping receipts and then respond to purchase-triggered surveys. We harnessed the resulting data to create a new, differentiated way to help brands understand consumer behaviors.

What made our solution different from legacy competitors? In short: more consumers uploading more shopping trips. We made it so fun and easy for people to report their purchases that it became a habit. Suddenly, we captured ten times as many shopping trips as the incumbent competition. Moreover, our data tracked the full shopper journey, gathering in-store and online purchases. No one else was able to do that.

The enriching user experience made it easy to recruit more panelists at a lower cost, thanks to strong app store ratings and happy panelists who referred their friends. More panelists participated, allowing Numerator to overcome the primary challenge brands had with consumer purchase panels: small sample size.

With this superior data, Numerator quickly landed Procter & Gamble, Unilever, PepsiCo, Kraft, and Anheuser-Busch as its first five clients. By meeting—even exceeding—their expectations in our engagements with them, we won repeat business. These industry-leading clients with the most sophisticated needs for panel data told their counterparts at other CPG companies about our work, making it easier for us to win even more new clients. Today, Numerator has over one thousand clients who rely on the company's comprehensive market intelligence and deep consumer insights to grow their brands.

Along the way, we experienced firsthand why it's not enough just to win new customers; we had to delight them so they would become repeat customers and provide validation for others to follow suit. But this wasn't unique to Numerator. As you'll soon see, this is a key ingredient in the recipe for brand growth regardless of the industry.

## WHAT TO EXPECT

While this book is based on scientific research, it is not a science textbook. It's not simply a book of theories or a history of marketing science. Such books have their place, but they are rarely practical. My goal with *Breakout Brands* is to give you a pragmatic field guide that shows through data-backed examples the tactical mechanics by which brands grow year over year. By the end of this book, you should better understand the levers you can pull and how those levers work together to help you increase revenue and gain more market share.

This book reveals how to engineer brand growth. It is informed by peer-reviewed research but moves beyond the science to show you what you can do with the empirical evidence—how to take simple, rational, and down-to-earth steps to grow a brand year after year sustainably.

As a brand manager, you are like a sound engineer in a music studio. You need to know how all the knobs and levers on the soundboard interact with each other. None stand alone. If you want lush, pleasing results, you must adjust the various levers to balance the instruments for maximal effect. You have to know how everything fits and works together.

By reading *Breakout Brands*, I want you to leave with a real sense of the key factors and how they combine to drive brand growth. Ultimately, all the parts fit together in a big reinforcing feedback loop that I call the Brand Growth Flywheel.

# 1

# A NEW KIND OF STUDY

n 2005, while with the Silicon Valley startup Retail Solutions, I used point-of-sale data to help brands measure how promotions, pricing, assortment, and product placement affected their sales. This information also helped retailers collaborate with the brands to grow their sales and improve operational execution. The approach seemed like a win for everyone.

There was only one problem: many of our brand clients wanted more data than we gave them. For example, they wanted to know how consumer behavior changes during a promotion. We could tell them how much sales rose when their product was on sale, but we couldn't tell them *why* these consumers behaved as they did. Were the sales coming from existing buyers of the brand choosing to stock up at a discount, or was the brand picking up entirely new customers who decided to buy their product thanks to the lower price? What brands were they switching from?

Retailers are notoriously secretive about that kind of customer data. These are *their* customers, after all, and retailers don't like sharing information about them with the brands. What if Walgreens, Kroger, and Walmart shared their shopper-level data with a brand like Heineken? Heineken could discover that it's more profitable for them to promote their beer to, say, Walmart customers rather than Kroger customers. That would hurt Kroger's business. Consequently, retailers prefer to control the relationship with the shopper. It's not in their best interest to hand that control over to brands.

We realized that the only way to get the data we needed for our brand customers was to go directly to the consumers. We had to convince them to share their shopping lists, spending decisions, and lifestyle information so we could develop a true, unified view of their behavior and answer the bigger questions brands had. This need for bigger answers prompted me to leave Retail Solutions and start Numerator with Jon.

Little did we know that Numerator would go on to reach unicorn status by disrupting the market research industry and enabling a new brand growth paradigm to emerge.

## BUILDING A NEW DATABASE

Numerator's basic premise was to develop smartphone apps that used gamified incentives to encourage shoppers to take pictures of their everyday shopping receipts. Previous shopper panels used by research firms like Nielsen required consumers to go home and scan in barcodes via clunky devices and transmit them. Our gamified apps allowed consumers to simply take a picture of their receipt and collect points they could later cash in. We made it fun. Our most popular app was Receipt Hog. You'd start with a baby runt, and when you "fed" the pig with your receipts, your piggy bank would grow into a weaner, a sow, and eventually, a hog, earning more and more along the way.

To gain even greater insight, we'd ask users questions about themselves each time they uploaded a receipt. If they answered the question, they would earn a little extra reward. In this way, we learned about their demographics, interests, values, and lifestyles—full psychographic profiles that we could correlate with purchases to build a rich understanding of what type of consumers bought particular brands.

The apps were addictive, and we started capturing hundreds of thousands of shopping trips every day—even quick stops to buy a soda or a six-pack. At the same time, we were creating an incredibly deep database, far more detailed than any previous consumer panel.

Our apps were unique in that we kept user information anonymous. We never sold people's data or marketed to users based on shared data. Consumers understood that we only used their information for market research—we wanted to observe their purchases, not influence them.

And, of course, we appreciated their help. As the data poured into our system, we quickly realized that the rich trove of information had the potential to help us rethink brand management and marketing.

Consumer panels date back to the fifties, starting just after World War II. Arthur Nielson, the Founder of Nielsen, began by sending physical diaries to people's houses. Participants would write down what they bought, how much they paid, and other relevant information about their shopping experience. Then they would mail these diaries back each month.

In the next major phases of consumer panels, companies utilized phone modems and in-home barcode scanners. When I launched the Numerator OmniPanel in 2012, researchers used scanners connected to home internet routers. Participants had to scan each item, type in the price, and record any coupon or promotional details. Once users realized how much time it took for a 10-cent or 15-cent reward, many dropped out. As a result, the sample size was incredibly small, and the data about household penetration, purchase frequencies, and high-level switching behaviors were sketchy at best. And when you considered the amount of work involved and the scant reward consumers received, you had to wonder: could these people possibly be representative of America's shoppers as a whole?

So we made it easy and fun, and within a year, we collected ten times as many shopping trips as Nielsen, our top competitor. We hoped to collect hundreds of thousands of receipts but quickly had hundreds of millions (now billions). With this information, we could see consumers' major trips to the store and what they bought at a convenience store after filling their gas tank. What did they get at the grocery store just before dinner at a friend's house? How did their weekend purchases differ from their midweek buys? We were starting to see consumers from every angle. We narrowed down on the *what*, the *when*, and the *why*.

Brands ate up the insights. They could look at specific stores and see where their products were underperforming. They might notice Walmart wasn't carrying individual six-packs like other retailers where their products were selling much better. They could then go to Walmart, present the evidence, and ask them to start carrying their six-packs. Brands could also see what kind of advertising or promotions lured new consumers. They could see what an army of consumers liked and didn't like about their purchases or how often they bought the same product.

Ultimately, we gathered a staggering volume of data about how people shop. We expanded our findings by integrating this purchase data with our comprehensive ad tracking across TV, digital, radio, etc., and promotion data from 1,500 retailers.

## BEYOND ASSUMPTIONS TO BETTER ANSWERS

Why were some consumers buying hard seltzers like White Claw? What were consumers switching from when they bought Liquid I.V.? With our database, we could now answer these broad questions in a way never before possible. For example, if a new product launched, we could provide the fastest read on who was buying the product. We could see if they were trading up or trading down. We could quickly see if they would buy it again, and we'd use surveys to gather further insight into what led to their initial purchase decision. With all this information at our fingertips, we could tell within a few weeks how successful a new product would be in the market or even at a specific retailer. Meanwhile, our competitors needed six months to deliver a detailed read on how new products were performing.

Our information allowed brands to know better where to allocate their marketing budgets. They would know if they should aggressively push to get the new product into more retailers. They would have evidence to convince current retailers to keep carrying a product line. They would be able to convince a major chain to carry their product in three thousand of their locations instead of fifty. They could even go in and tell a retailer that their store would sell more shampoo in total if they carried their specific shampoo product.

Our data was not only useful for the biggest brands but small brands as well. We had a big enough sample size to offer smaller brands real value. A niche brand like King's Hawaiian bread or an upstart health and beauty brand like Yes To had no consumer-level data to take to retailers until we came along.

## THE BIGGER PICTURE

Our panel business snowballed, and in 2017 I merged the company with Market Track to form the basis of what Numerator is today—a market intelligence firm that combines omnichannel purchase data with extensive multimedia advertising and in-store promotion tracking.

Since 2012, Numerator's consumer purchase panel surpassed one billion shopping trips, with over eight million distinct advertisements and nearly 375 million unique in-store promotions from nearly every brand and retailer, regardless of the channel. This massive data set, along with the company's work with over one thousand brands, served as the launching point for this book. The merger also allowed me to step back from my day-to-day operational responsibilities as CEO to devote my time to my true loves: family and data.

I had always wanted to take a giant step back to examine the bigger picture and ask the bigger questions. Does loyalty even matter, or is it a fool's errand? How effective is advertising versus just dropping the price or running in-store promotions? Was it true, as some leading brand experts claimed, that the best way to increase sales was to appeal to "light" category buyers? Some experts also proclaim that if we want to grow a brand, we should market to all category buyers equally. Is *that* true? Competing paradigms argue that brands grow by getting more people to buy their products *or* getting those who already buy to spend even more—which one is right?

Around this same time, I read Jim Collins's *Good to Great*. I was captivated by how he studied companies for multiple years to compare and contrast the fundamental differences between winning and losing companies. His analysis was a great model for me to follow with my research, so I decided it was time to step up and do something similar for brands. We needed to understand what makes a winning or losing brand and what specific actions explain the great performances of some and the decline of others.

I recruited a couple of analytic consultants from Numerator (the dynamic duo of Paul Stanley and Jake Grocholski), and we devoted the next two years to answer some of the biggest questions in the industry. I pored over hundreds of peer-reviewed articles. I listened to claims made by our clients, brand managers, and academicians researching brand marketing and management. I had no theory of my own; I simply wanted to discover scientific truths by putting every credible hypothesis to the test. We ultimately ran tests against thirty-nine of these high-level and broadly accepted (yet often conflicting) hypotheses.

Too often, researchers form theories and then look for data to reinforce their worldview. Our study was different. We came to this process without an ax to grind. We didn't have a theory to prove. So instead of forming a theory and then trying to back it up with data, we started with the theories of others and used our unparalleled data set to put those theories to the test. We didn't come in saying we knew the formulas that worked. We simply challenged existing paradigms and probed for fresh insights.

One of the first—and most surprising—things we learned is that there aren't many brands that grow market share by even 1.5 percentage points over three years. All brand managers and executives are incentivized to grow market share, so we figured there'd be some real movement among brands in this regard. There wasn't. Hundreds of brands grow, but very few have a net gain of 1.5 percent or more. Was this a sign that very few brand managers had cracked the code? Was this a sign that the prevailing paradigm of brand growth was inherently flawed? You had to wonder.

## FINDING OUR ANSWERS

As we examined the data for the four years from 2016 to 2019, we found only fifty-eight brands that grew retail sales by more than $30 million from 2016 to 2019 while also growing their category share by at least 1.5 percentage points. We call these the *winning brands*.

We paired each winning brand with a corresponding *losing brand* from the same category. Many of these losing brands also showed increased sales in dollar terms—particularly if the overall product category was experiencing strong growth—but they lost market share during the study.

Our research closely examined why certain brands outpaced their competitors. For example, Mission Foods increased market share and sales in the tortillas, pitas, taco shells, and wraps category to become a winner. But a quality competitor, Guerrero, had fallen behind, despite extraordinary sales among the fast-growing Hispanic consumer segment. Why? In the alternative meat category, venture-backed startup Beyond Meat had overtaken category mainstay Tofurky, which twenty years ago had almost single-handedly invented the category. Was it through innovation, advertising, pricing, or something else?

In the end, my team and I discovered a clear set of principles. And in the process of linking these principles in a causal graph, we found that our findings fit together like a flywheel, where the different factors affecting brand growth flowed naturally into each other in a continuous, reinforcing feedback loop. Winning brands, we saw, had a higher rate of consecutive repeat purchases than similarly sized brands, and the momentum behind their growth stemmed from a flywheel that revolved around great products that repeatedly won one purchase occasion after another. The resulting Brand Growth Flywheel I developed depicts the first visual representation in the marketing industry of how all the critical growth levers dovetail to explain the momentum-building activities that propel a brand to the top of its category.

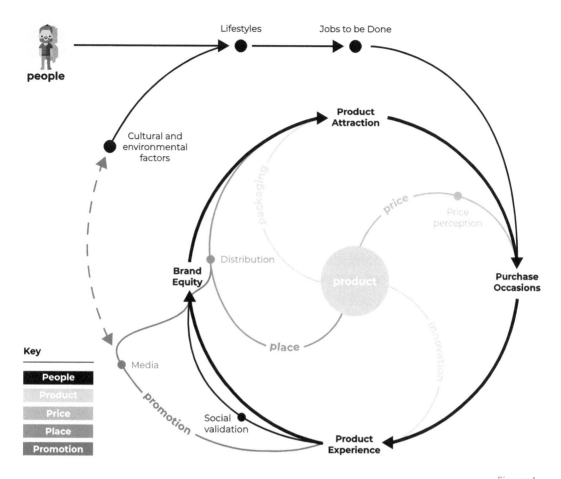

## THE BRAND GROWTH FLYWHEEL

*Figure 1A.*
The Brand
Growth
Flywheel

The accompanying image of the Brand Growth Flywheel shows how these different factors work together to create the repeat purchase loop that propels brand momentum. We'll detail each element chapter by chapter, but let me give you a brief, high-level summary of how the flywheel works.

Demographics and psychographics influence consumers' purchases and lead to distinctive lifestyles. Cultural, economic, and environmental changes shape those lifestyles. Life stage events, such as the birth of a child, starting a new job, or moving to a new city, also play a role.

Besides lifestyles, other factors influence our shopping. For example, we often decide what to buy after thinking about what we'll be doing, with whom, where, and in what context. These thoughts reflect what the industry already refers to as "need states," "demand moments," or "jobs to be done," and these have a significant impact on what we decide to buy on any given purchase occasion.

And, as I noted earlier, we rarely think of what brands we'll need, just what categories we need to shop in. We want a product that'll get the job done. This is our *category intent*. When consumers ultimately choose a product, they are mostly "satisficing"—buying something that's "good enough" rather than expending more energy to find the perfect solution. This is especially true of the fast-moving consumer goods we buy most frequently. As they shop, consumers are more likely to notice and be attracted to products that trigger a viscerally favorable response—that's *Product Attraction*.

When we start thinking about which brand we'll purchase at the store during the *Purchase Occasion*, we typically evaluate several criteria—mostly subconsciously. These criteria can change depending on who we're buying for, what we'll be doing, and how our product choices affect others' perceptions. The basic question is: what do I need for this specific occasion that I have in mind? Bang energy drink, one of our winning brands, capitalized on this curve in the flywheel big time. Bang understood that fit people often want a preworkout energy boost that is low in calories and rich in vitamins and supplements. These were pretty specific criteria, but they weren't met well until Bang came along. This enabled Bang to outperform all other energy drinks in our study.

How much does pricing affect our product choices? Quite a bit. How much does pricing affect brand growth? Not as much as you might think. Price levers may act as a short-term sales incentive, but they're not a long-term growth lever, and consumers will typically pay more for a product they're confident will get the job done. Conversely, our data show that brands with a strategy of being the everyday low-price leader in their category have been suffering through continuous share losses to retailers' private-label brands.

Consumers' *Product Experience* is a much more important driver of long-term brand growth, if not the most important. The more we purchase a brand, the more experience we gain with it. The more positive those experiences, the greater the *Brand Equity*.

Brand equity is roughly equivalent to the value a brand generates when compared to a generic equivalent. So when you choose to pay more for Advil over the store's private label brand (which contains the same amount of ibuprofen) because you think it will work better on your throbbing headache, you're demonstrating the value of Advil's brand equity. Some key ways that brands generate equity are by making their products more memorable, more attractive, and better at getting the customer's job done. BERA, the firm that provided the equity measures used in our study, continuously tracks over a hundred metrics when measuring brand equity and its drivers.

When we used those BERA metrics to compare our winning brands to our losing brands, we found the winners outscored the losers most significantly in consumers' perceptions of innovation, honesty, intelligence, and quality. Winning brands were seen as more relevant and demonstrated a better understanding of consumers' desires, lifestyles, and usage occasions—what the consumer will be doing when using the brand—than their competitors. They made more trustworthy claims and delivered on them. And the value they delivered was superior—they weren't cheap, but in the consumer's eyes, they were worth more.

As we round the corner of the flywheel, we see that gains in *Brand Equity* feed into and increase *Product Attraction*, making it more likely for the brand's products to be noticed and considered among the sea of competing products. This helps brands win more *Purchase Occasions* that lead to more positive *Product Experiences*, which leads to greater *Brand Equity*, which further increases *Product Attraction* at the shelf. This leads to brands winning even more *Purchase Occasions*, adding additional momentum as the flywheel begins yet another rotation around the *Repeat Loop*.

This gives you the basic dynamics of the flywheel. Later in the book, we will discuss how other factors—such as innovation, distribution, advertising, and social validation—contribute to accelerating the momentum of the Brand Growth Flywheel.

## KEY FINDINGS THAT EMERGED

Although many of our key findings ran counter to popular wisdom about brand growth, they were largely backed up by previous peer-reviewed research. What was different about our research, though, was that we looked at *all the possible effects*. Most academic and industry research tended to be narrowly focused on individual topics, such as pricing, distribution, or advertising. But our data allowed us to look at all the different drivers and clearly see how those drivers work in concert to build a brand's momentum over a long period of time.

Here, then, is a quick rundown of our key findings. In future chapters, we'll go deeper into each of these principles and show how you can use them to increase sales and win market share.

1. **Winning brands have significantly higher consecutive repeat rates than their similar-sized losing competitors.** Consumers are more likely to buy a winning brand again the next time they shop the category than if they initially purchased a losing brand. For instance, winning brand Rao's consecutive repeat rate[1] was 42 percent while losing brand Barilla's was just 25 percent. Winning brand Beyond Meat's consecutive repeat rate was 36 percent, while losing brand Tofurky's was just 19 percent.

---

1     Consecutive repeat rate differs from the traditional repeat rate metric in that it focuses on whether consumers repeat buy the brand on their very next category purchase occasion. The traditional repeat rate metric measures whether they purchase it again anytime in the next year.

Higher consecutive repeat rates are primarily the result of delivering a great product experience that people want to enjoy again and again. To build that experience, it helps to pay attention to cultural waves. If speed and convenience are important to consumers in your category, for example, your brand should align with the trend. Jimmy Dean's frozen breakfast foods are a great example. People are too busy in the morning for a sit-down meal, which is when breakfast sausages are normally eaten. Jimmy Dean won with microwavable breakfast sandwiches, breakfast burritos, and breakfast bowls that overcame the time and hassle barriers to enjoying morning sausages.

2. Growth never comes from either acquiring more customers or earning greater loyalty; it always comes from both. There has long been a debate about whether brands grow by acquiring more customers or by earning greater loyalty among existing customers. However, our study revealed that this is a false choice. It's not an either-or equation; it's both, or it's nothing at all.

I recently participated in "The Great Growth Debate" series coordinated by the Mobile Marketing Association where industry thought leaders argued differing perspectives on how best to grow a brand. As part of the debate, Dr. Peter Fader, a marketing professor at Wharton School of the University of Pennsylvania, whose research has been cited over twelve thousand times, argued that to grow, brands have to focus on taking care of their customers to win more loyalty from their existing base. At the other end of the spectrum was Dr. Byron Sharp, the author of *How Brands Grow* and perhaps the most influential marketing scientist at work today, who argued that to grow, brands must focus on acquiring more new customers. The more people who buy your product, the more sales will go up, he argued. From his perspective, loyalty is a naturally occurring outcome of acquiring more customers.

What got lost in the debate is that to a large extent, both claims are true. Brands don't grow from only one or the other. They grow from both because brand growth stems from a continuous feedback loop that plays on itself. It's not a question of the chicken or the egg. It's both, or it's none at all.

3. **The recently popularized notion that in order to grow, brands should focus on acquiring new, light buyers is misguided.** When we tested the hypothesis that growing brands would win disproportionately among lighter category buyers, it simply did not hold up. Growing among light category buyers is not what distinguishes winning and losing brands. Many of our losing brands (especially those that grew sales but lost market share) performed quite well among light buyers on a year-over-year basis. On the other hand, our winners' ability to retain heavy category buyers was a critical factor distinguishing them from the losers.

Moreover, the argument that it's a fool's errand to pursue heavy category buyers because today's heavy buyers are tomorrow's light buyers and today's light buyers are tomorrow's heavy buyers is patently false. Only 5 percent of a category's heavy buyers in one year will fall into the ranks of the category's light buyers in the following year. (In this case, we rank every category buyer according to their annual dollar spend in the category. The top one-third of spenders are heavy category buyers, and the bottom third are light category buyers.)

For example, we examined the behavior of consumers who were heavy buyers of chocolate in 2017. Did a large number become light buyers in 2018?

No. Seventy-four percent of heavy buyers of chocolate in 2017 remained heavy buyers of chocolate the following year. Twenty-two percent became medium buyers (falling to the middle third of all chocolate buyers), and only 4 percent slipped to the bottom third of light buyers. On the flip side, only 3 percent of the light buyers of chocolate in 2017 suddenly became heavy buyers the next year. This kind of year-over-year behavioral consistency can be found across all categories of fast-moving consumer goods. The bottom line is that heavy buyers remain heavy and light buyers remain light—this is highly predictable and highly actionable for targeting purposes.

We found that brands that grow year over year hold onto or even grow sales from the heaviest category buyers who buy their products. Furthermore, these heavy buyers attract light buyers. Heavy buyers are more likely to influence the purchases of lighter category buyers through word of mouth and online reviews (among other forms of social validation) than the other way around. Heavy buyers work for the brand without even knowing it. Brands in decline, meanwhile, see their greatest losses among these heavy category buyers.

This finding severely undercuts Dr. Byron Sharp's argument that brands should not focus on heavy buyers. In fact, it's essential that they do. One of our winning brands, Michelob Ultra, illustrated this point in the beer category: the top 33 percent of households that spend the most money on beer each year accounted for 62 percent of Michelob Ultra's retail sales. In monetary terms, the sales growth of winning brands comes predominantly from heavy buyers of the category, and these heavy category buyers remain heavy buyers year after year.

4. **Many brands develop greater appeal among particular demographics and then double down on their marketing efforts toward those high-affinity demographics. This is a losing strategy.** A clear example of this finding is when you compare Mission Foods, a winning brand, with Guerrero, a losing brand, in the product category that encompasses tortillas, pitas, taco shells, and wraps. Guerrero performed particularly well among the fast-growing Hispanic demographic, and so did Mission. But Guerrero focused heavily on positioning itself to win among this lucrative demographic. At the same time, Mission broadened its appeal to *all* buyers of the category, allowing them to gain market share while Guerrero lost market share. Other similar examples from our study include Mac's win over Krave in the meat snacks category and Modelo's growth in the beer category.

The difference between Mission and Guerrero is best illustrated by their product packaging and on their respective websites. For example, Guerrero's site features an interactive map of Mexico that allows customers to click on a region to get authentic recipes from that area. Mission's website also offers a wide variety of recipes, but theirs are more "Americanized," with recipes for chicken avocado ranch wraps and turkey apple cheddar wraps. It's no surprise that Mission's consumers resembled buyers of the category as a whole, and as a result, the brand increased its market share while recording outstanding sales growth of nearly $200 million in three years.

Modelo is another great example. This Mexican beer rose to become the number two import beer in America by strengthening its Hispanic consumer base. But it had an "affinity gap" with other consumers of the category, so it intentionally broadened its appeal to a wider audience, leveraging a hard-working, blue-collar image to reach a broader base of demographics without alienating its core consumers. The brand's "fighting spirit" campaign helped Modelo close its demographic affinity gaps, leading to outstanding sales and market share growth.

5. Winning brands win occasions that grow categories. Most companies focus too much energy on identifying discrete types of consumers and not enough effort on pinpointing the usage occasions in which consumers might use their brand to perform a certain job. Brands give consumers 80 percent of the attention and give usage occasions only 20 percent of their focus. This should be flipped. Segmenting potential usage occasions for your brand and the category and discovering how you can outperform your competitors on those occasions is a winning strategy.

You still need to pay attention to consumers and overall demographic trends, but usage and purchase occasions matter so much more. The same consumer may differ from one type of occasion to the next. So, ask yourself: *what are the most important occasions for our category and for our brand?* Then ask, *How do we position ourselves to win those occasions?*

Take White Claw, for example. White Claw was a winning brand in the beer category, and it's technically not even a beer—it's a hard seltzer. But it won in the beer category by fulfilling an underserved need and growing the "beer" category. In particular, White Claw filled the need beer buyers have for variety. When stocking the cooler for guests or friends, beer buyers need an assortment, and White Claw delivers a light, flavorful, and refreshing alternative to beer during beer-drinking occasions.

Bang energy drink and Caulipower frozen pizza also used differentiated ingredients to win occasions that competing products in their category had failed to win at all. If your brand drives consumers to a category and you are consistently delivering a good experience, your brand will win. Period.

6. **Brands that use price and trade promotions to accelerate short-term sales velocity often hurt long-term brand momentum.** Since the advent of point-of-sale-based retail measurement in the 1980s, $100 billion per year in the US has shifted from brand advertising to funding retail sales promotions. This has been a colossal mistake.

Our study found that overreliance on trade promotions (especially their most common implementation, temporary price reductions) is a hallmark of declining brands. Consumers interpret price as a sign of quality, value, and competitive positioning. Too often, trade promotions lead consumers to see a brand's regular everyday price as expensive. We found that consumers are more likely to switch away from a brand on the next purchase occasion if the price "increases" back up to its regular price. This steals brand equity to boost sales velocity temporarily, and overall it causes the brand's flywheel to lose momentum. Winning brands in our study also scored higher than their competitors in Price Performance—one of the metrics BERA tracks to measure brand equity. Price Performance measures consumers' willingness to pay more than they already do for the brand. Winning brands deliver value, helping consumers to realize the benefit of their product far in excess of its perceived cost.

Instead of trade promotions, focus on better distribution and merchandising. Winning brands Caulipower, Health-Ade Kombucha, and Rao's all used their initial success at a limited number of outlets to convince more retailers to carry their products. Once you're on the shelf, leverage your early success to win better shelf positioning and more shelf facings. If your brand's products truly increase category sales and margins for the retailers, you'll have little difficulty winning over retail buyers to start carrying your products.

7. **The biggest difference between winning and losing brands' equity drivers is the extent to which consumers see their products as "innovative" or "unique."** This finding challenges Byron Sharp's contention that differentiation is a fool's errand and supports an emphasis on differentiation as advocated by marketing pioneers such as Philip Kotler. Being seen as innovative and unique is a function of actually having differentiated products and effectively marketing the unique benefits they deliver.

For example, Bang relentlessly focused its marketing on people working out and using their product to get more energy for their workouts. They didn't show people drinking it at work instead of coffee or at a bar instead of beer. Everything in their positioning and marketing focused on people being fit and looking good, and this positioning allowed them to win where competing energy drinks were falling short.

8. **Most industry people believe that advertising is the main driver of brand equity. That's false.** Product experience, not advertising, is dominant in shaping our perceptions of brands. If a consumer has a bad first impression of your product, no amount of advertising will change their mind. Advertising is much more effective at reinforcing

in consumers' minds what a great experience your product delivers—reminding them to buy rather than convincing them to buy in the first place. The one critical exception to this is the advertisement of new product innovations—a topic we will cover in later chapters.

## WILL YOU WIN OR LOSE?

What follows is the complete list of the fifty-eight winning brands that met our criteria for exceptional increases in sales and market share to outperform the twenty-five thousand other brands tracked in our study. They are paired with brands from the same category that lost market share during the study period, even if their absolute dollar sales increased due to overall category growth. When you see a loser listed as "Private Label," that means it's a generic brand created for the retailer.[2]

| Product category | Winning Brands | Losing Brands |
|---|---|---|
| Sports & Energy Drinks | Bodyarmor | Gatorade |
| Kombucha | Health Ade | Live Soda |
| Household Batteries | Energizer | Duracell |
| Beer | Michelob Ultra | Miller |
| Incontinence | Always Discreet | Poise |
| Frozen Pizza | Caulipower | Digiorno |
| Meal Combo-Kids | Hillshire Farm | Kraft |
| Stop Smoking Aids | Nicorette | Private Label |

*Figure 1B.* The 58 Pairs of Winning and Losing Brands Emerging from This Study

2    In many product categories, retailer Private Label brands collectively met the sales and share growth criteria to qualify as Winning Brands. They were excluded from our analysis so that we could focus on the learnings applicable to brand managers and marketers for national and international brands.

| Product category | Winning Brands | Losing Brands |
|---|---|---|
| Tortillas, Pitas, Taco Shells & Wraps | Mission | Guerrero |
| Performance Shakes | Premier Nutrition | Muscle Milk |
| Women's Deodorants & Antiperspirants | Dove | Degree |
| Meat Alternatives | Beyond Meat | Tofurky |
| Sports & Energy Drinks | Bang | Rockstar |
| Dish Detergent | Dawn | Palmolive |
| External Pain | Biofreeze | Bengay |
| Dusting | Swiffer | Private Label |
| Probiotics | DSM | Renew Life |
| Dental Floss & Between Teeth Cleaners | Oral-B | DenTek |
| Sleep Aids | Olly | MidNite |
| Cold, Cough & Flu | Zarbee's | Breathe Right |
| Pet Health & Wellness | Feliway | Comfort Zone |
| Flushable Wipes | Cottonelle | Charmin |
| Spirits | Tito's Handmade Vodka | Grey Goose |
| Barbecue Sauce | Sweet Baby Ray's | KC Masterpiece |
| Mouthwash | Listerine | Colgate |
| Hair Color | L'Oreal | Clairol |
| Weight Loss | Slimfast | Weight Watchers |
| Nuts & Seeds | Fisher | Diamond Foods |
| Baby Formula | Similac | Gerber |

| Product category | Winning Brands | Losing Brands |
|---|---|---|
| Drinks & Mixes | Liquid I.V. | Gatorade |
| Lip Care | Blistex | Eos |
| Hand Soaps & Sanitizers | Kleenex (wipes) | Germ-X |
| Pasta & Pizza Sauces | Rao's Homemade | Barilla |
| Frozen Appetizers | CJ Bibigo | Pagoda |
| Snack Cakes | Hostess | Tastykake |
| Men's Deodorants & Antiperspirants | Old Spice | Right Guard |
| Meat Snacks | Mac's | Krave |
| Toothpaste | Sensodyne | Colgate |
| Butter & Margarine | Kerrygold | Blue Bonnet |
| All-Purpose Cleaners | Fabuloso | Windex |
| Frozen Desserts | Edwards | Marie Callender's |
| Laundry Detergent | Persil | All |
| Hair Accessories | Conair | Goody |
| Baking Mixes | Kodiak Cakes | Bisquick |
| Performance Powders | Orgain | Eas |
| Dried Fruit & Fruit Snacks | Welchs | Ocean Spray Craisins |
| Milk, Cream & Milk Substitutes | Coffee Mate | Land O'Lakes |
| Frozen Breakfast Food | Jimmy Dean | Kellogg's |
| Stocks & Broths | Better Than Bouillon | Swanson |
| Eye Care | Refresh | Opti-Free |

| Product category | Winning Brands | Losing Brands |
|---|---|---|
| Beer | White Claw | Redd's |
| Popcorn | Smartfood | Pop Weaver |
| Fabric Softener | Downy | Purex |
| Continuous Action Air Freshener | Febreze | Glade |
| Non-Seasonal Candy | Reese's | Snickers |
| Toothbrushes | Oral-B | Sonicare |
| Nutrition and Wholesome Bars | Kind | Kellogg's |
| Hair Removal Tools | Harry's | Gillette |

In addition, Modelo, Mary Kay, and Cheez-It met the criteria for being selected as a winning brand but were left out of the final study due to the lack of a comparable losing brand.

In the coming chapters, we'll examine these brands more closely and explore how they embodied the key findings of our study. We'll use positive examples from our winning brands and negative examples from the losing brands to illustrate how you can put these concepts into practice to drive sustainable growth.

The key is for you to understand that we've entered a new world of consumer understanding. While the data I used to write this book was unprecedented, in the coming years it will become the table-stakes market intelligence that brand managers and marketers require to navigate the competitive landscape successfully. And the first step for many will be developing a better understanding of who their consumers really are and how they live their lives. So, if you're ready, let's dive in and find out what the data tells us. Let's begin assembling the flywheel so you can build *your* momentum and grow your brand.

**2**

# PEOPLE AND LIFESTYLES

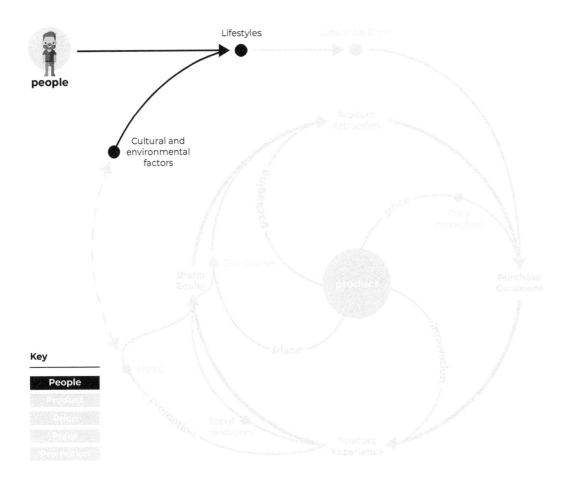

people

Lifestyles

Cultural and
environmental
factors

Key

People

While visiting my parents in Arizona recently, I went to the supermarket to pick up flour tortillas for some enchiladas we were making that night. The store carried two brands—Mission and Guerrero. Both brands produce excellent products and experienced sales growth during our study, each benefiting from the growing Hispanic population in the US.

But Mission had emerged as a winner by increasing sales and market share—sales grew by $200 million, and market share was up 2 percent—while Guerrero had emerged as a losing brand. Although Guerrero's sales grew by $35 million from 2016 to 2019 due to overall growth in the tortillas, taco shells, and wraps category, its market share had slipped by nearly 1 percent.

Why?

Standing before the shelves of flour tortilla packages, I got a clue. Guerrero's package was primarily in Spanish—*Un pedacito de Mexico* (A little piece of Mexico), the package proclaimed—while the Mission package was in English. Hmmm. Then I went to each brand's website. There, Guerrero doubled down on its appeal to the Hispanic market by emphasizing the brand's authenticity and connection to Mexico. Its website said such things as "get inspired by the flavors of Mexico" and featured traditional dishes like "enchiladas verdes" and "carne guisada tacos." Its site also presented an interactive map of Mexico and invited me to "choose a (Mexican) state and find out the recipes that suit you best."

Mission's website, meanwhile, seemed to appeal to a broader audience. It, too, offered some Mexican recipes, but many other menu ideas were a long way from being "authentic" Hispanic dishes. These recipes included such items as the Cuban Press, Greek Chicken

*Figure 2A. Sample Packaging for Guerrero and Mission Tortillas*

Wrap, or the Vegetarian Bean and Roasted Butternut Squash Tacos. Mission's home page also emphasized the line's low-carb, whole wheat, and organic offerings.

*Figure 2B.*
Comparison
of Websites
for Mission
and Guerrero

All this helped explain how Mission became a winner and Guerrero—despite its increased sales—became a losing brand. Guerrero focused on a high-affinity demographic, particularly its popularity in a Hispanic community that grew by 10 million over the four years we studied. Meanwhile, Mission focused on an ever-broadening range of *category buyers*. Over the course of the study, Mission's customers grew to look more and more like the category's customers as a whole. Sales soared, and market share increased.

*Massive Affinity Gap!*

| Ethnicity | % of Tortilla Category Buyers | % of Mission's Buyers | % of Guerrero's Buyers |
|---|---|---|---|
| White / Caucasian | 67.8% | 69.7% | 46.8% |
| Hispanic / Latino | 15.3% | 14.9% | 36.8% |

*Figure 2C.* Differences in Demographic Appeal between Mission and Guerrero Tortillas in 2019

What our study and this comparison of two top brands reveal is that winning among particular demographics doesn't matter as much as most brand managers think it does. In fact, targeting specific demographics at the exclusion of a broader set of category buyers is a losing strategy—it's one of the clearest ways losing brands lose.

Winning brands want their customers to resemble all buyers in their category. In Mission's case, they appealed to Hispanic customers, but they also wanted to appeal to the 85 percent of category buyers who were non-Hispanic, who wanted to use tortillas to make kid-friendly meals, quick-and-easy dishes for dinner, and authentic *carne guisada* tacos.

Mission's approach underscores that winning brands rarely win different demographics than their competitors. Winners understand that any strategy or tactic focused on winning a particular demographic subset of category buyers is likely to fail.

As we've said before (and will say again), winning brands want their customers to resemble the category as a whole. In the case of the tortillas, taco shells, and wraps category, around 16 percent of all buyers are Hispanic. Mission's customers reflected this; from 2019 to 2021, around 16 percent of the brand's sales (15.9 percent in 2019, 15.9 percent in 2020, and 15.3 percent in 2021) went to Hispanics. During the same period, around 60 percent of Guerrero's customers were Hispanic. Guerrero was excelling with that demographic group, but that didn't give Mission heartburn because their brand was gaining market share and increasing sales by drawing in customers from *all* the buyers in that category, not just Hispanics. In Mission's view, if anybody was buying products in the tortillas, pitas, taco shells, and wraps category, they should be buying their products.

There's a reason brands like Guerrero fall into the trap of focusing on a single demographic and missing out on a host of potential category buyers. After all, if a brand can't appeal to its main demographic, how can it appeal to anyone? And in Guerrero's case, they were capitalizing on the expansion of the Hispanic demographic, which grew by 6 percent per year during this four-year period. Guerrero went after those customers and got a lot of them. The only problem was that Mission was also capitalizing on this growth. Mission grew sales within the Hispanic demographic by 9 percent per year but did so without ignoring all the other potential buyers of their products.

The contrast in results between the two brands provides the first clear answer for us: if you don't maximize appeal among all the people who buy your category, you'll have trouble winning in the market.

## WHY YOU NEED TO STOP TARGETING DEMOGRAPHICS

Why do so many brands behave as if they are seeking a relationship with a single white male, age twenty-five to thirty-five, with a college degree and a full-time job? Isn't that strategy about as dated as personal ads in the newspaper classified section?

Yes, it is.

Brands fall into this trap when they notice a greater appeal among a certain demographic. It's hard not to double down on your marketing efforts toward high-affinity groups. After all, if something works, you should do more of it, right? Well, no. Growing via specific demographics (such as the Hispanic population) might help you record more sales in the short run, but you have to remember that all brands in your category will likely reap those rewards. It's nearly impossible to win overall market share based on a single demographic increase.

Demographic marketing works as well as identity politics. As political parties have learned, by overtly attempting to appeal to one subgroup, you effectively exclude or alienate others. Your brand must transcend demographic identity by appealing to what people value.

Marketing professor Scott Galloway of New York University often quotes nineteenth-century French sociologist Auguste Comte, who is credited with saying "Demography is destiny."[1] There is a good reason for this. Demographic trends move entire categories up and down, like the tide. This category movement makes it very unlikely that your brand will rise any faster than your competitors'. Again, you must instead appeal across the demographic spectrum of your category's buyers. But how do you grow your buyers so that they become indistinguishable from buyers of the category?

## CLOSING AFFINITY GAPS

One way to ensure your consumers look more like the consumers of the category as a whole is to actively close affinity gaps.[2] We already saw how Mission did this as they reached beyond the Hispanic demographic and appealed to other audiences, including parents who pack lunches for their kids and culinary adventurists experimenting with authentic recipes.

Another great example of a brand that closed an affinity gap is Modelo. Initially, the brand must have assumed it should focus its marketing efforts on appealing to Hispanics as their authentic Mexican beer of choice. However, to truly become a winning brand, they would need to appeal to blue-collar white guys in the South, yuppies in Chicago, and every beer drinker in between.

---

1 Many, many writers attribute the quote to Comte, but others have questioned whether Comte said this.

2 What's an affinity gap? Let's say Hispanics account for 20 percent of the total sales in a category, but they account for only 10 percent of your sales. You're getting half as many sales from Hispanics as you might expect based on the entire category. You have an affinity gap.

Modelo took action and began to run marketing campaigns targeting this wider spectrum of people. Their beer started showing up in bars and tasting contests well outside of their core Hispanic markets. Their TV ads showed white working-class people getting off the job and meeting up to drink Modelos. Their "Fighting Spirit" ads featured three-time Olympic swimmer Nathan Adrian, who is of Asian heritage, and basketball star Damian Lillard, who is Black.

In turn, Modelo effectively closed its affinity gaps and broadened its appeal far beyond the Hispanic market.

Of course, a brand may need to close affinity gaps based on all kinds of factors, not just race. For example, they might need to look at customer segments based on income, age, or preferably psychographic differences. The benefit of identifying affinity gaps and taking steps to close them is that more buyers in the category will consider buying your brand—maximizing its market potential.

Think of your customers as an investment portfolio or a mutual fund. When your portfolio is balanced (a mix of growth and value stocks, small-cap and large-cap stocks, international and domestic stocks, etc.) you're best positioned to win in all market conditions. You're also less susceptible to periodic drops or volatility in any area. However, if you focus on one specific demographic (stock), your growth is capped by that one stock, and you miss out on a wider range of growth—and the potential to become a "winner." The same thing occurs when a brand closes its affinity gaps, and its customers resemble the buyers of the category as a whole.

To be clear, Modelo didn't stop marketing to the Hispanic population that had been its core. One of their primary campaigns in recent years was about unsung heroes within the Hispanic community. Still, the brand knew it couldn't only appeal to this segment, or it would be missing out on a huge market opportunity. So, they diversified.

An example of a winning brand that focused on the overall category rather than a certain demographic was Mac's meat snacks. Their approach starkly contrasted with the loser in the category, Krave.

Mac's initially skewed toward Black and Hispanic populations, whereas Krave skewed toward a White population. But while Krave never closed its affinity gap with other groups, Mac's noticed its gaps and, by 2019, had achieved strong appeal across all demographics.

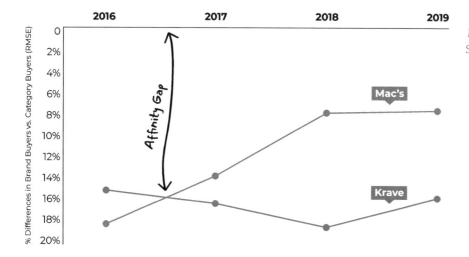

*Figure 2D.* Mac's Shoppers Better Resembled Overall Category Buyers as the Brand Grew

The accompanying chart (Figure 2D) shows how Mac's performed. The closer its brand got to zero, the closer its customers resembled the category's consumers as a whole. As you can see, Mac's customers in 2016 were quite different from those for the meat snacks category as a whole. Krave was closer to the ideal but still a ways away from being perfectly lined up with category customers. As time went on, Mac's closed its affinity gaps and got steadily closer to having its customers resemble the customers of the overall category. Krave, on the other hand, got farther away before making a course correction in 2018. As a result, Mac's numbers for sales and market share allowed it to become a winner in the meat snacks category, while Krave's emerged as a loser.

When brands understand the importance of closing affinity gaps, they change their approach to marketing. A good brand marketer will move beyond ads focused only on demographics or personas—the suburban mom or the middle-income White professional—and focus more on the distinguishing lifestyle and psychographic traits of the category's core consumers.

## PSYCHOGRAPHICS

Psychographics is the study of people's values, beliefs, attitudes, emotions, interests, and aspirations, and how these factors affect behavior, such as buying habits and choices. Psychographic data do a much better job explaining consumer behavior and consumer choices than demographics. They also provide far more clues about consumers' motivations to act. By focusing on psychographics—as opposed to demographics—you increase your chances of reaching *all* potential buyers in your category, and you decrease your chances of alienating any particular demographic group.

For example, if we highly value our health and fitness, we're drawn to different products. If we treasure the environment and want to protect it, we are more likely to choose brands that clearly share this concern. If we value history and tradition, certain product packages and messages will better resonate with us. These values will influence our purchase decisions and consumption choices[3]—maybe not consciously but certainly subconsciously. Another advantage of psychographics is that they provide insights into more significant consumer trends. Several of the winners in our study—Caulipower, Kind, and Michelob Ultra, for instance—all capitalized on the growing number of consumers who are increasingly conscious of what we put in our bodies. Meanwhile, several losing brands, such as Colgate (Total) and Muscle Milk, suffered from rising consumer concerns over perceived health risks associated with consuming their products.

---

3    Pamela M. Homer and Lynn R. Kahle, "A Structural Equation Test of the Value-Attitude-Behavior Hierarchy," *Journal of Personality and Social Psychology* 54, no. 4 (April 1988): 638–46, https://psycnet.apa.org/doi/10.1037/0022-3514.54.4.638. Homer and Kahle found that values predict a significant percentage of the variance in attitudes toward brands, which then partially predict the variance in consumption behavior.

Health-Ade Kombucha is an excellent example of a winning brand that leveraged psychographics as fundamental to its marketing strategy. By the time Health-Ade Kombucha started its business in 2012, a large spectrum of the population was paying more attention than ever to what they put in their bodies and how it made them feel. In addition, consumers were becoming more aware of probiotics and gut health.

This cultural rise led to an increased interest in kombucha drinks, which are full of antioxidants and probiotics that boost intestinal cell health, improve immune function, and aid in food digestion. As a result, the category as a whole took off during our four-year study. Health-Ade Kombucha realized early that the winning strategy was to focus on this psychographic trend, not on a particular consumer demographic. One of their advertisements stated, "Get Happy, Get Healthy, Get Health-Ade Kombucha." They essentially connected their name and brand to health and happiness. In turn, they won. Retail sales grew from less than $6 million in 2016 to more than $60 million in 2019—a 900 percent increase in three years! At the same time, the brand's share of the kombucha market grew from 3 percent to more than 10 percent.

Beyond Meat, a Los Angeles-based maker of meat substitutes launched in 2012, also capitalized on psychographic trends. Beyond Meat's founders, taking note of consumers' growing concern with their diet and the environmental and health dangers posed by the

*Figure 2E.*
*Health-Ade*
*Kombucha*
*Billboards*

farming and meat-processing industries, developed plant-based alternatives to beef, pork, and chicken.

*Figure 2F.*
Beyond Meat's
Psychographic
Appeal

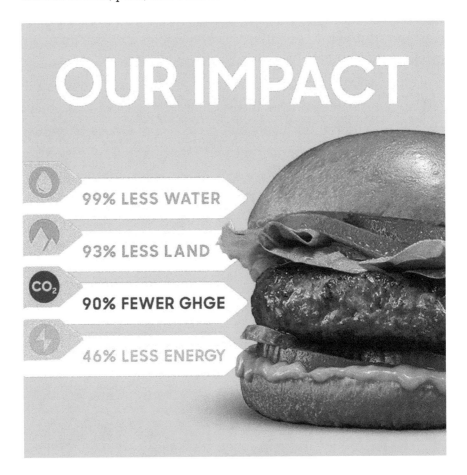

In its messaging, Beyond Meat explicitly stated how it responded to these issues, with explicit claims of "99 percent less water, 93 percent less land, 90 percent fewer greenhouse gas emissions, and 46 percent less energy used than industrial farming of cattle." By outlining these numbers in detail, the brand showed consumers how they could make consumption choices consistent with their worldview. That kind of smart branding set them apart from the category's longtime leader, Tofurky, which took a much more subtle (less obvious) approach to its positioning (see below) and became a losing brand in the category. Meanwhile, Beyond Meat grew from $7 million in annual sales to

$115 million, a 1,517 percent increase, while gobbling up market share—growing from 6 percent to 42 percent in just three years.

*Figure 2G*. The Contrasting Example of Tofurky's Positioning

Of course, psychographics go beyond health concerns. They could be connected to a person's religion or how often they go to church. They could be connected to someone's politics or personal opinions. Psychographics are based on what a person values and they play a prominent role in how a person *behaves*.

The success of Beyond Meat and Health-Ade Kombucha underscores what can happen when brands recognize large cultural shifts in psychographics. Psychographic data often reflect consumers' aspirations more than their actual behavior. That data makes psychographic intelligence particularly useful in helping brands spot unmet needs and develop products that close the gap between what their customer is and what the customer wants to be. In the case of Beyond Meat and Health-Ade Kombucha, both brands capitalized on the trend toward being more health-conscious and making better choices about what to put in our bodies. If you look at all our winning brands, I don't think you can find one that was selling products that are worse for your health or the environment than the loser in the same category. Caulipower is healthier than DiGiorno. Bang beat Rockstar by reducing calories while adding nutritional supplements. BodyArmor had fewer calories and sugar than Gatorade. There are many examples, and most relied heavily on psychographic appeal as part of their messaging and competitive positioning.

## WINNING BRANDS IN ACTION

While America's Hispanic population grew by 20 percent over a decade (from 50 million to 60 million), America's elderly population (65 plus) grew almost twice as fast. They went from 40 million to 55 million in the same period. That's the baby boom, baby!

Always Discreet incontinence pads rode this massive demographic wave to outstanding sales growth of 59 percent. While taking advantage of the upward demographic trend, Always Discreet also grew its market share by a staggering 220 basis points (or by 14.5 percent) from 2016 to 2019 to become a breakout brand.

The real difference between Always Discreet and competitors like Poise (the corresponding losing brand in our study) was the messaging to consumers. Always Discreet focused its ads on maintaining an active lifestyle. They showed people dancing and exercising with joyous expressions that suggested they weren't holding back anything. On the other hand, the messaging by Poise was much more functional. For example, their ads emphasized statements such as "Poise absorbs 2X faster" or "Pads are for periods. Poise is for bladder leakage." Always Discreet addressed what people in this group wanted (freedom to be active), not just what they needed. Their ads offered, "Enjoy dance-all-you-want bladder leak protection," and featured mature women enjoying an active lifestyle.

## LIFESTYLES

The figure at the beginning of this chapter illustrates how cultural, economic, and environmental factors combine with people's demographics and psychographics to influence lifestyles. Whether it's COVID disrupting where we eat or go to work, or simple changes to the seasons, our lifestyles are in constant flux—and those changes impact how we shop and what we buy.

A primary driver of changing lifestyles are major life events such as the birth of a new child, moving houses, or starting a new job. Before embarking on the primary study that serves as the basis for this book, Prabhath Nanisetty (who led product management for Numerator) and I wanted to understand how changing lifestyles triggered by significant life events impacted consumers' shopping behaviors.

For example, Figure 2I shows how five thousand consumers spent more or less on Amazon in the six months following a life event than they had during the six months prior. While it may not be a surprise that families having their first child suddenly increased their spending by 46 percent, we were stunned to see that people who had just stopped dating someone increased their Amazon spending by almost as much. Apparently, even retail therapy has moved online. Meanwhile, consumers entering retirement spent about 45 percent less on Amazon. A new lifestyle defined by a fixed income and loads of free time clearly makes a trip to the store more appealing than paying a slight premium for the convenience of online shopping.

*Figure 2I.*
Changes in Shopping Behavior on *Amazon.com* after a Life Event

| | Amazon Spend Index (Pre-Post) |
|---|---|
| Had/Expecting my first child | 146 |
| Stopped dating someone | 144 |
| Bought my first house / condo | 130 |
| Got divorced | 120 |
| Upsized: moved into a larger place (house, condo, apt.) | 112 |
| Started school | 112 |
| Got my first job | 101 |
| Received promotion | 98 |
| Had / Expecting another child | 97 |
| Started dating someone | 94 |
| Got married | 94 |
| Child moved out of house | 92 |
| Faced major financial hardships | 91 |
| Got a new job | 86 |
| Downsized: moved into a smaller place (house, condo, apt.) | 84 |
| Became an empty-nester (all kids out of house) | 75 |
| Moved 50+ miles away | 74 |
| Went on maternity / paternity leave | 73 |
| Retired from work | 55 |

It's not just where and how much people shop that gets impacted by changing lifestyles and major life events. When we looked at differences in purchasing behavior of particular product categories, we were amused to find that people starting a new job buy just as much beer as they did before but significantly increase their intake of spirits. Perhaps we shouldn't have been surprised, though, because a separate study we performed found that when people buy spirits, they rate their overall shopping experience more positively than when they buy any other product category.

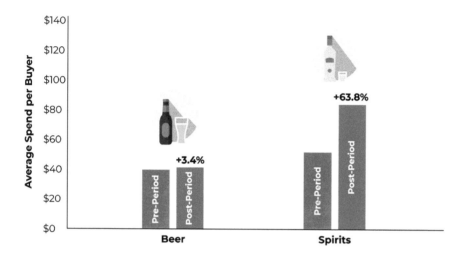

Figure 2J. Purchases of Beer and Spirits in the Six Months before and after Getting a New Job

So, what's the point of all this? Differences in lifestyles can go a long way toward explaining differences in consumer preferences and purchasing behaviors. A marketing manager can leverage a better understanding of lifestyle influences on your consumers' journey to improve the relevance and effectiveness of your brand's communications.

## GOING TOO NARROW OR BROAD

To effectively reach all the customers who might be interested in your products, you must notice when you're going too narrow or too broad in your marketing and actively make changes to achieve better results.

One winning brand, Olly, in the sleep aids category, almost fell into one of the most common delusional traps brands fall into—defining their target audience too narrowly. Olly's CEO, Brad Harrington, said in one interview, "We really want to create an iconic brand that connects lifestyle and millennials." In our study, however, we found that Olly moderately outperforms the category when generating sales from millennials yet performs significantly better among Gen-Xers.

*Figure 2K. Olly's Appeal by Age and Income Relative to Category Norms in 2019*

| Generation | % of Sleep Aid Category Spend | % of Olly's Retail Sales | $ Sales Above↑ / Below↓ Category Norm |
|---|---|---|---|
| **Gen Z** [> 1996] | 2.5% | 4.2% | $1,809,946 ↑ |
| **Millennials** [1982-1995] | 17.1% | 21.0% | $4,314,108 ↑ |
| **Gen X** [1965-1981] | 33.0% | 41.7% | $9,442,288 ↑ |
| **Boomers+** [< 1965] | 47.4% | 33.1% | -$15,566,342 ↓ |

| Income Bracket | % of Sleep Aid Category Spend | % of Olly's Retail Sales | $ Sales Above↑ / Below↓ Category Norm |
|---|---|---|---|
| **Low Income** (Under $40k) | 25.1% | 20.1% | -$5,429,715 ↓ |
| **Middle Income** ($40k-$80k) | 28.2% | 21.0% | -$7,890,603 ↓ |
| **High Income** (Over $80k) | 46.6% | 58.9% | $13,350,491 ↑ |

If you're looking only at demographics, the brand's strongest demographic by far is higher-income households ($80k+). This fact is not unique to Olly. Income level (in reality, it comes down to the capacity to engage in discretionary spending) is the demographic distinction that tends to have the greatest power in explaining differences in brand choice among consumers within a category. Income level also explains why the most common segmentation of product categories is by price tier: premium, midrange, and budget. Income levels directly affect consumers' willingness and ability to pay a premium for quality (or at least the perception of quality). It also explains why many consumers—particularly those with lower incomes—shop as if the price were their only consideration when choosing among brands in a category.

Olly managers got lucky; their overemphasis on demographics didn't get in the way. Why not? Because Olly followed the flywheel in one important way: they positioned their product around the job to be done—sleep—rather than the ingredients or other focal points competitors used.

Some brands are not so lucky. For example, some brands focus so narrowly on a demographic that they only run ads on TikTok, or they only run their ads during reruns of *Seinfeld*. These approaches will keep any brand locked into a certain demographic range, and the brand will miss many segments of the population that are also category buyers.

In some cases, brands take the opposite approach; they try to appeal to too broad a spectrum of people—well beyond likely buyers of the category. In these cases, a brand's message is either ignored or muddied because, to appeal to everyone, the brand appeals to no one in particular.

While you never want to market to only a single "ideal consumer," defining your ideal consumer can help focus your brand's marketing and communications. Just don't fall into the trap of confusing your brand's ideal consumer with the people who should buy your product. Yes, you want to be clear in your messaging, but never to the exclusion of someone who should want exactly what you have.

## THE GOLDILOCKS APPROACH

Procter & Gamble (P&G) seems to be particularly adept at avoiding the trap of going too narrow or too wide and getting it just right in marketing its brands. In fact, the company produced seven of the fifty-eight winning brands in our study, while the next closest competitor delivered only two of our winning brands.

I wanted to know more about Procter & Gamble's approach, so I reached out to Joan Lewis, who led Consumer and Market Knowledge, Media Transformation, and Brand Building Reinvention for P&G globally.

She explained that the idea of a "target audience" is often misapplied among marketers. In her view, most brands should not have a single target audience, but should instead define two audiences. To explain, she used the example of Red Bull.

This popular brand's first target audience is the inspirational consumer—the kind of person who inspires the brand's messaging and its innovation pipeline. Red Bull's branding is inspired by people who participate in extreme sports. The brand's tagline is "gives you wings," and they sponsor events that bring this idea to life, like Red Bull Flugtag, Air Race, and SuperSkicross. Having a strong idea about what inspires the brand helps it both internally and externally. Inside the company, the brand's inspiration helps everyone stay "on brand," building the equity of the brand by being consistent in all aspects of the brand's creative properties. Outside the company, the brand's consistency helps build a strong resonance with buyers by reinforcing iconic assets.

The second target audience is the consumer the brand must reach with marketing and distribution to build a large, solid business. For Red Bull, this group includes everyone who wants a pick-me-up beverage. Millions of people drink Red Bull—from college students to truck drivers to busy executives—and most don't participate in or even watch extreme sports. Red Bull buyers may like the idea that a drink "gives you wings," but they are drinking it for the benefit it provides.

Joan's theory makes sense, and I tend to agree with her perspective. Brands benefit from building a persona—often built around the most ideal consumer—but this ideal persona should not be confused with the brand's target audience. If you're a beauty brand, you might use beautiful people to advertise. You shouldn't confuse them with your actual market, but you can leverage them to gain that inspirational advantage. Consumers want to associate themselves with certain people and lifestyles. That's just how we work.

Procter & Gamble has obviously succeeded with this approach time and time again, so it's worth taking note and being clear about the role and distinction between your ideal consumer and your target consumer.

## THE HAPPY MEDIUM

Again, the key is to never go too narrow (e.g., a small niche of buyers) or too broad (e.g., an audience for whom your product is irrelevant). A good place to start is to make sure your messaging isn't alienating any potential buyers. If a certain group of people buys your category but your messaging is alienating that group, that's the most important issue to address. For example, Axe (also known as Lynx in some markets) alienated many potential customers because of the "toxic masculinity" and "objectification of women" in the way they advertised. Too many category buyers (including women who shop for their male partners) preferred to dissociate, rather than associate, with Axe, which was impacting its market share and future prospects. As the brand's new creative director put it, the brand "didn't correspond to where culture was moving."

Axe and its agency partner performed purposeful consumer research to guide the repositioning of the brand. After discovering that 90 percent of women are attracted to men who are "true to themselves" and that nearly half of all men were afraid to look different for fear of being judged, the brand team found their North Star. According to Fernando Desouches, Senior Global Brand Director for Axe/Lynx at Unilever, those insights helped them realize, "We wanted to empower men to be the most attractive man they could be—themselves." And they found this quote by Judy Garland particularly inspirational: "Always be a first-rate version of yourself, not a second-rate version of someone else."[4]

*Figure 2L.*
Scenes
from Axe
Commercials
Repositioning
the Brand

Through a series of ad campaigns and by partnering with social media influencers, the brand successfully changed its image and saw a tripling of its global growth rate as a result.

---

4    Nicola Kemp, "Case Study: How Axe Redefined Masculinity," *Campaign*, April 10, 2017, https://www.campaignlive.co.uk/article/case-study-axe-redefined-masculinity/1430092.

In our research, we learned that winning brands found a way to appeal to heavy category buyers *and* people who normally don't buy the product category. Not enough sales growth will come from new buyers in the category, so it's crucial that a brand do the job for heavy buyers while luring new consumers. This is core to our study's key findings: *winning brands grow categories.*

A great example of such a winner is Bang energy drink. Bang not only resonated with heavy buyers of energy drinks but also poured gas on sales by resonating with a bunch of buyers who *would* buy energy drinks more regularly *if* the right product came around that fulfilled their needs. These nonbuyers found Bang and fell for Bang—big time.

For Bang or any category newcomer, answering the needs of ardent energy-drink consumers was table stakes. But Bang's differentiation—it's low in calories and full of vitamins and supplements—allowed it to bring in enthusiastic new buyers and thus expand the category.

### WINNERS CAPTURE MORE NEW BUYERS

One of the most striking findings in our study was that winning brands attract 43 percent more new category buyers than you would expect based on their market share. For example, a hypothetical winning brand with a 10 percent market share would win 14.3 percent of purchases made by first-time buyers in the category. In marketing lingo, they are getting much more than their "fair share" of sales from consumers who weren't already buying the category.

Bang realized that fit people want a healthy, preworkout energy boost. The problem was that traditional energy drinks have all kinds of sugar, calories, and additives that exercisers *don't* want. Bang solved that problem with a beneficial, clean-burning beverage. This highly differentiated value proposition resonated with consumers across various usage occasions. Bang effectively met the distinctive criteria for this group, many of whom wouldn't otherwise buy energy drinks.

A category's biggest brands might have broad appeal and be the default option for most people, but they don't always meet the needs of valuable consumer segments or get the job done in all types of usage occasions. When leading brands fall short, upstart brands like Bang see daylight and rush in.

In our study, winning brands didn't acquire much of their share gains from their category's leading brand. They stole some share from the big guy, but that gain was 45 percent less than expected based on the two brands' relative market shares. Instead, the winners gobbled share gains from their category's smaller, niche brands. This dynamic suggests that the winning brands' new customers were buyers who had already ruled out the leading brands and were considering the smaller brands when they came upon their solution—an alluring alternative that gave them what they were looking for. This is a key insight we'll make actionable when discussing product innovation in Chapter 10.

## HEAVY CATEGORY BUYERS

Rather than appealing to particular demographic segments as many brand managers do, pay more attention to the heaviest buyers of your category—the top one-third of spenders, who typically account for more than two-thirds of retail sales.

Heavy category buyers come from all kinds of demographic segments. They rarely emerge from a specific demographic. What often distinguishes heavy category buyers from light category buyers is their psychographics. These buyers have particular values, interests, and aspirations that lead to lifestyle choices that influence their purchasing behaviors. The key is to determine what jobs these buyers need and deliver a product that does that job exceptionally well. While psychographics are key, demographics are often misleading. Take facial cleansers, for example. In 2018, 38 percent of all households purchased a facial cleanser on at least one occasion, and 22 percent bought the Neutrogena brand. When we looked at facial cleanser buyers who were among the top half of spenders in the category—a group that includes heavy buyers and some medium-level buyers—we found that 27 percent of them bought Neutrogena. We wondered, *Were there any demographic segments more likely to buy Neutrogena?*

To answer that question, we analyzed five thousand combinations of demographic attributes in search of a demographic segment that purchased Neutrogena at a higher rate than the heaviest 50 percent of category buyers. We found only one: wealthy white moms with at least four kids living in rural America. That's right; the *Duck Dynasty* family represents the only demographic in America that's more likely to buy Neutrogena than simply targeting heavier category buyers.

*Figure 2M.* The Demographics of Neutrogena's Highest Affinity Consumers

So, if you were Neutrogena, would you try to appeal to that group?

That wouldn't be wise. That demographic represents just 0.1 percent of the category's buyers. The top half of buyers—all heavy and some medium buyers—is five hundred times bigger. It just doesn't make sense to spend a lot of money to identify that 0.1 percent and then craft messages that appeal to them. You will not move the sales needle or market share dial that way. Wouldn't you be much better off identifying why heavy category buyers make their purchases and ensuring that you appeal to them?

Yes.

Neutrogena is not the exception. It's the rule. Across the dozens of categories we studied, it's nearly impossible to generate a sizable target audience via demographic segmentation that will have a higher propensity to buy than heavy category buyers. Can you target ads to heavy category buyers? Oh, yes. We'll tell you how in Chapter 8.

## CANARY IN THE COAL MINE

Part of our study tracked purchase behaviors of heavy-, light-, and non-buying consumers over time. Would winning brands grow disproportionately among light buyers of the category, as Dr. Byron Sharp and others have suggested? Or would loyalty gains among current customers explain the difference between winners and losers?

The answer: none of the above.

Both winning brands and losing brands tend to see similar year-over-year sales growth among light category buyers. And while winning brands tend to convert more nonbuyers of the category into first-time buyers, the sales contribution from these previous nonbuyers is often negligible and doesn't explain the winning brands' overall sales growth from one year to the next.

The most significant difference in the performance between winning brands and losing brands among buyer groups is among the heavy category buyers. Losing brands hemorrhage sales from heavy category buyers year over year while winning brands find a way to at least hold their ground among heavy category buyers. Even Bang, highly successful at bringing new buyers into the energy drink category, sourced 61 percent of its sales growth from already heavy buyers of energy drinks.

To illustrate the point with a representative example, let's look at the rise of Reese's (winning brand) and the fall of Snickers in the chocolate category from 2016 to 2017. Reese's saw retail sales grow 22.3 percent year over year, while Snickers grew just 1.7 percent in sales but lost market share as the category grew even faster.

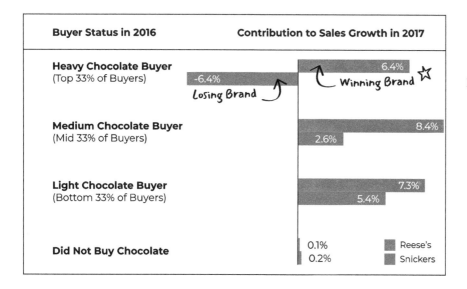

*Figure 2N.* Contributions of Heavy/ Medium/ Light Buyers to Brand Growth and Decline

The pattern we see for Reese's and Snickers is the same pattern we saw over and over again across our winning and losing brand pairs. The clear difference in performance came from winning brands growing and maintaining sales from heavy buyers of the category (the top one-third of spenders in the category) while losing brands hemorrhaged sales from this cohort in particular.

In short, the behavior of heavy category buyers is the "canary in the coal mine" for brand performance. If your brand is doing well, then you are maintaining or growing sales among the cohort that buys the category most often. If your brand is faltering, it is because you are experiencing a significant drop-off in the purchase behavior of heavy category buyers.

## KEY TAKEAWAYS

- Winning among particular demographics doesn't matter as much as many brand managers believe. Targeting specific demographics at the exclusion of a broader set of category buyers is a losing strategy; winning brands want their customers to resemble all buyers in their category. Spot and close affinity gaps so that all buyers in the category will consider buying your brand, thus maximizing your brand's market potential.

- By appealing to one "ideal customer," you risk alienating most category buyers. Your brand must transcend demographic identity by appealing to what people value.

- Understand and emphasize lifestyle's role in your consumer's journey to increase the relevance and effectiveness of your brand's communications.

- Psychographics better explain consumer behavior than do demographics. Psychographics reveal the values and interests that directly shape consumers' buying habits and choices and help you understand consumers' motivations to act.

- Winning brands appeal more to people who normally don't buy the product category. Winning brands grow categories.

- Winning brands shine when the leading brands fall short. When consumers have ruled out the category's leading brands and are searching for a better solution, winning brands can gobble up share gains from smaller, niche brands by delivering what these consumers are looking for.

- Pay more attention to the heaviest buyers of your category. Determine what jobs these buyers need and deliver a product that does that job exceptionally well. Losing brands hemorrhage sales from heavy category buyers year over year while winning brands hold their ground. If your brand is faltering, it is because you are experiencing a significant drop-off in the purchase behavior of heavy category buyers.

# 3

# USAGE OCCASIONS AND THE JOB TO BE DONE

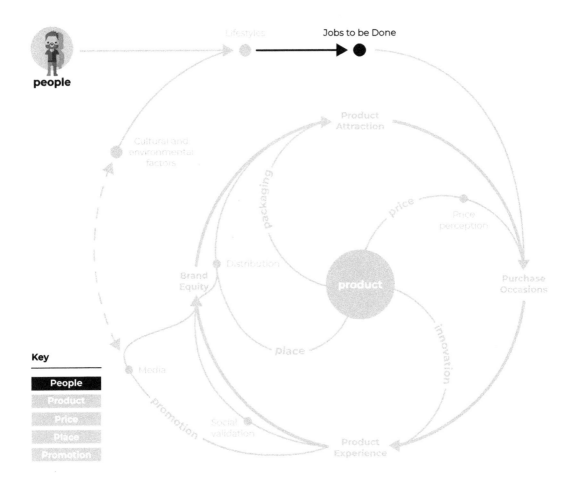

Key

| People |
|---|
| Product |
| Price |
| Place |
| Promotion |

E very weekday morning, millions of parents have a job to do: make their kids lunch for school. In our house, that's a job I've recently taken on for my kids, including my beast-of-a-child son, who grew seven inches (eighteen centimeters) and twenty pounds (nine kilograms) last year.

When I shop for groceries, I keep my lunch-making job in mind. I need food that can go without refrigeration for a few hours. I need items that aren't messy and don't require silverware or containers from home because I know they won't come back. I prefer options that are quick to prepare with minimal or no cleanup afterward. It's got to be both tasty and nutritious. And it can't be my son's favorite quick meal—canned tuna with rice and beans with peppers mixed in—because his friends at the lunch table will make fun of him for how it smells. Canned tuna may check the box on almost every criterion, but it will not work for this occasion. So I make him four sandwiches and add a protein bar and a bag of healthy lentil chips. No utensils are needed. Minimal mess. No smell.

It seems simple, right? Not really. When I shop, I avoid processed foods high in fat, sugar, and preservatives. I buy denser, whole-grain bread that still tastes good, has a soft texture, and doesn't fall apart. I buy mustard I can squeeze from a tube (Americans have no idea what they are missing—it's amazing) rather than spoon out of a jar because it saves time in the hustle-bustle of getting out the door for school on time. I shop precisely for this occasion and buy products I know will get the job done.

To be clear, usage occasions and jobs to be done are not synonymous. Usage occasions describe what the consumer will be doing when using the brand (making lunch), and jobs to be done are the things a consumer needs during that usage occasion (a tasty, nutritious, filling, and fast lunch with minimal cleanup). Every usage occasion has a corresponding job to be done.

## THE SIGNIFICANCE OF OCCASIONS

The importance of identifying and studying key usage occasions is a lost art that is only recently reemerging as a primary tool of the marketing trade. It's been entirely too easy for brand managers and marketers to fall into the trap of focusing on demographic segments without fully considering the needs and criteria arising from consumers' different usage occasions. Packing a school lunch is a very different occasion in our household than eating lunch at home (especially during the COVID pandemic) or having a minimeal that bridges the hunger gap between lunch and dinner.

Nuno Teles, the President of Diageo Beer USA and the former CMO of Heineken USA, best described it during a Mobile Marketing Association event I participated in: "Marketers want to believe that the brand is the most important factor, but everything starts with an occasion."

I couldn't agree more.

One thing that became clear during our study of winning and losing brands was how successful products address usage occasions. Whether they were established brands or new to the category, many of our winners took market share and increased sales by addressing specific occasions—the way Jimmy Dean did when it developed its hearty breakfast options for hungry people in a hurry.

## WHAT IS THE CONTEXT?

Defining different contexts—and the specific needs arising from those contexts—is another way of looking at occasions. The context of an occasion describes the circumstances under which goods will be consumed. It involves what you'll be doing, with whom, where, and why.

Take a moment to think about the most recent Thursday night dinner you made at home.

How did you go about deciding what to have that night? How much mental effort did you put into planning? Was the purchasing process complicated or simple? Maybe you repeated a meal you've made many times. When you grocery shopped for the occasion, you might have been inclined to reflexively grab the same food products you usually choose or pick a new product that caught your eye.

Now consider another Thursday meal planning scenario: the entire extended family is coming to your house for Thanksgiving dinner (or some other annual feast you celebrate in your country). The social and emotional dimensions are much more present, right?

In this scenario, you likely ask yourself entirely different questions. If guests are traveling from far away, you might feel extra pressure to meet social expectations. You'll go out of your way to buy enough to accommodate everyone's particular tastes and sensitivities. And if you want to impress your guests, you might splurge and think less about price than you typically would for yourself or your immediate family.

No matter how complex your typical Thursday dinners might be, the Thanksgiving meal will likely take much more thought and preparation. After all, the context is completely different. Remember: the way a consumer thinks about buying is largely dictated by the occasion, and occasions are largely dictated by context.

The criteria we use to evaluate products change significantly depending on the occasion. White Claw exemplifies how powerful this insight is.

White Claw was a winning brand in the beer category. Even though White Claw is a hard seltzer, it's carved out a healthy space in the beer aisle by understanding the job beer buyers need done and fulfilling that need. Here's how:

Say you're hosting a party at your place and inviting friends. You want a variety of drinks, right? Your beer aficionado friends will want a hearty microbrew, but others will want Budweiser or Michelob. Still, others will want something lighter than beer but still alcoholic. So what will you buy to put in the ice chest for these guests? Here comes White Claw to the rescue.

White Claw uses the same packaging as beer to fit the setting (glass bottles and aluminum cans), plus it's light and refreshing with distinctive flavors. It does the job of adding variety to the beverage cooler and does it better than competitors such as Redd's Apple Ale, the comparable losing brand of beer that previously filled the role of adding variety to a cooler full of beers.

Want further proof that this nonbeer beer did the job for this usage occasion? White Claw soared during our study. From 2016 to 2019, the brand grew from $10 million in sales to $374 million and from 0.1 percent in category share to 2.2 percent. During the same period, Redd's dropped from $170 million in sales to $100 million and from 1.2 percent in category share to just 0.6 percent.

White Claw is a great example of how winning brands win occasions that grow categories. I, for one, don't drink much beer because it leaves me feeling heavy and bloated. I don't experience that issue when drinking White Claw, and as a result, I end up drinking more than if beer were the only option. For other consumers, White Claw became a substitute for wine coolers that were too sweet or glasses of wine that contained twice the alcohol content. The point is that it's a winning strategy to segment usage occasions and understand why the category as a whole is falling short on those occasions. In doing so, our winning brands swooped in, met the underserved needs, and became as popular as a hard seltzer at a summer barbecue.

I'm not suggesting that White Claw and Bang won only on a discrete type of occasion. Their stratospheric growth suggests that by meeting the distinctive needs of consumers on those discrete occasions, they also earned the right to be considered for all kinds of beer-drinking and energy-drink occasions. If you're not the best at something, you don't stand a fighting chance of becoming a Breakout Brand.

## NEED STATES AND THE JOB TO BE DONE

In his highly acclaimed book *Competing against Luck*, Harvard's Clayton Christensen argues that companies succeed because they focus on the job customers are hiring your product (or service) to do. Companies that don't do that are more likely to fail. "What (brands) really need to home in on is the progress that the customer is trying to make in a given circumstance," Christensen wrote in 2016. "What does the customer hope to accomplish?"

When we purchase a product, Christensen noted, we "hire" it to do a job for us.[1] If it performs well, we tend to hire it again the next time the job comes open. If the product fails to do the job, we fire it and look for an alternative.

---

1    Clayton M. Christensen, et al., "Know Your Customers' 'Jobs to Be Done'", *Harvard Business Review*, September 2016, https://hbr.org/2016/09/know-your-customers-jobs-to-be-done.

Customers don't want features; they want the benefits associated with getting the job done. They have needs that must be met. As Bank of America Senior Vice President Lou Paskalis said, "Need states are the true north that guides us to which customers to market to and in what way."

Winning brands understand that doing the consumers' job exceptionally well is more critical than other factors that brand managers pay much more attention to, such as customer characteristics, product attributes, new technologies, or media trends.

The truth is that brand managers rarely think enough about usage occasions and the jobs to be done. I know this because I read the briefs brand managers send to their agency partners. The briefs often include plenty of demographic attributes along with a few psychographic hints about their target customers, but they rarely include much about how those customers think about the job to be done. This oversight is a massive blunder that we'll discuss more in Chapter 8, Media & Advertising.

Say, for example, that your yogurt brand does very well with shoppers who need a quick-and-easy breakfast to take to work. But that's just a portion of all the consumers who buy yogurt. People buy yogurt for a light, midafternoon snack. They buy it to put in their kids' lunches. They buy it to have a tasty dessert in the evening. People hire yogurt for several jobs, but the only one they hire you for is breakfast. Why? Maybe it's your packaging. Maybe it's your messaging. Maybe you need to add a chocolate or cheesecake flavor that piques consumers' evening cravings. If you truly look, maybe you'll discover something completely unexpected.

One of the most impactful bodies of work I ever performed for a client was to measure category sales and market share by brand by usage occasion. The client was a yogurt brand, and we found that a new usage occasion was emerging in that category: yogurt as a dessert. A competitor was already aware of this new job and was doing the job with flavor selections (such as strawberry cheesecake) that made them appealing to folks eating yogurt as an after-dinner treat. Our client had to adjust to compete in this new usage occasion.

This new perspective on market share—looking away from *when and where* people shop but instead looking at *how and why* people consume—was completely illuminating to the brand. It suddenly became clear why their competitor was on the rise. It also became clear how this new job to be done created new opportunities for my client. and just how big of an opportunity my client had to close the gap in a couple of higher-volume usage occasions for their category. As I learned with my client, brands that develop a deeper understanding of these occasions also gain a better understanding of the different criteria consumers use to choose products for each occasion type.

## THE SHOPPING LIST

While consumers may have certain jobs, they don't necessarily go to the store with a specific brand in mind for that job. We know this from the data we collected from Out of Milk, the world's largest shopping list app, which was acquired by Numerator and used for our study. When an Out of Milk user was also a Receipt Hog user, we could see what they had gone into the store to purchase and then compare it to what they bought. We could also trigger surveys to these people. "Hey, we noticed you bought Tide detergent. When did you decide to make that purchase?" Their list had said "laundry detergent," not "Tide," which would have been easier to type into their list, so we were curious when they decided to select that brand.

People, we learned, go to the store knowing what category they want to shop for—such as "laundry detergent"—but the actual brand they buy is a decision they make when they are standing before the shelf of products and surveying the options. Consumers rarely—as in almost never—think in terms of brand names when they create their shopping lists.

Out of Milk users added around ten million items to their shopping lists each month. Bread, bananas, yogurt, pasta, you name it. If you rank the most popular shopping list items, you have to go down to the 150th position to see the first brand name—Kleenex. Coke comes in second at around the two hundredth most common shopping list item. Yet even when shoppers go into the store with Kleenex or Coke on their shopping list, we found that didn't mean the person actually intended to buy that brand. They just bought from that category in general. Kleenex has become synonymous with "facial tissue" just as Coke has become synonymous with "soda pop." It wasn't until you encountered the brand names of Cheerios and Benadryl way down the list that the brand name actually signified the shopper's premeditated intent to buy that particular brand.

One 2015 study found that three-quarters of Americans use shopping lists to plan most of their shopping trips.[2] Our research backed that up; in 2015, we surveyed five hundred thousand consumers immediately after they completed a shopping trip by randomly selecting an item from their receipt to find out when they decided to purchase that product. We found that 72 percent of the category-level purchase decisions were made before the shopper stepped foot in the store. Whether it's in an app, on a scrap of paper, or simply in their head, consumers predominantly plan even their most mundane grocery shopping—at the category level.

### WINNING OCCASIONS, STEALING SHARE

Another phenomenon we saw across our winning brands was that they win significantly more new category buyers than their fair share (what you'd expect them to attract based on their market share) while stealing a smaller share of sales from the category's biggest brands. This occurs when a brand appeals to people whose psychographics and lifestyles lead them to occasions with distinctive criteria that aren't served well by existing competitors. Here are a few data points that fortify that conclusion:

---

2    Statista Research Department, "US Consumers' Grocery Shopping List Usage 2015, By Generation," Statista, August 5, 2015, https://www.statista.com/statistics/490730/us-consumers-grocery-shopping-list-usage-generation/.

- When consumers switch from one brand to another on their next occasion, we measure the frequency of switching between these two brands with something called an Interaction Index.[3] Winning brands interact with top and second monthly shopping lists less than we'd expect but interact more with smaller brands in the third quartile (13 percent more than expected) and incredibly 6.5 times more than expected with their category's smallest, bottom quartile brands.

- Winning brands sourced 45 percent LESS sales value from the category's highest market share brand than we'd expect based on the two brands' relative market shares.

- Conversely, winning brands source 42 percent MORE sales value from the third quartile of brands within their category and a whopping 55 percent MORE than expected from bottom quartile brands.

A key takeaway is that winning brands tend to meet needs that the largest competitors can't while far outperforming the category's smaller niche brands. We also learned that a key element of their success is these brands' understanding of the "why" consumers are buying their brand for a particular usage occasion.

## THE WHY BEHIND THE USAGE

Michelob Ultra and Febreze are winning brands that pay close attention to *why* consumers buy their brand.

Michelob Ultra, for instance, has positioned itself as the beer for athletic types who run, swim, ride bikes, have fun outdoors, and

---

3   See the Appendix for more detail about normal switching behavior and the Interaction Index.

socialize around those physical pursuits. Their product is a low-carb, low-calorie, light beer, of course, but they don't talk about that. Instead, they talk about taste and ingredients and promote active lifestyles. Where Michelob Ultra says it's "brewed for those who understand that it's only worth it if you enjoy it," other light beers lead with "low-carb" messaging. As a result, Michelob Ultra is flourishing while other light beers are struggling. By competing on flavor first, Michelob Ultra beat out other light beers and stole share directly from the category's regular beers—particularly in line with the broader cultural and psychographic shifts in favor of a healthier diet.

The brand had to win on even more occasions to continue its rapid growth. To do this, the brand continued to invest heavily in encouraging healthy and active lifestyles while extending that positioning into the broader world of sports.[4] As Ricardo Marques, Michelob Ultra Vice resident of Marketing, put it: "Bringing our brand into different occasions, namely sports viewing, (has been) instrumental in helping us accelerate the momentum of the brand." His words, not mine.

Febreze also bucked the trend in its air freshener category to become a winning brand. Unlike brands like Glade (our losing brand in the category), which primarily focuses on advertising the pleasantness of their different scents, Febreze focuses on the way their product eliminates odor and creates the feeling of a clean environment. As a result, consumers are drawn to the product because it's a substitute for doing all the hard work. If they can have the essence of a clean home without having to mop all of the floors or dust every corner, they'll take it.

How did Febreze meet the consumers' why so effectively? They did the research. They looked at how the air freshener actually affected

4    Michael LoRé, "How Sports Helped Fuel Michelob Ultra's Growth, Especially during the Pandemic," *Forbes*, September 3, 2021, https://www.forbes.com/sites/michaellore/2021/09/03/how-sports-helped-fuel-michelob-ultras-growth-especially-during-the-pandemic/?sh=1810d6246bc1.

people in their homes. Why would consumers actually use one product over another? The study went beyond smell and focused on how consumers felt after using the product. Febreze discovered that consumers don't want to use air fresheners that smell like they're covering something up. They want a space that feels fresh and clean—that was the job to be done.

---

### USING THE FIVE WHYS

The concept seems simple, doesn't it? All you need to know is *why* consumers need a certain type of product. Unfortunately, most brands aren't willing to go deep enough to find the real answers.

One of my first managers was an advocate for the Five Whys approach to problem-solving.[5] The Five Whys approach was created by the founder of Toyota as a means of finding both the root cause of a problem as well as its solution. If you want to get to the root of a problem (so you can develop a product that solves that problem) keep asking, *Why?* By the fifth *why* you should be at the core reason. Sometimes you get to the root cause and solution with fewer *whys*, but rarely does it take more than five.

Here's an example of how Febreze might have used the five whys in consumer interviews to find a deeper level of motivation for why consumers buy air fresheners:

*Interviewer:* Why do you buy air fresheners?
*Consumer:* They make my house smell better.
*Interviewer:* Why do you want your house to smell better?

---

5    Mind Tools Content Team, "5 Whys: Getting to the Root of a Problem Quickly," *Mind Tools* (blog), accessed August 30, 2022, https://www.mindtools.com/pages/article/newTMC_5W.htm.

*Consumer:* It's just nicer to smell pleasant smells than dirty ones.

*Interviewer:* You mentioned "dirty" smells. Why the word "dirty"?

*Consumer:* If I don't spend all my time cleaning up after the kids, the dog, and the dishes, the place smells "dirty" to me.

*Interviewer:* So is that why you buy air fresheners, to cover up those dirty smells?

*Consumer:* Yes, but no. If the scent is too strong, it's obvious that it's just "covering up" something stinky—it has to get rid of the stink, or otherwise it's just going to bug me.

*Interviewer:* Why would it bug you?

*Consumer:* Well, I guess because then I know I still have to clean it up. The problem's not gone, it's hanging over me.

By asking why five times, you get a sense of just how Febreze could figure out that what consumers really wanted was a product that eliminates odors to make their home feel clean. These consumers don't want their house to smell like lilacs or pine. First and foremost, they want it to smell clean. So let's offer them a solution that eliminates odors and leaves behind a clean, fresh, unperfumed environment.

## THE CONSUMER'S JOURNEY

We've discussed the usage occasions and the jobs to be done. But how does the shopper ultimately decide?

Winning brands know how to think through a consumer's journey. How is the consumer thinking about what they need, and how does that thinking lead them to buy and use a specific product? While consumers may not follow a clear and consistent rubric for making their purchase decisions, we know that they tend to follow a loose hierar-chy of criteria that must be "satisficed."

## WHAT IS SATISFICING?

You don't hear people use this term much, but it is a behavior we all regularly engage in.

Satisficing is a decision-making strategy where you settle for an acceptable or adequate result rather than investing time and mental energy in finding an optimal solution. When confronted with tasks (like shopping), satisficing results in making a prag-matic choice that simply satisfies your basic criteria. You're not bothering to find the optimal solution, just one that works.

The term was coined by American scientist and Nobel laure-ate Herbert Simon in 1956.

In our work with clients, we have found that attribute-based analy-ses of purchase occasions can reveal how consumers follow different choice hierarchies. Consider the accompanying graphic, "Dimensions of Choice Analysis for Shampoo." The diagram breaks down the dif-ferent benefits consumers might look for when purchasing shampoo and the related attributes that help inform their choice. For example, if they are motivated by a desire to preserve or emphasize their hair col-oring, they'll give more weight to factors related to "Color Treatment". If they're shopping for the best value, they'll care more about the price and the size of the shampoo container. For each consumer, on each occasion, these attributes carry their relative weights when influenc-ing a final purchase (or usage) decision.

Through advanced modeling of millions of purchase occasions by hundreds of thousands of consumers, we estimate the relative importance (weight) of each of these attributes. For example, we can establish the percentage of consumers for whom dandruff relief is an absolute requirement: 9.8 percent in this study. In the second graphic, we break down the choice hierarchy of these dandruff-relief-motivated shoppers even more. About half of them also want a shampoo that will leave their hair feeling clean at a reasonable price. Meanwhile, the other half of dandruff-driven shampoo buyers are primarily seeking additional therapeutic benefits while also considering the use of natural ingredients.

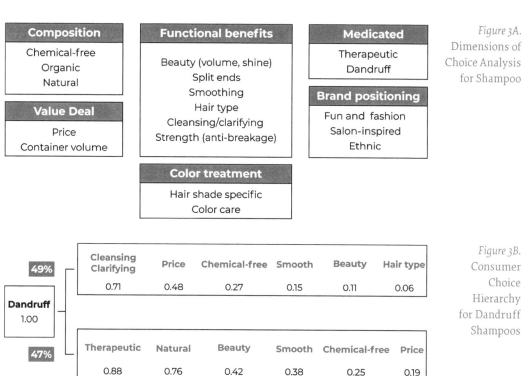

Figure 3A. Dimensions of Choice Analysis for Shampoo

Figure 3B. Consumer Choice Hierarchy for Dandruff Shampoos

While this analysis was performed from the perspective of purchase occasions, there are even more important attributes that tend to reveal themselves only through the lens of a performance-based analysis of usage occasions: how well the cap or spout works, how easy it is to dispense the desired amount, how the shampoo smells, how it feels as you wash your hair, how your hair and scalp feel after showering, how easy it is to style your hair, how your hair looks after you style it, how confident and attractive you feel after using it, and if and how others take notice. These experiential benefits often reveal what consumers truly look for when they buy (and most especially repeat buy) shampoo.

In the next chapter, we'll dive much deeper into how consumers behave during purchase occasions.

## FINAL THOUGHTS

I'm not the first person to recommend occasion-based segmentation and marketing, but our study shows just how powerful that approach can be when brands prioritize it. All brands do some kind of demographic (and hopefully psychographic) segmentation. Still, I can count on one hand the number of brands I've worked with that use occasion-based segmentation as a primary basis for their go-to-market. Have a look at your agency briefs. Do you emphasize who your target consumers are instead of what they are trying to accomplish and the challenges they face?

If you as a brand manager or marketer get a deeper understanding of the occasions for which consumers might need your product, you can better understand the criteria consumers use to choose among the available products. The study of usage occasions must also be tied to how people shop for each type of occasion (e.g., customer journey mapping). Too often, these studies focus on usage occasions and product experience—which are critically important—but fail to connect these demand moments with how consumers then shop for these products. They fail to ask, "Exactly when and how did you decide to buy this product to begin with?" You must unify these things into a customer journey—the usage occasion, the job to be done, and the criteria the shopper uses to choose a product.

This unification isn't easy, and splitting "consumer insights" and "shopper insights" into separate functions with their own research budgets and priorities makes it more challenging. As the head of shopper insights for a top-tier CPG company recently confided in me,

"The work our consumer insights team does to segment "Demand Moments" (think usage occasions) is probably the best in the industry. It's led to some great product innovations and hugely successful media campaigns. But we've had a hard time translating that into success at retail."

Why? Because retailers don't think in terms of usage occasions. They think in terms of shopping occasions. They want to know how people decide when and where to shop based on those future usage occasions, along with how they choose particular products over others in the store. Linking usage occasions with shopping occasions is critical to retail activation, which involves getting the retailer to carry your products, merchandise them well, and coordinate shopper marketing with your national brand marketing efforts—topics we'll discuss in greater detail in the chapters to come.

### KEY TAKEAWAYS

- Identifying and studying key usage occasions is a lost art. Brand managers and marketers must focus on the needs and criteria arising from consumers' usage occasions.

- Winning brands understand that doing the consumers' job exceptionally well is more critical than others such as customer characteristics, product attributes, new technologies, or media trends.

- Winners segment usage occasions and understand why the category as a whole is falling short on those occasions. Then they swoop in, meet the underserved needs, and gain sales and market share.

- Think through a consumer's journey. What triggers their need, and how does that lead them to buy and use a specific product? Consumers tend to follow a loose hierarchy of criteria that must be satisficed.

- Learn why consumers seek a certain type of product. Most brands don't go deep enough to find the real answers. Agency briefs rarely examine what customers really think about the job to be done. This oversight is a huge mistake. Apply approaches like the Five Whys to gain a deeper understanding of what consumers want from your product.

- When you measure category sales and market share by usage occasion, it often becomes clear why a particular competitor is climbing. Aggregate measures of market share fail to explain the most fundamental drivers of consumer behavior.

# 4

# PURCHASE OCCASIONS

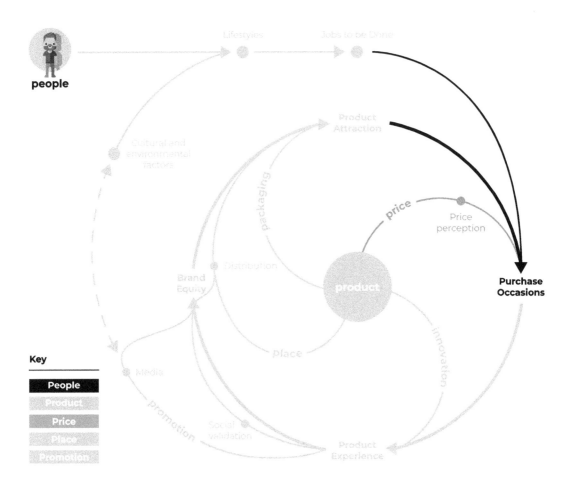

**people**

**Key**

| People |
| Product |
| Price |
| Place |
| Promotion |

W hat convinces people to put items in their shopping cart? Do they buy the same basic products over and over again? Or do they "shop around" and try new products to see if they're any better than the old standbys? How important are price and packaging? Do they read the labels to compare ingredients or nutritional information?

While it seems we should be able to answer these questions by asking shoppers, the unfortunate truth is that the shoppers themselves *don't know*. They don't know why they switch brands, or why one jar of applesauce appeals to them and another doesn't. They'll tell you that environmentally friendly business practices drive them to buy certain brands. Still, when you look at the items on their receipts, it's clear that an entirely different set of values are taking priority when they choose what to buy.

Managing a brand in a world of uncertainty and misdirection is difficult. But our study of a billion shopping trips and our review of the latest studies on consumer behavior detected certain truths that could help you increase sales and gain greater market share the way our fifty-eight winning brands did over four years.

In this chapter, I'll explore how shoppers make purchase decisions, how emotions (much more so than rational thought) influence those decisions, and how you can become the architect of your customer's choices. We'll explore what motivates shoppers, how they use mental shortcuts to make decisions, and why dropping your price is not the best way to grow a brand.

## SUBCONSCIOUS DECISION-MAKING

Let's be clear: shoppers rarely analyze the pros and cons of competing products before making a choice. Nearly one in five grocery store trips results in purchases of more than twenty products. Think about how exhausting shopping would be if you had to evaluate which brand of product you would purchase in each category by reading all the labels (or online reviews) about the product. That's simply not how we go about making 99 percent of our purchase decisions.

Most of the time, shoppers buy a product that meets their basic needs. They'll consider the product against a loose set of criteria, but they won't expend the energy required to choose the absolute best solution (i.e., *satisficing*).

PepsiCo's former marketing executive Will Leach, who is a student of both marketing and cognitive science with years of firsthand practical experience, concluded, "When it comes to buying decisions, most consumers are simply not thinking at all."

According to the Nobel Prize–winning research of Daniel Kahneman and Amos Tversky, we have two "systems" for thinking. System 1 tells us *how we should feel*. System 2 (when we engage it) tells us *what we should do*. Many of us might believe our lives are governed mostly by System 2, but for most purchase decisions where we don't need to consciously evaluate each product's features versus a set of buying criteria, System 1 is in charge. We let our emotions make these quick decisions for us, and we don't spend much time engaging System 2's more rational thinking.

"We are not rational beings influenced by emotion," Leach explains in his excellent book *Marketing to Mindstates*. "Instead, we are emotional beings who hope to rationalize our behaviors after we make them."[1]

Shoppers can tell you why they chose one product over another, but their explanations are unreliable. Beer buyers surveyed immediately after a purchase will claim that the brand they just bought represents their preferred brand more than 90 percent of the time. Yet, our data shows that less than 50 percent of those same shoppers will buy that "preferred brand" again on their next shopping trip. The data reveals that we buy our preferred brand in any product category barely half the time. So, unless our brand preferences are constantly changing—and they're not—we must not fully understand why we choose the brands we do.

This uncertainty doesn't mean consumers don't have brand preferences or loyalty to those brands. But it does suggest that human curiosity, a hardwired desire for variety, and the constant need to validate preferences by actually trying alternatives are even stronger motivators.

Why do 71 percent of consumers claim, "It is important to me that companies I buy from align with my values," while remaining completely oblivious to a company's values when they make purchase decisions? Because they're rationalizing. After all, they do not want to face the ugly truth that their actions don't align very well with their beliefs.

---

1    Will Leach, *Marketing to Mindstates: The Practical Guide to Applying Behavior Design to Research and Marketing* (Lioncrest Publishing, 2018), 50-52.

Consider this survey that reports "Price/Value" is of little importance to consumers relative to a company's environmentally friendly business practices and social responsibility.

Environmentally-friendly business practices

71%

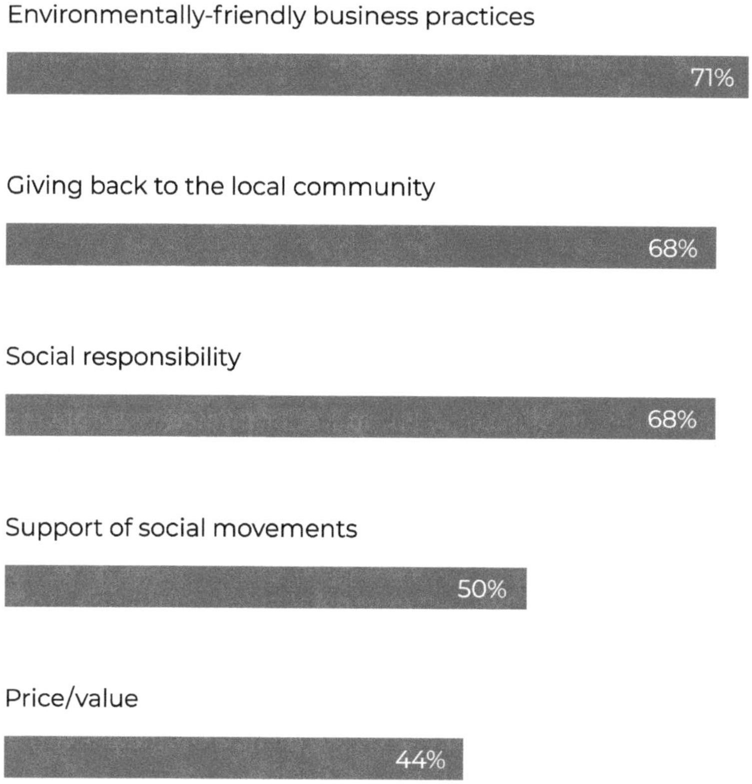

*Figure 4A.*
Consumer
Claims
about Which
Company
Attributes They
Find Most
Important

Giving back to the local community

68%

Social responsibility

68%

Support of social movements

50%

Price/value

44%

Percent of total respondents: N=420 people who made a purchase online or in-store in last six months. Source: Clutch 2019 PR and Corporate Social Responsibility Survey.

While the surveyed consumers probably believe their claims, their behaviors reflect an entirely different set of values that predominantly ignore social good in favor of personal gain.

As the legendary science fiction author Robert A. Heinlein penned in a 1953 novel that explored human nature, "Man is not a rational animal; he is a rationalizing animal." If only this had remained science fiction rather than having been proven beyond a shadow of a doubt by countless experiments in recent decades. Social scientists now believe that rationalization allows us to hide our truest, deepest motives from others by hiding them from ourselves (so as to not get caught) while at the same time remaining able to impress others with our judgment while maintaining our moral integrity, self-concept, and self-worth. The alternative is to face up to the incredibly uncomfortable feeling of cognitive dissonance—when our actions contradict our beliefs.

## THE VALUE OF THINGS

If asking people directly what motivates them results in misleading answers, how can we truly understand what motivates shoppers to make purchase decisions?

In his book *Kotler on Marketing*, Philip Kotler posited that "buyers think in terms of the value for the money: what they get for what they pay."[2] There's only one problem: their notion of value is always changing. Marketing professor and author of *Irresistible*, Adam Alter, put it this way: "(Shoppers) just have a set of general guiding principles that are very malleable, that change across time."[3]

One way to counter so much unpredictability is to become the architect of your consumers' choices. Guide them, and make it easier for them to find and choose your brand. You'll be doing them a big favor; in recent years, behavioral economists have shown that presenting consumers with too many choices can lead to a "tyranny of choice." You would think that having more choices allows consumers to get precisely what they want. Still, the research shows that buyers with more options to choose from experience more regret (*Did I make the right choice?*), decreased satisfaction (*I bet the other product would have tasted better*), unmet expectations, and indecisiveness.

---

2    Philip Kotler, *Kotler on Marketing: How to Create, Win, and Dominate Markets* (New York: The Free Press, 1999).

3    Adam Alter, *Irresistible: The Rise of Addictive Technology and the Business of Keeping Us Hooked*, (New York: Penguin Press, 2017).

Choice architecture, a term introduced by behavioral economists Richard Thaler and Cass Sunstein in their book *Nudge*, involves the conscious design of how options influence consumer decision-making.[4] Choice architecture includes reducing choice overload by eliminating trade-offs, limiting choices, or providing guides that ease consumer decision-making.

A great historical example in marketing is Aquafresh. Before Aquafresh hit the market, toothpaste was positioned to meet one of three objectives: protection from cavities, better breath, or whiter teeth. You could buy a product that whitened teeth, but it wasn't designed specifically to fight cavities. The product that fought cavities didn't include high-quality breath fresheners. The breath-freshening product did little to fight cavities or whiten teeth.

Aquafresh reasoned that consumers don't want to choose which benefit they value more, so they designed a product that would satisfy all three objectives. The problem was convincing consumers that a single product could deliver on all three simultaneously. To drive that value proposition home, they created a toothpaste that flowed from the tube in three distinct colors, one for each benefit. This simple design tapped into consumers' subconscious decision-making by eliminating an unnecessary trade-off, and the brand took off.

Another way to use choice architecture is to consider how your product looks on the shelf. Its merchandising and packaging and how its price is displayed relative to other products heavily influence consumer choice.

Similarly, claims you make on the packaging influence choice. Claiming "Italy's number one brand" on a sauce label will impact a shopper differently than "Just like Grandma used to make." The claims you make dictate the criteria you want to be judged on, and your criteria may not align with the shopper's criteria.

---

4    Cass R. Sunstein and Richard Thaler, *Nudge: Improving Decisions About Health, Wealth, and Happiness*, (New York: Penguin Books, 2009).

It's crucial to remember that each factor of choice architecture primarily influences consumers at the subconscious level. Whether you're trying to win a purchase occasion through price, merchandising, or messaging, you want to connect at the emotional level without having to explain all the rational reasons why your brand is the right choice.

## BREAKING DOWN SHOPPING BEHAVIOR

Shoppers look through a variety of emotional lenses when making purchase decisions. These include higher-order goals, motivations, regulatory focus, and cognitive heuristics. Let's take a look at each one of these.

### HIGHER-ORDER GOALS

Products and services address four needs: functional, emotional, life-changing, and social. Generally, the more needs a brand can handle, the greater the customers' loyalty (i.e., probability of repeat purchases) and the higher the company's sustained revenue growth.

While all of these needs are important, you must be able to tap into the higher-order emotional goals. Beyond the functional benefit of this product or service, what's the benefit to someone's life? How will your product make their life better?

Many of the winners in our study effectively targeted higher-order goals over functional goals and soared over competitors as a result.

For example, Nicorette and Always Discreet appealed to the quality of the consumer's future life, thus tapping into their emotions. Nicorette's marketing says little about how the product helps customers stop smoking. It focuses instead on how the product helps customers reduce anxiety and improve their wellness so that they can live a long life of meaningful experiences. Nicorette encourages consumers to consider future moments that really count, thus tapping into their subconscious desire to be there for those moments. Similarly, Always Discreet moved beyond the function of their

## The Elements of Value Pyramid

Products and services deliver fundamental elements of value that address four kinds of needs: functional, emotional, life changing, and social impact. In general, the more elements provided, the greater customers' loyalty and the higher the company's sustained revenue growth.

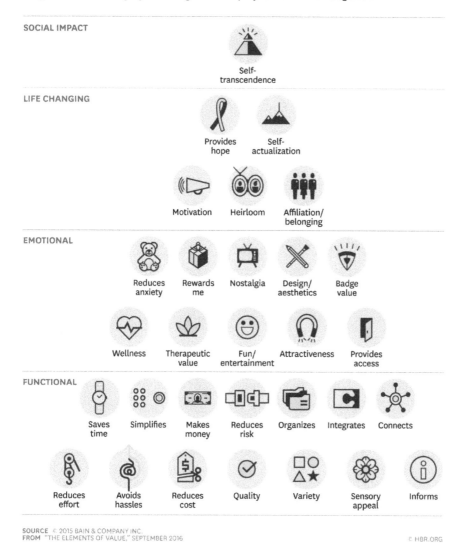

SOCIAL IMPACT

Self-transcendence

LIFE CHANGING

Provides hope · Self-actualization

Motivation · Heirloom · Affiliation/belonging

EMOTIONAL

Reduces anxiety · Rewards me · Nostalgia · Design/aesthetics · Badge value

Wellness · Therapeutic value · Fun/entertainment · Attractiveness · Provides access

FUNCTIONAL

Saves time · Simplifies · Makes money · Reduces risk · Organizes · Integrates · Connects

Reduces effort · Avoids hassles · Reduces cost · Quality · Variety · Sensory appeal · Informs

SOURCE © 2015 BAIN & COMPANY INC.
FROM "THE ELEMENTS OF VALUE," SEPTEMBER 2016

© HBR.ORG

product and focused instead on how the product allows customers to maintain an active lifestyle.

David Aaker did an extensive case study on Michelob Ultra and revealed how the brand responded when light beers were getting a bad rap for being a watered-down version of beer. Michelob Ultra focused less on having fewer calories and more on athletic performance. The brand's marketing went beyond the functional benefit and appealed to the way many consumers hope to live their lives while still enjoying beer. Michelob Ultra also made clear how its product helped consumers avoid this unnecessary trade-off between enjoying beer and staying fit.

Febreze beat out Glade in a similar way. The brand focused less on scents and more on how the product made customers feel about their homes. While Glade was promoting the way their product could fill a space with its vanilla almond scent, Febreze focused on the higher-order emotional goal of how customers actually wanted their homes to feel clean and inviting. Of course, Febreze could only reach this conclusion by doing deep ethnographic studies and continuing to ask why (see the breakout in Chapter 3). Febreze knew their customers would not be able to give a rational explanation of why they prefer Febreze because the true reasons are emotional.

Even the show *Mad Men* regularly tapped into the importance of higher-order emotional needs. In one episode, a lipstick maker presented different shades of lipstick. But instead of talking about all the shades, Don Draper and his colleagues developed a simple tagline: "Mark your man." Subconsciously, the tagline pointed to the way a woman could leave a distinctive mark on their man, which would have an emotional benefit. It was a bit animalistic, but the episode effectively made its point.

The bottom line is this: any time you assume consumers are thinking rationally about functional benefits, you leave yourself open to a competitor who can appeal to higher-order emotional and life-changing benefits.

## MOTIVATIONS

If goals provide us with a destination, motivations move us to action.

Research shows that nine primary motivations drive people to pursue their goals: achievement, autonomy, belonging, competence, empowerment, engagement, esteem, nurturance, and security. While these motivations may interact, we often have a primary motivation in pursuing a particular goal.

In *Marketing to Mindstates*, Leach encourages brands to ask: "Which motivations best describe how my customers want to feel in the moment of buying or using my brand?"[5] I would expand this to consider which motivations describe how customers want to feel when buying or using any product in the category. The answer to that question can inform how best to position your brand against the competition.

Leach argues that you must understand the consumer's underlying motivations for buying your brand, and I agree. Understanding consumer motivations for buying your product category (and your brand in particular) could be one of the most valuable pieces of research you will ever conduct. The caveat, of course, is that directly asking consumers what motivates them is fraught with rationalizations that have little bearing on reality.

For this reason, Leach offers a clever image-sorting exercise that helps you identify consumers' hidden motivations without triggering peoples' needs to rationalize their responses. In the exercise, he offers various photographs with emotional connotations for people. For example, there might be a photo of two people hugging, a family dinner, a person driving in a stressful situation, and many others. No words, no context, just an image. He then gives an example of needing to buy a product for a certain job, such as unclogging a drain. He asks readers to choose five or so pictures that are most closely associated with how they feel about that need and five pictures that have little to do with the job of unclogging the drain. From those choices, he can better discern the emotional motivations driving the person on that type of occasion.

If you're a marketing manager, you can't simply ask your customers what emotional benefits your products should deliver. Consumers

5    Leach, *Marketing to Mindstates*, 118.

probably don't know or won't be able to give an honest answer because they aren't fully tuned in to why they feel what they feel.

## REGULATORY APPROACH

If you ask consumers to tell a friend about why they use your brand's product (or products in your category), they will likely focus on how it allows them to gain benefits or avoid negatives. This insight is the basis for understanding consumer behavior in the context of regulatory focus theory (RFT). RFT examines the relationship between the motivation of a person and how they go about achieving their goal.

If consumers in your category predominantly focus on what they gain, you should focus your brand's messaging on maximizing the positive benefits. If consumers focus on how the product helps them avoid negatives, your messaging should focus on helping people minimize these pains.

When I interviewed Nicorette's brand director, Scott Yacovino, about the changes that led to the brand's breakout success from 2016 to 2019, he told me the following story:

> We conducted an A&U (Attitudes and Usage) based segmentation, including an understanding of where consumers were on their journey in terms of stopping smoking. For example, were they looking to reduce smoking versus trying to quit entirely? Had they tried to quit before but failed? The key insight from this study was that our consumers love smoking, and it's a big part of their life. Nicorette had been oriented around a consumer message of "I feel a prisoner to smoking," which was a negative framing. Instead, we needed a more empathetic orientation which led us to, "I love smoking, but I realize it's time to make a change."

Nicorette wants to encourage and empower its consumers to let them know, "We're with you on the journey." Their "What's your why?" campaign that resulted from this discovery was so successful because it captured their consumers' feelings and focused on the positive rather than the negative that had historically been a feature of their communications.

RFT is simple but has profound effects. The consumer is shopping because they have jobs that need to be done. They need products for those jobs. And as they examine products on the shelf, they evaluate them according to their desired gain or their pain relief.

According to Philip Kotler, *positioning* is the effort to implant a product's key benefits and differentiation in the customers' minds. The *full positioning* of the brand is called the brand's *value proposition*. The consumer's regulatory approach and mindset will influence whether they're receptive to one particular value proposition over another.

Brands within the same category could go in two different directions here. Take the shampoo category, for example. Some brands focus on how their products provide more voluminous or shiny hair. Presumably, they understand that their customers buy their brand to *gain* those benefits. Other shampoo brands focus on how the product fixes oily or damaged hair. Their customers are motivated to relieve the pain of limp, greasy hair.

In *Delivering Profitable Value*, Michael J. Lanning argues that a brand's value proposition is its promise to deliver a particular resulting experience. This relentless focus on communicating and delivering "a particular resulting experience" has been at the core of Olly's incredible success as an upstart dietary supplements brand.

In a 2016 interview, Olly's CEO, Brad Harrington, said that among supplements, "most products are ingredient driven, so you didn't know what to choose." Olly decided to simplify things for the shopper and "make everything about the end benefit versus the individual ingredients."[6] In the words of Brad's co-founder, Eric Ryan (who also founded the highly successful Method brand of cleaning products),

6    Connie Loizos, "Olly Has Built a Breakout Brand in a Crowded Space: Here's How," TechCrunch, June 8, 2016, https://techcrunch.com/2016/06/08/olly-has-built-a-breakout-brand-in-a-crowded-space-heres-how/.

"Instead of selling melatonin, we sell sleep. To me, it was such an obvious thing to do that I can't understand why no one had done it before."[7]

## COGNITIVE HEURISTICS

To avoid cognitive overload and overly time-consuming decision-making, consumers naturally apply heuristical shortcuts that help them find satisfactory solutions, rather than optimal ones. We often call these shortcuts "rules of thumb" because they are generally good guides to help us quickly attain an adequate result without the exhaustion associated with pursuing an optimal one.

Unfortunately, heuristics tend to bias our decision-making. Take a look at this Cognitive Bias Codex, which I keep hanging in my office to remind me of how easily biased and irrational our decision-making can be.

At the same time, heuristics can be a blessing because they simplify how we approach marketing. Most people are unaware of their biases, but cognitive biases are hardwired into the circuitry of our brains and act as an invisible hand directing almost every decision we make. As a clever marketer, you can benevolently leverage these known biases to influence consumers' decisions in your favor.

The phenomenon of cognitive biases is helpful in explaining exactly why certain marketing "tricks" work. For example, when consumers are given a choice between three products at three price points, where the top-level one is the "premium" option and much more expensive, most consumers will see the middle option as a bargain. If the premium option wasn't presented at all, the consumers typically choose the cheapest one.

The Cognitive Bias Codex can be a bit overwhelming to sort through and harness. This is why Will Leach's book *Marketing to Mindstates* summarizes the top twenty-one biases in consumer

---

7    Susan Caminiti, "How Method's Eric Ryan Is Disrupting the Vitamin Market One Gummy at a Time," *CNBC*, October 13, 2017, https://www.cnbc.com/2017/10/13/eric-ryans-newest-company-olly-is-reinventing-the-vitamin-market.html.

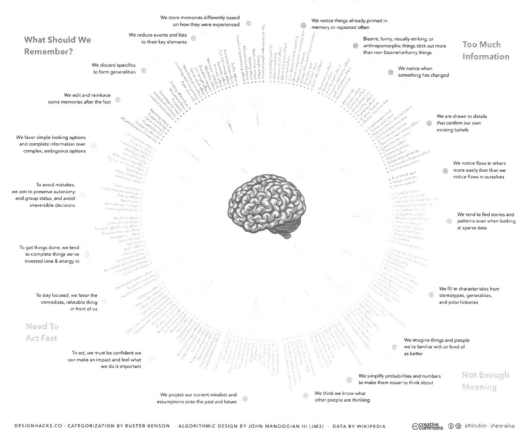

purchase decisions. For example, Elimination by Aspects (EBA) is a heuristic approach that consumers take to narrow the field of eligible candidates to get the job done. Consumers end up making a final choice through a series of eliminations. At each step, the consumer selects an attribute or aspect they consider important and eliminates any alternatives lacking that attribute. Then the next most important attribute is selected, and more brands are eliminated. The process continues until only one alternative is left. This is primarily done subconsciously for fast-moving consumer goods while often occurring more consciously for higher-value, less-frequent purchases.

Another common bias driving shopper behavior is the Status Quo Bias, Leach says. This bias is when a consumer wants to save the time

*Figure 4C.*
Cognitive
Bias Codex

and energy it takes to consider new products and instead opts to choose the product they've previously bought. This behavior is often attributed to brand loyalty driven by an emotional connection, but it's mostly driven by our lazy brains' status quo heuristic and the desire to avoid change.

## THE IMMUTABLE LAWS OF MARKETING

So, how can marketers grow sales using what we know about consumer motivation?

Jack Trout and Al Ries's timeless book, *The 22 Immutable Laws of Marketing*, offers some suggestions that dovetail nicely with the findings of our study, including:

1. In every category, "some attributes are more important to customers than others. You must try and own the most important attribute." Olly did this when they focused on delivering "sleep" while their competitors focused on melatonin.

2. "Once an attribute is successfully taken by your competition, it's gone...Your job is to seize a different attribute, dramatize the value of your attribute, and thus increase your share." Febreze did this beautifully by focusing on "odor elimination" and the smell of a clean home rather than on the artificial scents of their competitors in the air freshener category.

3. Sometimes the key to growth is to stop focusing on how to beat your direct competitors head-to-head and instead figure out why consumers who could or should choose your category for a given occasion don't.[8] Winning those occasions will grow

---

8 Al Ries and Jack Trout, *The 22 Immutable Laws of Marketing: Violate Them at Your Own Risk* (New York: HarperBusiness, 1994), 11.

the category and disproportionately favor your brand. White Claw discovered an unmet need in the beer category and became a winning brand—even though they aren't a beer.

The best way to find consumers who should buy your category but don't is through purchase-triggered surveys or ethnographies. Although consumers are biased, properly structured surveys can tease out valuable insights. With purchase-triggered surveys, you gain real-time insights into why a consumer bought a specific product for a specific occasion. In some cases, you might notice a customer has several items for a specific job but is missing an obvious one. For example, they might have chips and salsa and a bunch of beverages but not beer. In this case, you can ask why they didn't get beer. Another example: you notice a consumer with a particular lifestyle that often leads people like him to purchase products in your category. But that consumer doesn't shop your category. Here, you can again use a non-purchase-triggered survey, an interview, or a full ethnography to solve the deeper why's behind their rejection of your product's category.

Sometimes, shoppers told us that the product was too big to fit in their fridge or freezer. In this case, the problem was clear; there was a packaging issue. In other cases, the product was "too difficult to use." For example, some laundry detergents are in such large containers that it's difficult not to spill them while pouring. If a competitor has a drip-proof top, consumers will choose them to avoid the mess. In other cases, the messaging about the product did not break through to the consumer. While the consumer didn't articulate this directly, they did indicate the product wouldn't meet the criteria or values they have, even when it should.

BodyArmor and Bang are perfect examples of brands that made inroads in a category by noticing why consumers weren't purchasing any other brands in their category, such as their corresponding losing brands: Gatorade and Rockstar. Their research found that consumers were not happy with the amount of sugar and calories in their competitors' products, so the two brands eliminated both from their products and focused on messaging that indicated their healthier approach.

## MAKING SHOPPING EASIER

Though shopper behavior can be extremely unpredictable, we learned from our study that guiding shoppers through their shopping experience can go a long way in purchase decisions.

Nicorette was one of only two brands among our fifty-eight winners that clearly gained at the expense of private-label competitors. When I asked Nicorette's senior brand manager, Scott Yacovino, how Nicorette achieved such exceptional success, he said improved merchandising was key.

> It's an overwhelming category that's especially hard to shop. There are gums, patches, lozenges, and different dosage levels, and it's often behind the counter so you have to ask a clerk for help. We focused on in-store behavior—the decision hierarchy of how shoppers shop the category. As the most important national brand in the category, we were in a special position to collaborate with retailers and be a voice for the consumer. We want to convert at retail and not push people away. It was just too easy for people to get frustrated and walk away, so we added signage at retail that made it easy for consumers to navigate to the right product for their needs.

This approach helped their retailer partners grow private-label sales by 22 percent from 2016 to 2019. The real winner was Nicorette, which grew 55 percent over the same period and gained six points of share in the process.

Many brands could learn from Nicorette, even if their category isn't quite as complex. The truth is that consumers are rarely sure which product is best for them. How are they supposed to know without researching and trying each option? Any guidance they receive can go a long way, and how a product gets merchandised (displayed) can make it easier for consumers to choose the right product for their particular needs.

*Figure 4D.*
In-Store Display
Designed
to Help
Consumers
Choose the
Right Product

Though merchandising is rarely within a brand's control, you can influence your products' display by bringing data-backed insights to retailers. If you can help retailers solve their shoppers' problems through an improved layout or signage, then you are offering a path to increasing overall category sales—everyone wins. After all, retailers don't want shoppers walking away without purchasing a product or being unsatisfied because they've chosen the wrong product.

If Nicorette could partner with retailers to beat out the retailers' private-label brands, you can too. You just have to help deliver a shopping experience that will lead to overall category growth for the retailer. Making the category easier to shop is a great place to start.

### PRICE AND PRICE PERCEPTION

In his landmark book *Competitive Strategy*, Michael Porter suggested that being the low-price leader is one of just three primary winning competitive strategies companies use (along with "differentiation" and "focus"). So how could it be that none of our winning brands employed this strategy?

Dozens of CPG brands grew their sales by more than $30 million and increased shares by more than 1.5 percent from 2016 to 2019 using a price leadership strategy. However, **every single one of those brands was a private-label retailer brand.**

As noted earlier in the book, it's nearly impossible for national brands to win on price in the presence of private-label competition—especially as the perceived quality of private-label products continues to improve. As Kotler put it, "The art of marketing is largely the art of brand building. When something is not a brand, it will probably be viewed as a commodity. Then price is what counts. When the price is the only thing that counts, the only winner is the low-cost producer."[9] If you're a national brand and 35 percent of your revenue gets spent on sales and marketing, it's not possible to offer your products at a lower price than a retailer's private-label products.

Price is a crucial part of a brand's value proposition and competitive positioning, but there is little evidence that brands can change pricing or leverage promotions to drive long-term growth. There is, however, ample evidence that pricing missteps and over-reliance on trade promotions are the hallmarks of a brand in decline. Why? Because consumers learn to interpret prices as signals of quality, value, and competitive positioning. When brands "promote" themselves by temporarily cutting their price, they actually train consumers to value their products based on those temporary, promoted prices. These "reference prices" in consumers' minds lead them to see the more typical everyday pricing as expensive. In fact, in studying the effects of price promotions on our winning and losing brands' performance, we discovered that consumers are 10 percent more likely to switch away from a brand on the very next purchase occasion after having bought

---

9    Philip Kotler, *Kotler on Marketing.*

it on sale. We also found no evidence that changes in pricing or promotional activity could explain the success of any of our fifty-eight winning brands. However, those brands that relied more heavily on promotions to drive their sales were more likely to experience lower growth or sales declines year over year. This is entirely consistent with the findings of numerous scientific studies that have tracked the long-term effects of price reductions and promotions on shopper behavior.[10]

Consumers often interpret lower prices as indicative of lower quality and even value. If your brand competes on price, it's become tough to win against even lower-priced, private-label competition. In fact, according to our study, it's the most likely path a brand can take to becoming a losing brand. Palmolive dish soap, Colgate mouthwash, Barilla pasta sauce, Blue Bonnet margarine, and Bisquick baking mix are all examples of brands that lost head-to-head against private-label on price. In contrast, a branded competitor rapidly grew their sales and share with higher "premium" pricing.

Premium pricing conveys higher quality and greater value to shoppers—as long as the product delivers that value when consumers use it. Swiffer, Nicorette, Rao's, Liquid I.V., Biofreeze, Olly, Similac, and Kodiak Cakes are some of the clear examples of winning brands from our study that won with premium products at a premium price.

When you compare Walmart.com's prices of Kodiak Cakes with Bisquick and Walmart's Great Value pancake and baking mix (Figure 4E), you immediately notice that Kodiak Cakes' price is multitudes higher than the others.[11] Kodiak Cakes is achieving that premium price via a 24-ounce (680-gram) box while its competitors are charging so much less for a 40-ounce (1,100-gram) package. That's a whopping 58.7 cents per ounce compared to Bisquick's 9.5 cents and Great Value's 6.3 cents. Moreover, to further demonstrate that Kodiak Cakes

10   Dominique M. Hanssens, *Empirical Generalizations about Marketing Impact* (Cambridge, MA: Marketing Science Institute, 2015).
11   Prices were referenced on March 10, 2022.

does not compete on price, their product's price per ounce isn't even displayed—it's not part of how their products get merchandised. If someone's shopping based on price, they're not going to buy Kodiak Cakes. But if price is their primary factor for consideration, it's pretty obvious that Great Value is a better "deal" than Bisquick. And, in the modern era of private-label competition, competing on price is an extraordinarily hard game to win.

$14.09

Kodiak Cakes Flapjack And Waffle Mix Buttermilk And Honey, 24 Oz

$3.78  9.5 ¢/oz

Betty Crocker Bisquick Pancake and Baking Mix, 40 oz

$2.50  6.3 ¢/oz

Great Value All Purpose Baking Mix, 40 oz

*Figure 4E. Pancake Mixes as Merchandised on Walmart.com*

So what's the alternative? Charge a premium price for a premium product. Of the 144 different drivers of brand equity tracked by BERA, one of the single greatest differences between our study's winners and losers was found in "price performance," which means that consumers were much more likely to report a willingness to pay even more than they already do for the winning brands. For example, if Rao's raised their price from $7.19 to $7.99, most customers would still be willing to pay for the product. On the other hand, if Barilla raised its price from $2.49 to $2.99, most of its buyers would consider an alternative. Nonpromoted prices tend to be quite inelastic, but this is particularly true for products that are able to command premium pricing. They remain in demand even when the price increases, giving them an added advantage in weathering an inflationary economic storm.

Of course, there is a limit to price increases, and I am not advocating that premium brands raise prices continually. The key point is that if your brand is highly susceptible to price-based competition, it's in a precarious position.

## WINNING NEW CUSTOMERS

Where do winning brands find their new customers? Our study revealed that winning brands disproportionately steal market share from smaller brands rather than the largest ones in the category. When we look closely at the data, we typically find that the biggest brands in each category already cover consumers' primary occasions and criteria. However, when people have advanced or alternative criteria—when they're looking for a different option for a specific reason—this is where winning brands excel. They step in and fill the void.

Two types of shoppers tend to have more advanced and alternative criteria:

1. The heaviest buyers of the category (which makes sense because they are the most knowledgeable about their needs and how each alternative product fulfills those needs);

2. Nonbuyers of the category (who typically don't buy the category because they don't believe any of the existing products meet their needs. Example: Caulipower).

Some upstart brands take on their category's leaders and steal share. These are massive disruptions, and we saw this occur with Harry's razors (which stole share directly from Gillette in the men's razor category) and BodyArmor (which took sales away from PepsiCo's Gatorade in the sports drink category).

These disruptors reshape entire categories. Harry's is now a multibillion-dollar company, and BodyArmor was just acquired by Coca-Cola for $5 billion. Somehow, they could deliver on the primary criteria and jobs to be done more successfully than the category leaders for a significant share of the population.

BodyArmor noticed that Gatorade wasn't fully delivering on its promise for "sports nutrition." So, they stepped in and filled that gap for consumers, delivering a refreshing blend of electrolytes, potassium, and other vitamins while avoiding the artificial colors, sweeteners, and sodium used by the category's dominant brand.

Harry's capitalized on two primary opportunities to beat Gillette: price and ease of purchase. First, Harry's delivered shave quality comparable to Gillette's Fusion razors at a lower cost (about 30 percent lower). Second, Gillette Fusion's buyers had become increasingly frustrated by having to ask store associates to unlock the antitheft cabinets guarding Gillette's expensive blades. By comparison, Harry's monthly subscription eliminated the need to keep shopping for refill cartridges—they just showed up in the consumers' mailboxes. Even when Harry's expanded into physical retail, the brand avoided placement behind lock and key—giving it a huge advantage over its larger, more established rival. Harry's ability to capitalize on these market gaps wasn't an accident, as noted by an interview with Harry's co-founder Jeff Raider before their first retail launch at Target.

*Figure 4F.*
Harry's Direct
Challenge
to Gillette

"Our products won't be locked up behind plastic lock and key, something that frustrated the experience of buying razors in the first place," he

## Gillette

The Fusion5

## HARRY'S

The Truman

vs

said. "It'll be premium, have great packaging, and will be a lot more affordable than competitors."[12]

Olly (our winning brand from the sleep aids category) also started as a direct-to-consumer e-commerce brand in 2014. However, by June of 2016, just 3 percent of its revenue still came from online sales.

Why the shift? Olly's co-founder, Eric Ryan, explained: "If we had focused on Olly.com, the customer acquisition costs, infrastructure, and things like free shipping would have required a lot more capital. Focusing on our retail partners allowed us to reach profitability much faster."

Olly's willingness to give retailers one-year exclusivity was the key to gaining initial retail distribution. "We first launched in Target, which was an exclusive for a year. Doing channel exclusives has been our strategy," Ryan stated. Olly then expanded distribution via a drug store exclusive with CVS and a specialty store exclusive with GNC. In exchange for exclusivity, Olly was able to negotiate better shopper marketing and merchandising support from those retailers. "What's really cool about GNC is you have these storefronts with windows and passersby, so it's been great from a branding standpoint," Ryan explained.[13]

Gail Becker, the Founder of Caulipower, also discovered success through distribution in Whole Foods, the first retailer to carry their product. Whole Foods supports local products, so Becker capitalized on that. "I happened to live in Southern California, so I pitched local," she explained. "I literally just brought a Styrofoam case full of my first pizzas and left it there. I couldn't even meet with anyone. The assistant said, no, no, you can leave it with me. It's like leaving your child with a stranger. You never forget where you are. A week later, I

12   David Yi, "Online Razor Brand Harry's Is Coming to a Target Near You," Mashable, August 3, 2016, https://mashable.com/article/harrys-expands-to-target#:~:text=%22 Our%20products%20won't%20be,has%20become%20enticing%20for%20Target.
13   Caminiti, "How Method's Eric Ryan Is Disrupting the Vitamin Market."

got an email from the buyer at Whole Foods saying they really liked our product. We're going to bring it into thirty Whole Foods stores."[14]

The stores sold out. A few months after getting into Whole Foods, Caulipower was picked up by Walmart nationwide. After going to a food show for even more exposure to retail buyers, the brand exploded.

## KEY TAKEAWAYS

- Focus on your customer's emotional needs rather than their functional needs. Emotions at the subconscious level, not rational thought, drive their purchase decisions.

- Become the architect of your consumers' choices. Shoppers use higher-order goals, motivations, regulatory focus, and cognitive heuristics when making choices. Winners understand how consumers approach buying in the category and apply choice architecture techniques to ease decision-making in favor of their brand.

- Understand whether consumers look to you to deliver positive gains or help avoid negatives, then focus your messaging accordingly.

- Influence how your products are displayed by sharing data-backed insights with retailers. If you can help the retailer increase overall category sales with better placement, layout, or signage, everyone wins.

- Don't overuse promotional pricing. Consumers interpret price as a signal of quality, value, and competitive positioning. When

---

14    Gail Becker, "351: 0–$100m in 3 Years: How Gail Becker, Founder of Caulipower Changed the Game," in *The Foundr Podcast*, 45:34, https://foundr.com/articles/podcast/gail-becker-caulipower.

brands "promote" themselves by temporarily cutting their price, consumers become anchored to the lower price and become more likely to switch brands when your price returns to its original level.

- If you have a premium product, charge a premium price. One of the greatest differences between our study's winners and losers was that consumers said they would pay even more for the winning brands if they had to. Their purchase behaviors back it up. On the flip side, losing brands often resorted to price-based competition, which saw them consistently lose sales to private-label brands.

# 5

# PRODUCT ATTRACTION AND DISTRIBUTION

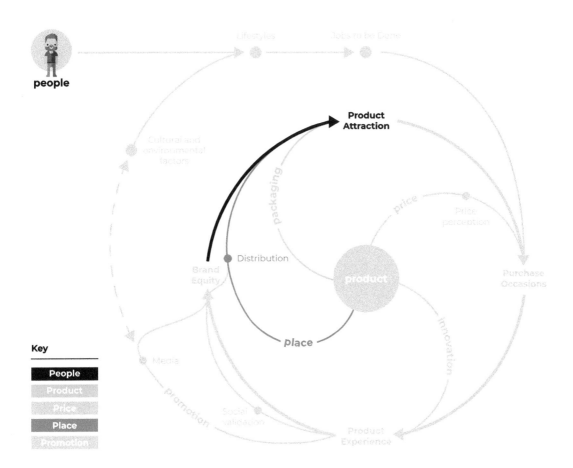

Product
Attraction

packaging

price

Price
perception

Distribution

Cultural and
environmental
factors

Brand
Equity

product

Purchase
Occasions

Innovation

place

Key

People

Product

Price

Place

Promotion

Media

Promotion

Social
validation

Product
Experience

Lifestyles

Jobs to be Done

hen Health-Ade Kombucha started showing up in small stores in Los Angeles in 2013, there were already several established kombucha brands on the market. What's more, many of those competing brands came in elegant packaging. There were clear bottles that showed off the colorful, thirst-quenching beverages inside, sturdy glass cylinders with European Quillfeldt stoppers, and even some tall, slender-necked carafes that almost resembled wine bottles.

Health-Ade was different. It came in a broad-shouldered, tinted glass shape that called an old-fashioned apothecary bottle to mind. It was practical and purposeful. It had a stout, ribbed cap that pleased kombucha drinkers who wanted to keep their beverage fresh as they sipped from it throughout the day. Designers even coated the label so it wouldn't peel after getting wet. The overall look—including the brand's distinctive ship's anchor—suggested a healthy elixir and matched the brand's assertion that Health-Ade is "handcrafted the old-fashioned way—the way nature intended."

But product attraction is just part of the battle. You can't attract buyers with attractive packaging if you aren't on the shelves, and for many upstart brands, gaining distribution often takes incredible persistence and hard work. Health-Ade Kombucha was no exception.

Health-Ade Kombucha won with hustle and grit. After getting their product into a few "mom-and-pop" stores in Los Angeles, they set their sights on more prominent stores. It took a dozen attempts to get their product carried in their first small retail chain, Erewhon Market's seven Los Angeles–area stores, but once they were on the shelves in 2013, Health-Ade's founders did everything they could to succeed.

"We weren't going to let this fail," co-founder Daina Trout said. "We knew that Erewhon had to be our success story."

They spent days at the store, handing out samples and explaining the benefits of their product to curious shoppers. Trout and two partners delivered product to the store in their cars and a rented refrigerated truck, piling up traffic tickets and burning gas navigating LA's choked freeways because they couldn't get a distributor to take them on unless a larger chain carried their products.

Dogged persistence and the brand's success at Erewhon led to Gelson's supermarkets agreeing to add Health-Ade Kombucha to their assortment for a limited trial. "They gave us sixteen weeks in eight stores. We did really well. That was how we unlocked our distribution problem," said Trout. "Once we had third-party distribution through Nature's Best, we started getting into more stores across the West Coast. When we opened up with Whole Foods in 2014, that connected us to another distributor. Now, we have 150 distributors across the US."[1]

---

1   Ronald D. White, "Kombucha CEO Says Company's Founders 'Were "Succeed at Any Cost" Types of People,'" *Los Angeles Times*, September 8, 2019, https://www.latimes.com/business/story/2019-09-06/health-ade-kombucha-tea-daina-trout.

Health-Ade Kombucha continued its shoestring approach to gaining distribution by leveraging small wins with retailers to gain new distributors. As they gained new distributors, they were able to land additional retailers. They continued to tinker with their design—adding a variety of colors to their label and squaring their bottle's shoulders while keeping its apothecary feel.[2] As they landed new retailers, they enlisted even more distributors. In this fashion, they zigzagged their way to distribution in more than twenty-six thousand stores across the country by 2019.

As Health-Ade Kombucha demonstrated, gaining distribution and paying attention to product attraction go hand-in-hand and were the most significant factors in the growth of many of our winning brands. Distribution problems also helped explain the declines experienced by many of our losing brands.

While you might think that winning distribution only matters for startup brands, the same holds true for legacy brands. Maximizing distribution for both existing and new products in the market is critical. Rao's Homemade pasta sauce has been selling the same core products through retail since 1992. Yet, the brand's rapid doubling of retail sales from less than $50 million in 2016 to over $100 million in 2018 wasn't due to a new product launch or increased advertising—they didn't start investing in advertising until 2019—it was due to gains in retail distribution.

## INNOVATION

Product innovations may be the primary enabler of most distribution gains, but it's important to note the flip side of that equation. As Dawn Hedgepeth, Unilever's General Manager and Vice President for Deodorants (including our winning brand, Dove women's deodorant)

---

2    Jessica Deseo, "Before & After: Health Ade Kombucha," *Dieline* (blog), September 8, 2014, https://thedieline.com/blog/2014/8/12/before-after-health-ade-kombucha.

told me, "Sometimes you need innovation to win distribution, but new products that fail to win sufficient distribution will fail."

As we reviewed the data for Dove deodorants during our study period, we found retailers making room for their innovative new "dry spray" products while showing much greater resistance to carrying their equally innovative "dry serum" products. The result: the introduction of dry spray deodorant grew both Dove's sales and the retailers' overall category sales. As for the "innovative" dry serum antiperspirants, let's just say that there's a reason you've probably never heard of them.

## SELLING IN AND SELLING THROUGH

Successful brands know they must both "sell in" and "sell through."

Selling in is about getting the retailer to carry the product in the first place. Will they carry the Modelo six-pack or only single bottles? Will they sell Modelo at all?

Selling through is about getting consumers to notice and buy the product once it's in the store.

Advertising and media efforts can help on both fronts. Suppose the retailer already knows who you are because of your advertising and knows shoppers will also be familiar with your product. In that case, they are more likely to not only carry it but to prioritize its placement on their shelves. Most brands think about advertising's role in winning the hearts and minds of consumers, but not enough attention gets paid to advertising's role in winning over the retail buyers who control distribution.

As the legendary David Aaker said, "A strong brand will have an edge in gaining both shelf facings and cooperation in implementing marketing programs."

## BRAND MEDIA

What's the single most valuable billboard in America? You might assume that it's a prominent billboard on Times Square, and you'd probably be correct if you defined value based on the cost of renting the billboard for a month. But, if you're a consumer goods company, I'd argue that the single most valuable billboard in America is this one located in a small town with a population of fewer than 50,000 people.

What's so special about this billboard?

It's the only one visible from the employee parking lot at Walmart headquarters in Bentonville, Arkansas. Walmart's buyers in charge of determining which products to include in their given category's limited shelf space see this billboard daily. There's no guarantee that if a product advertises on that billboard that Walmart will carry it at its four thousand stores, but it can't hurt to have your brand beaming out to the megaretailers' category buyers, can it?

When you're trying to sell your brand into Walmart stores (and gain access to 30 percent of the US market for many categories of consumer goods), even a tiny extra advantage can be of enormous value. This is a prime example of how brand media influences distribution, without which you cannot have product attraction.

Let's say that your product has the potential to generate $100 million in sales with full distribution across all relevant (e.g., grocery-related) retailers in America. It's likely then that Walmart would have the potential to account for $30 million in retail sales. If you rented that billboard for the month of your pitch to the Walmart buyer, it might cost you $2,000. If there were just one in one thousand odds that the billboard would influence the Walmart buyer in your favor, that investment would still have an expected value of $30,000 per year ($30 million divided by one thousand) in retail sales. Not bad for a $2,000 ad placement, eh?

If the product's not there to buy, you can't even think about merchandising or what makes the product stand out on the shelf. So, think carefully about how you can leverage your advertising budget to help your sales team win more retail distribution.

## THE ROLE OF ADVERTISING

Jeff Pinsker, CEO of Amigo Toys, said that advertising not only reaches consumers but it also reaches the retail store buyers who decide on what products to buy and where to merchandise those products.

"In our little branch of CPG, (retail) buyers purchase products that are advertised on TV, oftentimes just because they're advertised on TV," Pinsker said in the comment section on episode 440 of the *Freakonomics* podcast. "I can't blame them; if I rated two products equally and one had a $2.5 million TV campaign behind it, that's the one I'd buy for my limited shelf space.

"A solid majority of purchasing still goes through brick-and-mortar stores, and consumers shopping in stores don't buy products that aren't on the shelves. So, when companies spend money on TV budgets, they may reach consumers, but they will certainly reach the buyer who decides what products to buy and where to merchandise those products. And that can be worth many more millions of dollars than the cost of the TV campaign."

I'll talk more about advertising in Chapter 8, where we'll explain why buying ads is not the panacea most brand managers hope it will be.

## DISTRIBUTION IS THE KEY

If you could pull just one lever to drive growth of your brand, distribution should be the lever to choose. Among our winning and losing brands, distribution explained 87 percent of these brands' changes in sales. That far exceeds the explanatory power of changes in brand equity, advertising spend, promotion activity, price moves, or even the role of product innovation.

The head of analytics at a top ten CPG company recently confirmed this finding when he told me, "In our forecasting models, distribution carries 85 percent of the weight. Everything else in the marketing mix is minor in comparison."

It makes sense, right? Your product sales are limited to where your products are sold. Some may argue that is no longer true because, with e-commerce, your products are available everywhere. But if 80 percent of a category's sales happen in physical stores, then e-commerce will have a limited impact on improving your share of those sales.

## ONLINE SALES

Given the massive growth of e-commerce (especially for CPG products) in the last several years, we had a hunch that gains in online sales would be a leading indicator of in-store (and overall) brand performance. As it turns out, that was a false hypothesis. Winning via e-commerce did *not* turn out to be a leading indicator of success for our winning brands versus losing brands. That is, share gains online did not precede share gains in store.

Case in point: Harry's razors. Harry's was the exception that proves the rule. Harry's did start by gaining sales and share online—via a direct-to-consumer (D2C) business model. Simultaneously, Dollar Shave Club grew faster via its D2C go-to-market. So, how did Harry's catch up to and outperform Dollar Shave Club to earn its place among our winning brands? Retail distribution.

Harry's shocked the retail industry when it shifted gears by expanding beyond its online-only, D2C brand roots to be sold through Target stores in 2016. Harry's chose Target because Harry's research showed that 90 percent of their customers shopped there. Target gave Harry's four feet of retail space—with room for the brand's razors, aftershave, face wash, and shaving cream products—right next to traditional brands, including Gillette. But Harry's razors wouldn't be behind plastic lock and key, and although it was a premium product, its price would be lower than Gillette's. Two years later, Harry's could be found in Walmarts across the country. Those two retailers alone drove $100 million in sales growth for the brand by 2019.

So, distribution is key. But it's not the only thing. Once you're on the shelves, how do you get noticed? Consumers are open to a vast array of alternatives while they shop. When they are in the act of shopping, they are more attentive to relevant marketing, more receptive to a suggestive nudge, and less likely to forget the message before making a purchase decision.

Let's look at how the best of the best make that suggestive nudge.

### SHOPPER MARKETING AND BRAND GROWTH

Procter & Gamble and Unilever are two shopper marketing masters, having won far more Effie Awards for marketing excellence for their efforts to market with and through retailers than any of their peers. It's also no coincidence that these companies excel at shopper marketing and brand growth.

In recent years, both companies have leveraged the scale afforded by being a "house of brands" to generate cross-brand demand in store. One such example is Procter & Gamble's "Everyday Essentials" campaign at Walgreens, which combined several of our study's winning brands together in a single, prominent display that varied from quarter to quarter. If you planned to buy Tide laundry detergent and a to-be-determined brand of dish soap going into the store, this display made the choice of dish soap brand easy for you: there was Dawn (another winning brand of Procter & Gamble's). Since there's a bonus gift for spending $25 or more on P&G products, why not also stock up on Downy (another winning brand) and give Febreze (yet another winning brand) a try?

*Figure 5B.*
Procter &
Gamble's
Everyday
Essentials
Display at
Walgreens

It's a brilliant shopper marketing tactic that builds on P&G's house of brands strategy. P&G improved its execution so that the family of brands could be comarketed at retail through retailer circulars, cross-brand promotions, and multibrand displays and signage.

My hat's off to the P&G team for identifying and exploiting the advantage of their scale to strengthen their brands. Of course, most brands are not part of such a high-powered family and don't have the leverage to command such a premium display continuously. However, if you're representing individual brands, all is not lost. You will have to pay for such a premium display space, but that's a better option than simply paying the retailer to drop the price for a short-term increase in sales. Invest your trade dollars in displays that make your product more visible and attractive, not in price cuts.

Advantages of these secondary displays include:

- Their placement in high-traffic locations gets your brand noticed.
- You avoid competition because the shopper doesn't have to go down the aisle to where the entire category of competing products is merchandised.
- Display signage visually connects advertising campaigns and brand-building messaging to your products at the point of purchase.
- Displays encourage impulse buys.

P&G's Everyday Essentials display is an example of a suggestive nudge to buyers at the point of sale. Remember: consumers rarely go to stores with specific brands on their shopping list. They typically list categories they need to shop in (laundry detergent, dish soap, paper towels) and don't pick their brand until they see the products on the shelves. A display like this puts your brands front and center and inspires those hurrying to cross several items off their list in one convenient location.

"Any marketing that you do closer to the point of purchase, all else equal, is going to be more effective," says Dominique Hanssens, a professor at UCLA Anderson Graduate School of Management. The latter authored the metastudy: *Empirical Generalizations about Marketing Impact.* "That we know. You're more sensitive to these messages when you're walking around a store about to buy something versus when you're parked in front of your TV set far away from that store...The closer to the purchase occasion, the better the marketing works."[3]

## MERCHANDISING

I learned about the importance of merchandising firsthand. My first job in college was to work the sales floor at Big 5 Sporting Goods for the handsome wage of $4.25 an hour. Mostly that meant dressing up in slacks, a button-up shirt, and wearing a mandatory tie just to sell sneakers at rock-bottom prices. I quickly learned that even price-oriented shoppers are heavily influenced by merchandising—how and where products get presented in retail.

Our store displayed most shoe models on the store's back wall, which required me to run back and forth to the back room to grab shoes the customer wanted to try on. However, each week we would rotate a set of shoe models displayed in little islands on the sales floor along with all of the inventory (shoeboxes) we had in stock for the customer to grab.

Which form of merchandising resulted in greater sales for any given shoe type? The shoes displayed on the sales floor—regardless of whether they were on sale. The customer saw the display shoes before they saw ones on the back wall, and the display shoes had fewer competing options surrounding them. Customers were likelier to try on the display shoes because they didn't have to ask and wait for an associate to help them.

It didn't matter what shoes we placed on those little island displays. They were going to sell faster than they would off the back wall. This

---

3   Dominique Hanssens, "Long-Term Impact of Marketing: A Compendium," *The Great Marketing Debate with Dr. Dominique Hanssens*, MMA, July 29, 2020, video, https://www.mmaglobal.com/webinars/long-term-impact-marketing-compendium.

was just one of the dozens of merchandising tricks I'd learn while working in retail stores over the next many years.

## PRODUCT DISPLAY

Several years later, I found myself leading products and services for Retail Solutions, where we leveraged store-item-day level retail sales and inventory data to help brands partner with retailers to improve in-store execution and grow sales. We developed masterful algorithms to detect sales anomalies of specific products at specific stores, which alerted personnel to check and resolve the issues or report their findings.

I'll never forget the report from a third-party merchandising rep who visited a Walgreens store where sales of Q-tips had suddenly spiked to levels multiples higher than any other store in the country. What did he find?

He found shelf-hangers of Q-tips in more than 12 locations throughout the store. I had repeatedly seen how powerful a secondary merchandising location could be for a product within a store, but a dozen secondary locations? That was extreme—extremely successful at generating sales, that is. And without discounted pricing.

*Figure 5C.*
Nutella
Dominates
the Shelf

If you ever have the great fortune of grocery shopping in Europe, you may have difficulty finding peanut butter. Still, I have little doubt that you'll find hazelnut spread—or Nutella.

Nutella dominates the planogram regarding the number of facings, different product variants, and their premium placement at eye level. Each of these factors subconsciously conveys the brand's popularity, yet another form of social validation.

Did you notice the brand of hazelnut cream with the red packaging in the top left corner of the shelf set? Even though it has two facings, it might as well be out of stock. Why? There's no shelf tag displaying the price. That was another insight from my days working retail sales floors followed by years of algorithmically alerting merchandisers to check on sales anomalies: **a product without a price isn't for sale.** It's as if an impenetrable force field gets erected around a missing shelf tag that prevents all but the most determined shoppers from grabbing the product.

After issuing millions of "out-of-stock" alerts to store personnel and brand merchandisers, my team at Retail Solutions collected evidence that most stock-outs stopping sales weren't stock-outs. Missing shelf tags, a misplaced item blocking a product's only facing, a product turned around showing only its back side, a damaged package in front, a change in placement to the top or bottom shelf...all of these were more common than the store running out of a given product—at least before COVID-induced hoarding.

One of the brand managers for one of our study's losing brands confided in me, "Shelf space was a real challenge. It wasn't just that we lost facings at some retailers, but that the placement of those facings got shifted from eye-level down to the bottom shelf." These placement shifts at Walmart and Target turned out to be more detrimental to the brand's nationwide sales declines than fully losing distribution at other retailers had been.

In the case of Gillette, their declining share of the men's grooming category wasn't just because Harry's had won distribution at some key retailers but also because so many stores had merchandised Gillette products (which tended to sell at premium price points) behind lock and key to reduce theft. This made Gillette harder to buy, making it easier for shoppers to choose a competitor's products.

*Figure 5D.*
Gillette
Razors Locked
Away from
Shoppers

Another common merchandising issue that greatly impacts sales is where to merchandise crossover products that can find their home location in more than one category. Take this "Protein Cream" in the center of the picture below. It's a low-calorie, high-protein hazelnut spread.

*Figure 5E.*
Mismer-
chandising
a Healthier
Alternative
to Nutella

My local grocer merchandises it in a remote corner of the store with a handful of other fitness-oriented products. If I were the maker of that hazelnut protein cream, I would do everything in my power (including paying slotting fees and staffing merchandisers) to demonstrate to the retailer that this product should also be merchandised alongside Nutella. Doing so would undoubtedly multiply the sales of this product. Still, it would also grow the hazelnut spread category for the retailer because of its premium price point and appeal to shoppers who occasionally pass on Nutella as a sugar-filled indulgence.

Secondary, premium merchandising in the form of permanent end caps that were thematically refreshed each season played a clear role in the success of several of P&G's winning brands. The initiative went live in Walgreens stores in 2016 and grew sales of the brands there by 147 percent year over year.[4]

As a final example of in-store merchandising brilliance in action, I present merchandising nirvana. In the men's grooming section of my local drugstore, the entire top shelf, pleasantly placed just below eye level, is a permanent display of Braun electric razors. The display is constructed from high-quality materials and visually appealing with built-in lighting.

*Figure 5F.*
Merchandising
Nirvana

4    "Procter and Gamble: Walgreens for a Healthy Home," Effie, 2016, https://www.effie.org/case_database/case/SME_2017_E-115-997.

A selection of Braun razors is out on display, allowing consumers to see and hold the actual product. Accompanying each item on display is a fact sheet highlighting the product's points of differentiation and consumer benefits. Ready-to-buy boxes of each product are neatly organized directly behind each item on display. No need to hunt and peck or ask an assistant for help.

Finally, and most crucially, this display leaves no room for competitor offerings. If you want an electric razor, it's going to be Braun. This is a marketer's dream come true. And if you don't consider this type of work part of the marketing function in your organization, it's time to rethink marketing's role in facilitating brand growth.

## MERCHANDISING MOVING ONLINE

A recent McKinsey study discovered that up to 40 percent of consumers who shop for a product at a brick-and-mortar store change their minds because of something they see, learn, or do once they get to the store. The shift can occur due to packaging, placement, or even interactions with salespeople. "Consumers want to look at a product in action and are highly influenced by the visual dimension," the study found.[5]

Increasingly, however, the merchandising battle is moving online. And this trend provides us with incredibly insightful data. The search terms consumers type along with their click-stream navigation paths reveal new insights into how consumers choose between products and the quantifiable role of merchandising in influencing those choices.

Let's use dental floss and picks on Amazon as an example.

DenTek (our losing brand in the dental floss category) was a "Best Seller" in the category with by far the greatest number of product reviews. But it doesn't appear until scrolling down through several screens' worth of products. In a search for "dental floss," Amazon depicts fifteen competing products before showing the first DenTek

---

5   David Court et al., "The Consumer Decision Journey," *McKinsey Quarterly* no. 3 (June 1, 2009), https://www.mckinsey.com/business-functions/marketing-and-sales/our-insights/the-consumer-decision-journey#.

**Department**
Dental Floss & Picks
  Dental Floss
  Dental Picks
∨ See All 10 Departments

**Avg. Customer Review**
★★★★☆ & Up
★★★☆☆ & Up
★★☆☆☆ & Up
★☆☆☆☆ & Up

**Brand**
☐ Oral-B
☐ Reach
☐ Plackers
☐ Solimo
☐ DenTek
☐ Johnson & Johnson
☐ GUM
∨ See more

**Price**
Under $25

Sponsored ⓘ

Oral-B Glide Pro-Health Dental Floss, Original Floss, 50m, Pack of 6
**Pack of 6**
★★★★☆ ⌄ 2,813
$17⁸² ($2.97/Count) $19.76

Sponsored ⓘ

Colgate Charcoal Waxed Dental Floss, Non-Toxic and Non-Teflon, Mint - 2 Pack
★★★★☆ ⌄ 5,439
$11⁷⁹ ($0.24/Count)
Save 25% with coupon

Sponsored ⓘ

Glide Oral-B Pro-Health Deep Clean Floss, Mint, Pack of 6
**6 Count**
★★★★★ ⌄ 13,178
$14⁹⁸ ($2.50/Count) $17.99
$14.23 with Subscribe & Save discount

Best Seller

Oral-B Glide Pro-Health Comfort Plus Dental Floss, Mint, 40 M, Pack of 2
**Pack of 2**
★★★★★ ⌄ 10,638
$4⁹⁹ ($2.50/Count) $6.35

Glide Oral-B Pro-Health Deep Clean Floss, Mint, Pack of 6
**6 Count**
★★★★★ ⌄ 13,178
$14⁹⁸ ($2.50/Count) $17.99
$14.23 with Subscribe & Save discount

Amazon's Choice

Johnson & Johnson Reach Mint Waxed Dental Floss, 5 Count
**Pack of 5**
★★★★☆ ⌄ 3,738
$11⁶³ ($2.33/Count)
Ships to Hungary

askmen° **Editorial recommendations**
By Askmen | Earns commissions ⓘ

**Best Dental Flosses**

Mar 15, 2021 - 4 Recommendations

Oral hygiene is so important, as well as brushing your teeth twice a day. It's essential to floss too. Flossing provides better overall oral health, cleaning away bits of food and plaque that can accumulate after meals and cause all kinds of damage to teeth and gums. However, you have to choose the best care, as some forms of floss are much more effective and enjoyable to use than others. Here are some of the top options.

Read full article

**Top Pick**
Reliable Option

Glide Oral-B Pro-Health Deep Clean Floss, Mint, Pack of 6
**6 Count**
★★★★★ ⌄ 13,178
$14⁹⁸ ($2.50/Count) $17.99
$14.23 with Subscribe & Save discount

Coming from one of the best brands in the dental health industry, this dental floss offers a deep and thorough clean of the teeth.

*Figure 5G.* Search Results for Dental Floss on *Amazon.com*

product. Only a very determined shopper would exert the mental energy (i.e., System 2 thinking) in their search unless they were already a very loyal DenTek buyer.

In this example, I had searched for "dental floss" even though DenTek offers both floss and a pick. The problem is that consumers don't search the term "dental floss and pick." They search either "dental floss" or "dental pick," and according to Google Trends, they are nearly five times more likely to search for "dental floss."

That said, DenTek is still losing the merchandising game at Amazon even when consumers do search specifically for a "dental pick." DenTek products appear well below the fold (what is seen when a webpage first loads), and they're not even listed first among the organic (nonsponsored) search results.

DenTek Triple Clean Advanced Clean Floss Picks, No Break & No Shred Floss, 150 Count

★★★★☆ ˅ 40,574

$5⁹⁹ ($0.04/Count)
$5.69 with Subscribe & Save discount
**40% off** your first subscription order

*(top) Figure 5H. DenTek's First Listing Under "Dental Floss" on Amazon.com*

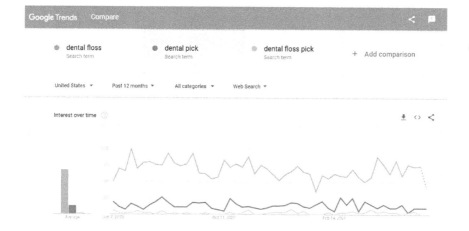

*(left) Figure 5I. Google Search Trends for Dental Floss versus Dental Picks*

It's no wonder that DenTek's share of the overall "Dental Floss & Picks" category at Amazon dropped from 7 percent in 2016 to 4 percent in 2019. It's not enough to have the best product and great distribution; merchandising matters.

Whereas DenTek is highly visible in its merchandising among dental flosses and picks in store, it's practically invisible online. It fails to appear where consumers search because it failed at SEO: search engine optimization. Competing brands optimize their online merchandising by appearing first in search rankings, including "dental floss" or "dental pick" in their product name and product description. That way, if a shopper searched on one of those terms, their product would be more likely to return as a top-most relevant result. By contrast, DenTek referred to its products as "floss picks" in the product name and description fields—a term that almost no online shopper enters into the search bar.

*Figure 5J.*
Search Results
for Dental Picks
on *Amazon.com*

*Figure 5K.*
YouTube
Merchandises
a Digital Shelf
of Videos to
Choose From

It's no coincidence that Amazon's product merchandising algorithms and YouTube's algorithms for which videos to display have started to look more and more alike. Amazon's digital shelf sure looks an awful lot like YouTube's page full of video recommendations.

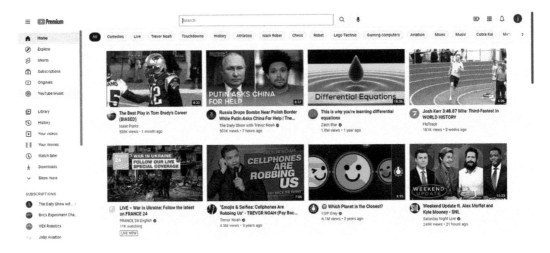

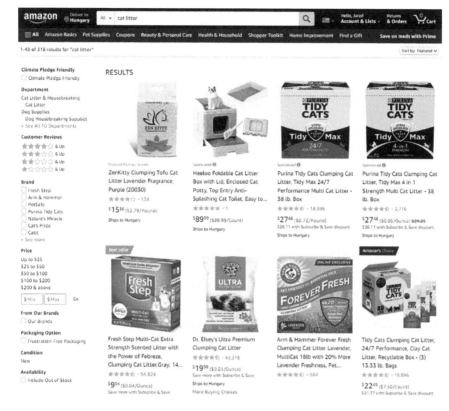

*Figure 5L.*
Amazon's
Digital Shelf
for Cat Litter

Why? Because the science behind consumer choice is the common theme between cat videos and cat litter. This means that lessons learned from how and why particular videos go viral (or languish) will deliver tremendous insights into how to grow product sales (and the brands they represent).

One of my favorite YouTubers, Derek Muller, recently explained the secrets of viral video growth on his YouTube channel: Veritasium. His explanation holds quite a bit of insight into the mechanics of exceptional brand growth. In his video "My Video Went Viral. Here's Why," he explains the criticality of two factors: 1) watch time and 2) click-through rate.

Watch time simply reflects the extent to which consumers watch most of the video. Think of it as a measure of how well consumers like the "product"—do they like it enough to keep using it? The equivalent in this book is the idea of delivering a great product experience that results in a consumer's intent to repurchase, tell others about it (word of mouth), and leave a positive review (social validation).

The importance of watch time didn't surprise Derek, however. What surprised him was the importance of the click-through rate.

"If you want a viral video, you must have a high click-through rate. So that is the total number of clicks on your title and thumbnail divided by the total number of times that title and thumbnail have been shown."[6]

Whether it's in store or online when someone is shopping in your category, you must understand how well you're performing in click-through rate, or the percentage of the time they choose your product compared to the number of times they shop the category. What is your brand doing to ensure that your products are visible and distinctively attractive?

What brands need to realize is that online merchandising through Amazon and Instacart looks more like the art and science of optimizing one's dating profile on Tinder and Bumble than anyone cares to admit. So, the next time you're looking for a little inspiration for improving your products' online profiles, have a little fun researching the latest trends and the world of online dating. You might improve your love life and career prospects in one fell swoop!

## PACKAGING

Stan Sthanunathan, Unilever's Executive Vice President of Consumer & Market Insights, recently told me, "The two least-understood dimensions of brand growth are the product experience and packaging."

It's true. Packaging's contribution to brand growth (and decline) is perhaps the most challenging variable to measure in our study. For

6    Derek Muller, "My Video Went Viral. Here's Why," Veritasium, May 19, 2019, video, 23:42, https://www.youtube.com/watch?v=fHsa9DqmId8.

one, most product package changes are implemented without introducing a new barcode number (UPC or EAN), so there's no way to track them. In addition, many of the younger brands that emerged victorious during our study took a different approach to packaging than their rivals from the beginning. Still, it's nearly impossible to tease out exactly how important those packaging differences were versus the role of factors such as price and promotion.

Yet, there's plenty of evidence that packaging influences not only product choice but also the product experience.

In *The Elephant in the Brain*, authors Kevin Simler and Robin Hanson describe an experiment where researchers sent subjects home with boxes of three "different" laundry detergents and asked them to determine which one worked best on delicate clothes. The subjects didn't know that all three boxes contained the same detergent. Only the boxes were different. One was plain yellow, another blue, and the third was blue with "splashes of yellow."

"In their evaluations, subjects expressed concerns about the first two detergents and showed a distinct preference for the third," the authors wrote. "They said that the detergent in the yellow box was 'too strong' and that it ruined their clothes. The detergent in the blue box, meanwhile, left their clothes looking dirty. The detergent in the third box (blue with yellow splashes), however, had a 'fine' and 'wonderful' effect on their delicate clothes."

The subjects liked the blue-and-yellow box best, influencing how they felt about the product inside. Researchers have gotten the same results with wine and pantyhose. Identical wines, but one tasted sweeter because of the type of bottle it was poured from. Same exact pantyhoses, but one felt smoother because of the packaging.[7]

My favorite example of winning with packaging comes from our winner in the frozen pizza category, Caulipower.

[7]    Kevin Simler and Robin Hanson, *The Elephant in the Brain: Hidden Motives in Everyday Life* (New York: Oxford University Press, 2018), 101.

Katie Lefkowitz, COO of Caulipower, explained to me that the company turned its packages into billboards with meme-worthy catchphrases. They wanted their package to stand out in the freezer, so they created packaging Lefkowitz called "very Instagramable."

"I think when an entrepreneur starts out, you have to figure out pretty early on what rules you're going to follow and what rules you're going to break," says Gail Becker, the brand's Founder and CEO. "For us, one of the rules we broke is we're not going to have our box look like everybody else's. We're going to put big black letters right over the pizza. I can't tell you how many times people said to me, 'You don't want to do that.' I had graphic designers say, 'Let me fix that for you.' But it really worked for us, and it was different, and we stood out, and I think that had a positive impact."[8]

*Figure 5M.*
Caulipower's
Packaging Acts
like a Billboard
for Its Products

Another example of winning with packaging, specifically labels, comes from Olly in the sleep aid category.

When the company's founder, Eric Ryan, started sketching out his idea of what a new kind of vitamin and supplement brand could be, he decided the product name would spell out the benefit it was delivering (the simply named "Sleep," for instance, is Olly's best-selling product).

Rather than typical round jars, Ryan made his square. As for the name, he wanted something friendly. "Everything in this category is either very pharma-sounding or very folksy," he said. Olly sounded like neither of those things, and Ryan explained the name "just looked so good on the bottle."[9]

---

8    Becker, "351: 0–$100m in 3 Years."
9    Caminiti, "How Method's Eric Ryan Is Disrupting the Vitamin Market."

Liquid I.V. took a similar approach to help them win against Gatorade in the drink mixes category. Prominently featuring the consumer benefit "Hydration Multiplier" (or "Energy Multiplier" for another one of their highly successful products) while also depicting that the consumer will need to drink much less to feel hydrated. Liquid I.V.'s use of single-use sachets was another packaging win—aligning the product with everyday usage occasions.

How a product looks may be important, just like the picture on your dating profile, but packaging isn't just about aesthetics—after all, it's what's inside that counts. "Millennials are reading labels, and they want cleaner labels," says Eric Skae, CEO of Rao's Homemade pasta sauce. "Rao's was a clean label before clean labels even existed. It's always been super-premium, all-natural, with simple ingredients, no preservatives, no added sugar, no fillers."[10] Featuring "All Natural" on the front of the label and having the ingredient list to back it up was a winning recipe.

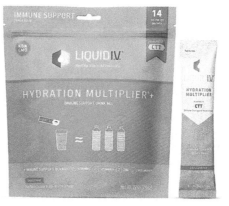

---

10   Watson, "Rao's Notches Up Double Digit Growth."

I previously worked with a mouthwash brand (sorry, I can't tell you which one) that used packaging to shift their results. First, the brand noticed customers were hiding away the original containers because they looked like old, unattractive medicine bottles. The brand added more attractive packaging and improved the ergonomics of their larger bottles. Right away, customers began putting the bottles on the bathroom counter and the constant visual reminder led to more mouth-washing and skyrocketing sales.

Harry's razors is another great example of a winning brand that influenced purchase decisions through its packaging. Harry's is a startup brand that initially sold only online, direct to consumers. In order to continue their growth, they knew they'd need to get into stores where the vast majority of razors are purchased. Their entire business shifted in 2016 when they signed a deal with Target to make the move to offline retail. Harry's already had great packaging design optimized for their subscription delivery model, but the brand knew they would need to develop new packaging to attract eyeballs away from competition at the shelf.

*Figure 5P.* Gillette Packaging versus Harry's Packaging

According to Harry's, "Breaking the model of locked-up razors and blister packs, we developed simple, clean packaging designs that resonate with modern shoppers. We sought to holistically connect with Target's guests using high-quality photographic imagery of our razor handles and forward-facing five-blade cartridges. Each handle color option matches the paper-molded tray inside, which holds a custom-fit bundle of Harry's products."

The brand's packaging was a clear contributor to its success in store. As one early reviewer noted, "I'll be honest, I pretty much bought it because the box looks cool." This reviewer wasn't alone; within weeks of launching at Target, Harry's commanded nearly 50 percent of all razor sales at the retailer.

## GETTING SPACE ON THE SHELF

As almost any brand manager will tell you, getting shelf space in a retail outlet is no simple task. If you're launching a new soup brand, how can you elbow onto a shelf clogged with fifty varieties of Progresso and Campbell's?

For most large retailers, planograms—the directive stores use to determine what to stock and where to place individual brands on their shelves—come from headquarters. These corporate planners take into account each store's size, geographic location, the consumers' shopping patterns, and other factors in determining product placement. Some brands can gain shelf space by paying slotting fees, and many retailers ask brands to buy advertising and do trade promotions in return for getting shelf space. Fledgling brands often don't have the capital to buy their way into the store, so they do other things—like provide product samples the way Health-Ade Kombucha's founders did.

Sometimes a store manager will have some flexibility and can stock a new product, but most brands have to contact a buyer at the store's headquarters and convince that person to carry their product. And the best way to do that is to come in armed with data that shows your product will increase sales in your category or even bring new buyers into the category. If the store is making $2 a bottle selling a competing brand and you can show that the store can make $4.50 selling yours, you have a better chance. Rao's used that strategy very effectively. Rao's was also able to show that if their product wasn't on the shelf, consumers would go to another store to buy it. That was a very convincing argument.

In Health-Ade Kombucha's case, they were able to convince retailers that their tasty recipe for fermented teas would not only get kombucha buyers to spend more but it would also get nonbuyers to start putting kombucha in their shopping carts. They told retailers, "Kombucha is picking up overall, and we have the best-flavored kombucha. Therefore, we're going to capture sales that other brands aren't because ours just tastes better."

## PRODUCT ATTRACTION

There are many prerequisites to product attraction that must be fulfilled for a shopper to notice and consider your products among all the options available in the category.

First and foremost, your product must gain distribution at the retail locations where shoppers shop for your category of products. Distribution means your product gets added to the planogram and that stores make room on the shelf for it. And not just any location, but the best possible location (preferably eye level, center-right, within reach, and ideally taking up as much shelf space as possible). An additional secondary display would be ideal.

You must also ensure the product stands out visually. No private-label look-alikes. The packaging quality conveys product quality, so color, shape, material, graphics, logo, font, and claims should all be considered to make the product distinctive and attractive. In physical retail, packaging changes are notoriously expensive and time-consuming to implement, but the rise of e-commerce allows brands a low-cost, low-effort means to experiment—changing a few pixels can fundamentally change performance on the digital shelf. Those online learnings can then be reapplied to the physical world of retail with much greater confidence.

## KEY TAKEAWAYS

- If you can pull just one lever to drive brand growth, choose the distribution lever. Distribution explained 87 percent of our winning and losing brands' yearly changes in sales, making it far more important than brand equity, advertising, promotion, price, or product innovation.

- Most consumers hold off their final purchase decision until they're in a store. Merchandising and packaging are therefore very important selling factors, a point that's not widely understood because it's so difficult to measure.

- Once you're on the shelves, make sure you get noticed. You may have to pay for premium display space, but that's a better alternative than dropping the price. Skip price cuts and invest your trade funds in displays that make your product more visible and attractive.

- Packaging influences both product choice and product experience. The same wine that is bottled two different ways, for example, may seem sweeter to consumers when they pour it from an amber bottle than when they pour it from a clear one. And packaging is about more than aesthetics; customers, particularly millennials, are reading labels and want cleaner labels.

- Packaging drives product attraction at the point of purchase *and* at the point of consumption. Great packaging gets noticed at home so that it gets chosen from the fridge, pantry, cabinet, or closet more often. The more it gets used at home, the more it gets repurchased at the store.

- Sometimes it takes a combination of approaches—great packaging, a favorable shelf position, forceful fixtures, informative signage—to attract consumers who enter a store with a strong attachment to their initial considerations. The research shows that in-store touch points provide a significant opportunity to beat the competition and win purchase occasions.

# 6

# BRAND EQUITY

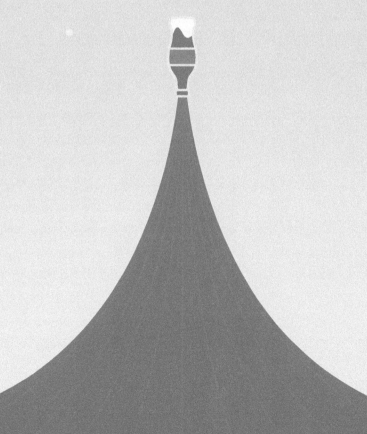

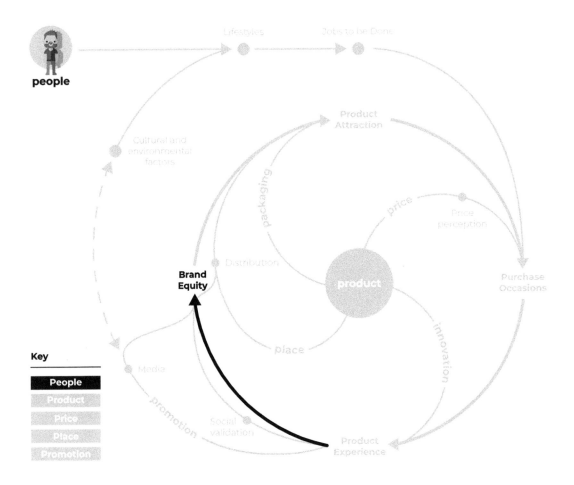

people

Key

People

Product

Price

Place

Promotion

'd like to introduce you to one of Hungary's most beloved brands: Túró Rudi (pronounced something like "Two-Row Roo-Dee").

The thing about "Túró Rudi" is that it's not actually a brand name, at least not in the trademarkable sense. Turo is the Hungarian word for "curd" (as in curds of sweet farmers' cheese), and Rudi is Hungarian for "rod" or "bar." So, Túró Rudi simply means curd bar, and many competing brands use the term to describe virtually identical products—finger-length cylinders of curd coated in chocolate.

Take a look at the picture of fifteen different brands of curd bars. Do you have any idea what makes any one of them better than the others? Any guesses as to which one dominates sales for this type of snack? (In case you're wondering, it's *not* the one in the very center with the name Túró Rudi clearly visible.)

There are more than thirty different brands that sell these little curd bars in Hungary, and they are as undifferentiated as can be. They are all packaged exactly the same way, and when you take them out of their little sachets to eat, they are completely indistinguishable.

Not only do they look the same, but they taste the same to most consumers, too. In a blind taste test, Hungarians can hardly distinguish the flavor of one brand from the next. However, there is only one curd bar *brand* that every store carries, and there is only one brand Hungarians think of when they hear "Túró Rudi." This one:

The funny thing is, the brand name Pöttyös (which translates to "polka-dotted") is hardly ever used; it's only referred to as "Túró Rudi." If you ask Hungarians a simple brand awareness question such as, "When you think of Túró Rudi, what brands come to mind?" they'll look at you like you're an alien. Every Hungarian knows that Túró Rudi makes turo rudi. And if you tell a Hungarian that the brand they are almost certainly thinking of—the one with the red polka-dotted package—isn't actually named Túró Rudi, they probably won't believe you. In fact, many are surprised to learn that there are different brands of turo rudi. My very own Hungarian wife didn't believe me when I told her; she immediately turned to Google hoping to prove me wrong.

So, here we are with a single dominant brand—among dozens of branded competitors offering nearly identical products—with a brand name that no one seems to know, yet everyone immediately recognizes. "It's the one with the red spots." Not only is this specific brand top-of-mind for consumers (despite not having a recallable name), it dominates in market share, selling at a higher price than its knock-off competitors.

How can this be? **Brand equity.**

As Philip Kotler once said, "A brand must be more than a name. It should invoke a set of associations, expectations, and preferences."

For Hungarians, the associations go well beyond a name. The moment that little curd bar gets draped by a red polka-dotted wrapper, it is instantly transformed. It's no longer just a tasty snack; it's a fountain of fond memories. It's the reward Grandma gave you and your cousins for "helping" in the garden. It's the extra energy you need to bounce around on the trampoline for another hour. It's what you shared with that cute guy or gal in your class as a way to flirt a little. And now as an adult, it's those same kinds of memories you want your kids to have and remember.

That's brand equity.

Awareness is the foundation of brand equity. Brand consultant David Aaker, who gave us the first widely accepted model of brand equity, said, "the value of brand awareness comes from its role as an anchor to which other associations can be attached" and is "a primary basis for consideration" when people are shopping.

Brand equity is the difference between otherwise identical products. It is the reason why retailers carry one brand and not another. It is why consumers are more likely to notice your brand's advertisements and your products' packaging in retail stores. It leads to more consumers choosing your brand over nearly identical competing products. It explains why some consumers are willing to pay more to buy your products versus lower-priced equivalents. And it's why consumers claim that your brand tastes better even though they prefer a competitor's product during blind taste-testing.

In this chapter, we will see there are many definitions for brand equity and even different ways to measure how much equity a brand has. We'll also see that if you want to increase your brand equity, your products have to tap into a consumer's subconscious and be perceived as holding a higher value than all other options.

## DEFINING AND MEASURING

The following list taken from ResearchLeap shows just how many definitions of brand equity have been used over time.[1]

---

1    Sanaz Farjam and Xu Hongyi, "Reviewing the Concept of Brand Equity and Evaluating Consumer-Based Brand Equity (CBBE) Models," *International Journal of Management Science and Business Administration* 1, no. 8 (July 2015): 14–29, http://dx.doi.org/10.18775/ijmsba.1849-5664-5419.2014.18.1002.

| | Researcher | Definition |
|---|---|---|
| *Figure 6D.* Various Definitions of Brand Equity | Farquhar (1989) | Added value endowed by the brand to the product. |
| | Aaker (1991) | Set of brand assets and liabilities linked to a brand, its name, and symbol that add to or subtract from the value provided by a product or service to a firm and/or to that firm's customers. |
| | Keller (1993) | The differential effect of brand knowledge on consumer response to the marketing of the brand. |
| | Simon and Sullivan (1993) | Cash-flow differences between a scenario where the brand name is added to a company product and another scenario where the same product does not have the brand name. |
| | Rangaswamy et al. (1993) | Favorable impressions, attitudinal dispositions, and behavioral predilections. |
| | Park and Srinivasan (1994) | The difference between overall brand preference and multiattributed preference based on objectively measured attribute levels. |
| | Lassar, Mittal, and Sharma (1995) | The enhancement in the perceived utility and desirability a brand name confers on a product. |
| | Yoo et al. (2000) | The difference in consumer choice between a branded and unbranded product, given the same level of features. |
| | Vázquez et al. (2002) | The utility that the consumer associates to the use and consumption of the brand. |
| | Ailawadi et al. (2003) | Outcomes that accrue to a product with its brand name compared with those that would accrue if the same product did not have the brand name. |
| | Baldauf, et al. (2003) | Reflection of the premium price the firm charges for a strong brand combined with the sales it is able to attract compared to other average brands in the same product category. |
| | Clow and Baack (2005) | Set of characteristics that make a brand unique in the marketplace. |
| | Kotler and Keller (2006) | A bridge between the marketing investments in the company's products to create the brands and the customers' brand knowledge. |
| | Yasin et al. (2007) | Consumers' favoritism toward the focal brand in terms of their preference, purchase intention, and choice among brands in a product category, that offers the same level of product benefits as perceived by the consumers. |

It's no wonder marketing has failed to graduate from an interpretive art form into a disciplined science. Imagine if financiers each decided to use their own "understanding" of owner's equity. Without an established definition of owner's equity (which equals total assets minus total liabilities), valuing company shares would be a nightmare. There's a reason clear definitions are given in most fields. Unfortunately, when it comes to brand equity, marketing scientists seem hell-bent on remaining artists.

To help us navigate this nebulous topic, let's stick with Farquhar's original definition: *Brand equity is the added value with which a brand endows a product.*

Even with this simple definition, it can still be difficult to quantify just how important brand equity is. Here are a few ways brand equity helps a brand grow:

1. Increases the odds of having your product chosen over alternatives during purchase and usage occasions.

2. Results in a better usage experience, which results in a higher repeat purchase rate than an "equivalent" product.

3. Customers pay more for your product without losing purchase occasions.

4. Reduces the amount of advertising spend required to achieve revenue and profit goals.

5. Lowers customer acquisition costs (CAC) and increases the lifetime value (LTV) of these newly acquired customers.

6. Reduces the amount of trade spend required to achieve revenue goals, increasing profits.

7. Lowers the barrier to entry (time and sales expense) to win distribution through retailers.

8. Improves the quality of shelf placement and merchandising in those retailers.

9. Increases the odds of success of new product launches by increasing both the likelihood of retailer adoption and consumer trial.

The importance of brand equity cannot be overstated. Next to top-line sales, market share, and profitability, it is one of the most important metrics brand managers and marketers can use to measure performance.

## CRITERIA FOR MEASURING

So, if brand equity is such an important metric, how can you effectively measure it?

Most brands use third-party market research companies. These companies use "proven" methodologies to give a brand a composite score or percentile.

If you are getting a score from a third party, it's important that they can show how your brand measures up against its direct competitors. Many research companies don't offer this kind of insight, however. They give you a score for your brand and leave you wondering how you stand among competitors in your category.

To reach a composite score or percentile, four key criteria are often used: salience, differentiation, meaningfulness, and loyalty.

Kantar's Millward Brown, a prominent market research company, scores brand equity using the first three.

**Salience:** To understand how salient your brand is, you ask: *Is it a brand that comes to mind when consumers think of the category?* Remember the polka-dotted Pöttyös (Túró Rudi) brand? It's an excellent example of saliency. It's the one that comes to mind in the category—as long as the researchers ask the question the right way.

**Differentiation**: To know how differentiated your brand is, you ask: *Is it better than competitors in some way?* What is the value proposition, not in a visible sense but in terms of expected benefit? To win here, consumers need to see the product as having more functional benefits than competitors.

**Meaningfulness**: This is the extent to which a brand builds an emotional connection with customers while also delivering against functional needs. What beneficial memories, emotions, or personal associations does the product evoke?

Other market researchers add **Loyalty**, a measure of consumer claims about how often they choose the brand over competitors. This recall-based measurement can be unreliable, but it can add some insight when used with the other three measurements.

To gain a more comprehensive understanding of brand equity's role in explaining the performance differences between the winning and losing brands in our study, we sought the help of BERA brand management. BERA continuously tracks over 144 different attributes of brand equity (e.g., familiarity, favorability, etc.) across thousands of brands via proprietary consumer surveys. I am particularly grateful for their contribution to this study because there is simply no other company that continuously tracks this kind of data. It is the only possible way in which we could retrospectively evaluate differences in brand equity and its drivers among our winning and losing brands.

Most market research firms only track brand equity for paying clients, but BERA tracks brand equity continuously for thousands of major brands using a syndicated approach. They will send a survey to one consumer, asking several questions about five brands, and then ask the next consumer about two of the same brands plus three completely different brands. Each month, hundreds of thousands of survey responses are gathered and scored.

Among the thousands of brands that BERA tracks, each brand is given a percentile based on where it ranks for each attribute. For any given attribute, the highest-scoring brands will be in the 99th percentile, and then you work your way down from there.

To normalize the data across 144 different attributes, BERA provided each winning and losing brand's percentile scores for every attribute from the beginning of 2017 through 2019. For example, over the course of the study period, Old Spice ranked among the top 5 percent of all brands (not just deodorant brands) in terms of consumers rating the brand as highly "original" and therefore received a percentile score of 95 for that attribute.

## FINDING OUR WINNERS

When we compared the winners to the losers, eight of the 144 different brand equity attributes emerged as having scores that were significantly higher for the winners versus the losers. In other words, these are the qualities that most distinguish winning brands from losing brands.

The most significant brand equity attributes that separated the winners from the losers were that consumers viewed them as much more **innovative** and **unique**. That means you offer differentiated products and value propositions, and consumers can expect qualities the other brands don't have. Your brand gets the job done in a way others can't. This gives consumers a positive perception of what they're getting compared to what they're paying—especially versus competitors. Kodiak Cakes pancake mix offers an excellent example of this dynamic. By positioning its product as protein-packed "Power Cakes," the brand makes clear that it's offering a differentiated product from the typically carb-heavy pancake mixes that have historically defined the category.

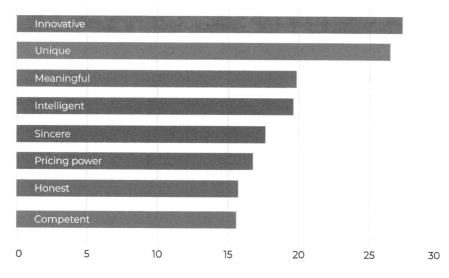

Figure 6E.
Brand Equity
Drivers:
Differences
between Winners
and Losers

Source: Analysis of BERA metrics; Average percentile difference
between matched winners & losers from Q1'2017 through Q4'2019

**BERA**

The next most significant brand equity differences between winners and losers were **meaningfulness** and **intelligence**. When you
score high on these characteristics, consumers believe your brand
understands their needs and desires. The brand has struck a chord
with the consumers; you understand what the consumer is trying to
achieve and why their goal is important. Your brand fits into the consumers' lifestyles and usage occasions.

Winners also scored high on **sincerity** and **honesty**, suggesting
that consumers believe these brands make trustworthy claims about
their products and live up to those promises. This is further evidenced
by the higher scores for **competence** (another word for quality), which
comes from delivering a quality product that gets the job done.

Finally, winners stand out when it comes to **pricing power**, which
measures the extent to which consumers are willing to pay more for
your product than they already do. The perceived value of your product is significantly greater than the price consumers pay for it. When
you score high on **pricing power**, your brand is more likely to retain
customers from one occasion to the next, even when a competitor is
being promoted at a discounted price.

## DISTINCTION VERSUS DIFFERENTIATION

**Brand distinction** describes how a brand stands out with its name, typography, logo, colors, packaging appearance, and tagline so buyers can easily identify, recall, and buy the brand. **Brand differentiation**, meanwhile, comes when you set yourself apart from the competition through product features and benefits that (should) result in a better usage experience for your customers.

While there is a very strong case to be made for the importance of **brand distinction**, our study makes clear that **differentiation** plays a major role in separating winners from losers. Winning brands offer a differentiated value proposition backed by real differences in their products versus the competition—even in the highly commoditized world of fast-moving consumer goods. Bang energy drink is differentiated because it has nutritional supplements that none of its competitors have. Caulipower is differentiated in the frozen pizza category by delivering a flavorful product that is also healthy and gluten-free. Real differences do more to explain the performance of our winners and losers than any stylistic distinctions we could identify.

## BRAND AWARENESS AND FAMILIARITY

Perhaps the most surprising finding from BERA's data is that the two great pillars of brand equity—awareness and familiarity—failed to rank among the metrics with the biggest difference between winning and losing brands. The average consumer "awareness" of our winning and losing brands was identical—both sets scoring high at the 85th percentile among all brands tracked by BERA over the course of the study. Our winning brands did not have an awareness advantage, and our losing brands did not suffer from a lack of awareness. Similarly, the familiarity percentile score for winners was 69 versus 65 for losers. Nearly sixty other brand equity attributes showed greater differences between the winners and losers than familiarity.

What this data shows is that consumers are aware of and familiar with losers; they're just not buying them because their products don't deliver on other, more important attributes of brand equity.

Heightened awareness may be table stakes for brand building, but it doesn't separate winning brands from losing brands. According to our study, what separated them was their uniqueness and inventiveness. Winners offered consumers something the other brands couldn't; they got the job done better than their competitors.

What role does advertising play in building awareness and brand equity? Not as much as many think. Empirical studies show two primary ways we learn about brands and their products: endogenous (product usage experience) and exogenous (advertising and other marketing) signals. Between the two, product usage experience is the dominant driver. The more a consumer buys and uses a brand, its equity will grow, and the more likely it is to become top-of-mind.

Our study backed this up, revealing that increased advertising did not strongly correlate with sales or brand equity growth. Like previous studies, we found that brand equity is primarily a function of the customer's own experience using or consuming the brand's products. Awareness (especially top-of-mind awareness) and familiarity grow stronger through repeated usage of the brand's products. I have yet to see any study showing that advertising has a greater impact on top-of-mind brand awareness than actual purchase and usage behaviors.

You can advertise to attract new customers, but repeat buying is still the key to growth. If you don't keep those repeat buyers, you aren't going anywhere fast. Advertising can remind consumers how much they love your product and to buy it, but ads are most effective when you are rolling out an intriguing innovation. This, too, has been repeatedly proven through peer-reviewed research and by the best practitioners.

Brand equity has much more to do with having a product that people love. People don't love it because of the advertising but because of the product itself. It gets the job done and delivers a delightful experience at a price consumers consider a good deal for the value they derive from it. A winning brand like Kind is top-of-mind in the nutrition bars category because many people genuinely love their products. They'd pay more for them if they had to.

Being top-of-mind in a category is important, but it's not as crucial to growth as people think. Just because a product is top-of-mind doesn't necessarily mean you will buy it. The actual causation is a great product experience, increasing awareness and someone's likelihood of buying it again.

## PRIVATE-LABEL BRANDS

Private-label brands, also known as "generic" brands, are products labeled by the retailer but made by some other manufacturer. As the quality of private-label products improves and consumers gain more experience with them, the "added utility" of a fully branded alternative declines. Shoppers looking for the lowest-priced product that gets the job done (a common criterion for consumers across all product categories) tend to buy private-label products.

Private labels are not as concerned about brand equity, and brands that try to compete on price with private labels are bound to get their asses kicked because the retailers don't incur the same sales, marketing, and trade costs that brands do. This is why some brands are "trapped" on the shelf next to low-priced generics. They can't raise their price and pretend to be a premium product when they're not, yet they can't afford to compete with equivalent private-label products on price.

So, what can brands do?

Well, you can't win on price because you have to spend money on sales and marketing while private labels don't. So, if you want to compete against private labels successfully, the proven path forward is to innovate and upgrade your products to deliver greater benefits and market those differences. Without a differentiated value proposition, you'll be limited to marketing gimmicks as your basis for overcoming the challenge of lower-priced rivals.

Did winning brands have strong equity that improved over the course of the study?

If you measure equity by looking at high consecutive repeat purchase rates relative to market share, the answer is yes. If awareness and familiarity are your benchmark measures of equity, then the answer is no.

We know the winners scored higher on brand equity attributes like uniqueness and innovation, but were there any measures where losing brands significantly outperformed our winning brands? Yes, and they all have to do with the behavioral types of consumers who prefer the losing brands.

As noted earlier, losing brands have significantly more consumers who are aware of the brand but choose not to buy it. In addition, consumers of losing brands are much more likely to be among the category's lighter buyers who do not have a significant brand preference. (These are called Low-Value Switchers in BERA's terminology.) This finding might come as a surprise, especially since figures like Byron Sharp assert that the key to brand growth is winning light buyers. But this is just one of our study's findings that undercuts this assertion.

| BERA metric | Loser | Winner | Delta | |
|---|---|---|---|---|
| Low-Value Switchers | 35 | 27 | | (8) |
| Non-Customers | 80 | 71 | | (9) |
| Non-Customers Aware | 77 | 67 | | (10) |

*Figure 6F. Brand Equity Metrics Where Losing Brands Most "Outperform" Winning Brands*

The accompanying graphic illustrates this. Losing brands tend to attract more Low-Value Switchers than winning brands (35th percentile versus 27th percentile). Also, more noncustomers (people who aren't buying the brand but are being asked about it) are more aware of the losers than the winners (77th percentile versus 67th percentile). This is further confirmation that consumers are actively rejecting the losing brand.

### RESPONDING AS A BRAND MANAGER

So, what should you do differently based on our brand equity study?

Most importantly, you need to care more about actual product performance. What is the product experience that gets delivered to your customers? How can you improve that experience through unique innovations?

Brand managers *and* marketers need to be part of the decision-making process regarding product development. You need to advocate for meaningful improvements to product experience and provide evidence to the research and development team showing why particular innovations matter.

Finally, remember that no amount of advertising will overcome a bad product experience. If you have a choice, improve your product rather than investing more into advertising, which is often the default behavior. There is a role for advertising, but it's not the panacea most brand managers think it is (or wish it were). Remember that advertising works best when introducing consumers to a brand-new innovation that does a job they need to get done and does that job better than any other brand in the category.

### KEY TAKEAWAYS

- Brand equity is primarily a function of product experience—not advertising, as many experts want you to believe. The dominant paradigm says advertising is how you boost brand equity, but brand equity grows when you have a product people love. Your product must make a promise and deliver on that promise.

- Premium innovation leads to Price Performance, which is when your customers love your product so much that they would be willing to pay more for it if they have to.

- To compete with private labels, you can't expect to win by beating their price. Rather, you have to identify the occasions (types of jobs) when your products are a better option and emphasize your ability to do that job.

- It's a popular assertion that differentiation doesn't matter because other brands can imitate your innovation. The data tells a different story. Brands that continue to innovate and create differentiated products are the brands that significantly outperform their peers.

- Many experts say that growing a brand requires increasing awareness through advertising, but our winning brands did not win due to gains in awareness. The awareness and familiarity metrics between winners and losers were equal and relatively steady over time. There was also a low correlation between changes in advertising spend and changes in either awareness, retail sales, or market share.

- Advertising is most effective at building brand equity when touting a new innovation. If you have a great new product, you should be advertising the hell out of it. Advertising is no substitute for product-led growth, however. Losing brands should improve their products before ramping up advertising to drive growth.

# 7

# SOCIAL
# VALIDATION &
# EARNED MEDIA

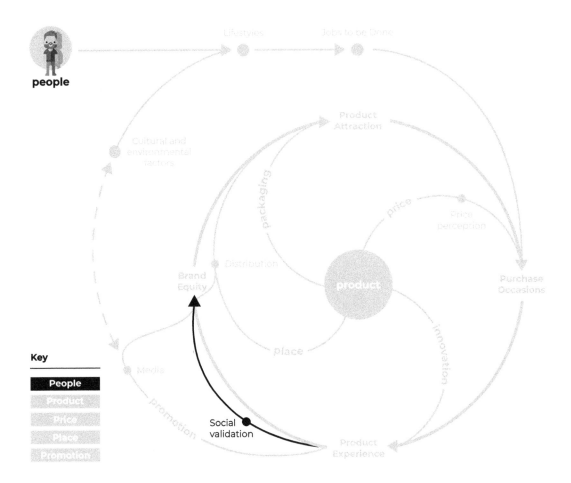

people

Key

People

Product

Price

Place

Promotion

Social validation

White Claw, an alcoholic seltzer water, burst onto the scene in 2016 and grew at a triple-digit annual rate over the next five years. Moreover, the brand claimed over half of all total hard seltzer sales in the US. And it did this with very little advertising.

What propelled White Claw were viral social media videos featuring the slogan "Ain't no laws when you're drinking Claws," a rallying cry coined not by the brand (thank goodness!) but by YouTube comedian Trevor Wallace.

Wallace wasn't the only one posting about White Claw. Fans generated more than four billion impressions for the brand in those first few years, delivering nearly fifty times as many social media mentions as any of White Claw's competitors. One man's tattoo of Baby Yoda drinking White Claw went viral on social media and generated stories in national magazines and countless websites and blogs.[1] In the summer of 2019, sales were so brisk that the brand pulled back on advertising to try and offset a product shortage. But the memes, videos, and hashtags continued rolling out unabated, and in 2020 and 2021, White Claw built a $250 million production facility in Arizona and another $400 million facility in South Carolina.

White Claw's success with social media had the compounding effect of generating tremendous earned media from prestigious publishers. Earned media is any material written about your product or business that you didn't pay for or create yourself. White Claw's viral success triggered dozens of articles in national media, from *Ad Age* and *AdWeek* to *People*, *Time*, and the *Washington Post*.

The White Claw experience underscored why social validation is so powerful; a stamp of approval from a person, rather than from an advertisement, is one of the best endorsements a product or service can get. When a friend or even a well-known figure we follow talks about a product they love, it can have a profound impact on us. If they love it, it must be worth checking out. By some accounts, Trevor Wallace's videos made it socially acceptable for college-age men to drink hard seltzer, which many previously considered a "girly" drink.[2]

At the heart of social validation and earned media is the product experience. Great product experiences lead not only to repeat purchases but also to social validation that generates new customers. If those new customers go on to have a great product experience, they'll repeat buy and recommend the product to others. It's a positive reinforcing feedback loop often referred to as a product's virality.

1    Megan Graham, "White Claw Will Make Its Biggest Ad Push Ever as Seltzer Space Heats Up," *CNBC*, April 1, 2021, https://www.cnbc.com/2021/04/01/white-claw-to-make-its-biggest-ad-push-ever-as-seltzer-space-heats-up.html.
2    "White Claw—Case Study," Professional Leadership Institute, accessed August 30, 2022, https://professionalleadershipinstitute.com/resources/white-claw-case-study/.

## SOCIAL VALIDATION

The concept of social validation as used in this book originates from Robert Cialdini's Social Proof Principle coined in his landmark 1984 book, *Influence*. It is based upon the psychological and sociological evidence that when people face uncertainty, they tend to follow the behaviors of others. Simply put, when faced with a choice, we often default to following the choices of others.

## GOING VIRAL

The term "viral" conjures up images of two things: something that gets widely shared (and insanely popular) on social media and an illness that is spreading rapidly through the population. When it comes to consumer goods, virality is a measure of the likelihood that existing customers will extol the virtues of a product and convince others to try it.

There's a formula (called the "k-factor") for calculating brand virality, which mirrors the math behind measuring the virality of communicable diseases such as COVID-19 or the common cold. It simply measures how often existing customers expose others to the product times the proportion of those exposed who convert to become new customers. If each existing customer exposes ten other people to the brand (e.g., by putting White Claw in the cooler at their party) and 20 percent of those people become new customers (e.g., by purchasing White Claw themselves), then the product's k-factor is two (ten people exposed X 20 percent conversion). This means that every existing customer will lead to two more new customers—just via word of mouth. That would result in insanely rapid growth for the brand—without having to advertise. As long as the k-factor remains above 1.0, the brand will grow from viral forces alone.

The big question for brand managers then is whether this phenomenon is just a matter of chance or if it's something that can be engineered. If you search Google for "engineering virality," you'll quickly see that virality is more than dumb luck—especially when it comes to branded media. Whether it's the virality of your products or your branded media, being intentional about delivering "surprise and delight" is a surefire way to harness viral forces.

## THE NEW WORD OF MOUTH

A McKinsey study of American, German, and Japanese consumers across several high-evaluation categories (e.g., autos, computers, and skin-care products) found that "internet reviews and word-of-mouth recommendations from friends and family" were the dominant factors determining which brands were actively evaluated—far outperforming all forms of brand marketing combined.[3] Word-of-mouth endorsements might have their greatest effect on highly considered purchases, but they are also highly relevant to the success of the winning brands in our study that compete in low-consideration categories. If someone says, "I tried Rao's spaghetti sauce and it's so worth the price, I can't imagine ever going back to the old stuff," you're much more likely to give it a try. It's that simple.

It's not just that word of mouth makes consumers more likely to try your product. Empirical research shows that customers acquired through word of mouth are longer-term and have a higher value than customers acquired through advertising.[4] This helps explain why word-of-mouth marketing delivers five times more sales than a paid media impression.[5] Why is the effect so powerful? Simple: trust.

3    Court, et al., "The Consumer Decision Journey."
4    Hanssens, *Empirical Generalizations.*
5    Khalid Saleh, "The Importance of Word of Mouth Marketing—Statistics and Trends," *Invesp* (blog), April 11, 2022, https://www.invespcro.com/blog/word-of-mouth-marketing/.

Consumers are 90 percent more likely to buy a brand recommended by a friend because they trust their friend's opinion far more than they trust claims made in a paid advertisement.[6]

In many cases, word of mouth has gone online, and consumers now learn about products from reviews, social media, videos, and other forms of shared content. For products involving greater levels of consideration (such as consumer electronics or even beauty-care products), online reviews have emerged as the modern proxy for word of mouth. Today, online reviews provide a way for consumers to share their experiences with others without having to talk face-to-face.

A study by McKinsey & Company found that even small changes in star ratings can result in eye-popping product growth—anywhere from 30 percent to 200 percent, depending on the category.[7] Even a small rise in score from 4.2 to 4.4 can dramatically increase sales. The likelihood of a sale peaks when the average rating is from 4.0 to 4.7 and decreases as the rating approaches 5. Shoppers distrust 5-star ratings, thinking every product has some room for improvement. A study at Northwestern University found that the sheer number of reviews—including negative ones—can also boost sales. Eighty-two percent of shoppers seek out negative reviews because they are viewed as more credible.[8]

Let's look at how this plays out for a winning brand such as Premier Protein relative to its losing counterpart, Muscle Milk. The accompanying screenshot shows the top search results for "protein shake" on Amazon.com at the end of this study. Does this screenshot from

---

6    Julian Villanueva, Shijin Yoo, and Dominique Hanssens, "The Impact of Marketing-Induced Versus Word-of-Mouth Customer Acquisition on Customer Equity Growth," *Journal of Marketing Research* 45, no. 1 (February 2008): 48–59, http://dx.doi.org/10.1509/jmkr.45.1.48.

7    Dave Fedewa, et al., "Five-Star Growth: Using Online Ratings to Design Better Products," McKinsey & Company, August 12, 2021, https://www.mckinsey.com/ industries/consumer-packaged-goods/our-insights/five-star-growth-using-online-ratings-to-design-better-products.

8    Spiegel Research Center, "How Online Reviews Influence Sales," Northwestern University Medill School of Journalism, accessed August 31, 2022, https://spiegel. medill.northwestern.edu/how-online-reviews-influence-sales/.

Amazon provide any clues as to why Premier Protein has been growing faster than its competition?

Figure 7A. Social Validation via Online Reviews for Premier Protein versus Muscle Milk

Premier Protein Shake, Vanilla, 30g Protein, 1g Sugar, 24 Vitamins & Minerals, Nutrients to Support Immune Health 11.5 fl oz, 12 Pack
**11.5 Fl Oz (Pack of 12)**
★★★★☆ ˅ 98,007

Pure Protein Strawberry Protein Shake | 30g Complete Protein | Ready to Drink and Keto-Friendly | Vitamins A, C, D, and E plus Zinc to Support...
**11 Fl Oz (Pack of 12)**
★★★★☆ ˅ 20,166

Muscle Milk Pro Series Protein Shake, Knockout Chocolate, 32g Protein, 11 Fl Oz (Pack of 12)
**11 Fl Oz (Pack of 12)**
★★★★☆ ˅ 10,450

Let's start with the obvious. Premier Protein shows up as the first result. While we don't have the data for Amazon, we know that the first search result on Google yields 31.7 percent of all clicks, and this is about 30 percent more clicks than the second spot, which itself is worth 30 percent more clicks than the third spot.[9] But why does Premier Protein show up first in this search result? Because it offers the most popular product in the category—the one consumers buy and review the most. If ten times as many consumers have reviewed Premier Protein versus Muscle Milk and it has slightly higher review scores, then it must be a better product, right? If you were buying the category for the first time, wouldn't you be more inclined to try Premier Protein first? And, if you liked it, would you even bother trying a competitor with fewer or less-raving reviews?

Online reviews have become more important than ever because consumers now check them before making first-time trial purchases in-store. Why trust the label over the wisdom of the crowd?

---

9    Brian Dean, "Here's What We Learned About Organic Click Through Rate," *Backlinko* (blog), last modified August 17, 2022, https://backlinko.com/google-ctr-stats.

This is not showrooming; it's more akin to webrooming, where shoppers evaluate options online before going to the store to make the final purchase. And given that shoppers like to know they are making a good product choice, you can expect retailers to further ease in-store decision-making by including online product review ratings on in-store shelf tags. I've already seen this practice implemented by several retailers in Europe, and as a shopper, I like it. I don't have to get out my phone and search for reviews before trying a new product; they're right there for me.[10]

*Figure 7B.*
Online Reviews
Are Making
Their Way onto
the Shelves of
Physical Stores

In the early days of e-commerce, retailers tried to simply replicate best practices from physical retail online. Let's call this era Shelf 1.0. Over time, brands and retailers realized several best practices specific to how consumers shopped online. For example, the addition of ratings and reviews, attribute-based search, and cross-category product suggestions are hallmarks of Shelf 2.0. But now we're entering a new era. The era of Shelf 3.0 is when learnings and capabilities from e-commerce begin to shape our in-store shopping experiences. A prime example is how online social validation via ratings and reviews is making its way into physical retail. Online reviews will no longer

---

10    Image: EllaRetail, "The Best Pricing Solution on the Market," accessed August 31, 2022, https://www.ellaretail.com/.

just influence the 10 percent of purchases that happen online or those webrooming occasions mentioned above; they will soon play a growing role in influencing our everyday in-store purchase decisions. Online reviews are rapidly supplanting traditional word of mouth as the most important way we learn about new products and overcome our fear of trying a product only to suffer buyer's remorse.

## EARNED MEDIA

There's an adage in the marketing world: *While advertising is what you pay for, public relations is what you pray for.* Public relations is a primary example of earned media: unpaid, third-party stories describing your product and why it stands out. You can't buy that kind of exposure, but when you get it, it's worth its weight in gold. When you gain exposure for your brand without paying for that exposure, you're doing something right. You've earned it.

Consider Tesla. Every car brand does ads, but not Tesla. In many markets, Tesla outsells Mercedes, BMW, and other high-end automakers by significant margins. They've sold millions of cars and have only been around for ten years. Yet, the day Tesla stops making news headlines (i.e., earning its media) will be the day we see our first Tesla ads.

Not only is earned media cheaper than paid media, but it also carries more influence because consumers' defenses aren't triggered by the obvious manipulatory efforts of a paid sales pitch. Consumers are more likely to think of earned media as an honest opinion, like traditional word of mouth.

In our study, four winners—Caulipower, Beyond Meat, Health-Ade Kombucha, and Dove—stood out for leveraging free earned media to drive viral growth.

### A HEADLINER

Gail Becker, the Founder and CEO of Caulipower (our winning brand in the frozen pizza category), had just won her first retail distribution with a trial at thirty Whole Foods stores when Trader Joe's launched its own cauliflower pizza crust in May 2017.[11]

She thought that was it for her brand, until a few weeks later when a miracle happened. An article appeared in PopSugar, a popular website that features beauty, entertainment, fashion, fitness, food, and parenting content. The PopSugar headline declared, "Meet the Cauliflower Pizza That Blows Trader Joe's Out of the Water."

Becker went straight to social media. "Holy shnikeys, fam. We have some news—you may want to sit down for this. We know that you all (and us, included) lost our minds when Trader Joe's came out with cauliflower pizza crust. It was a big deal, there's no denying it. But...there's a new cauliflower pizza in town...and...it's better. A lot better. The brand in question: Caulipower."

The PopSugar article said, "You can buy Caulipower cauliflower premade pizzas or just the crust—we tried the Margherita, Three Cheese, and Veggie premade varieties, and all three blew our taste-testers away in an unprecedented, unanimously positive review from over thirty of our colleagues, with a rare '6 out of 5' score." Not only did the article recommend Caulipower over the competing product from Trader Joe's, but it also placed Caulipower ahead of frozen pizza's number one brand: DiGiorno. "It's not delivery, it's not DiGiorno... it's better."[12]

According to Becker, the article had a huge impact on sales. "Our business exploded," she said. If we look at Caulipower through the Brand Growth Flywheel lens, we can see how its momentum built, starting with the initial distribution in thirty stores and increasing by getting the job done on usage occasions, attracting buyers with a billboard-like package, gaining social validation and positive reviews,

---

11    Zoe Bain, "Trader Joe's Latest New Grocery Item Is Going to Sell Out Fast," Refinery29, last modified August 19, 2017, https://www.refinery29.com/en-us/2017/05/154473/trader-joes-cauliflower-pizza-crust.

12    Dominique Michelle Astorino, "Meet the Cauliflower Pizza That Blows Trader Joe's Out of the Water," PopSugar, June 13, 2017, https://www.popsugar.com/fitness/Caulipower-Cauliflower-Pizza-43631318.

and leveraging all these piston punches and resulting momentum to gain wider distribution. Now that's a flywheel spinning with gusto.

When I interviewed Caulipower's chief operating officer, Katie Lefkowitz, about the secrets of the brand's success, she emphasized the impact of earned media, especially since the brand did not advertise during our study period. But this wasn't dumb luck. The earned media didn't just happen. Before founding Caulipower, Gail Becker had a successful career in public relations. She knew the value of direct outreach to journalists and media outlets, and she worked tirelessly to provide them with stories that would generate positive visibility for her fledgling brand.

"If you're doing something different, it's much easier to garner earned media, to be a story," Lefkowitz said. If DiGiorno had innovated—if it had come up with its own cauliflower crust or something else new or exciting—they too could have earned some media. But they didn't earn the story and ultimately had to rely on expensive advertising.

## NOVEL INNOVATIONS

Innovation isn't just a tactic for upstart brands like Caulipower. Oreo, which has been around for more than a century, has mastered the art of PR-worthy innovations. Although its classic cookie is by far the brand's most popular flavor, Oreo nevertheless loves to launch limited-edition flavors. Birthday Cake Oreos, anyone? Or perhaps you'd prefer Wasabi Oreos?

According to Justin Parnell, senior director of the Oreo brand, these limited-edition Oreos sell "reasonably well." But that's not why they are brought to market. The brand rolls out these novelty flavors to help drive sales of "our classic Oreo cookie, as well as the sales of the limited edition," Parnell said.[13]

---

13   Jonah E. Bromwich, "We Asked: Why Does Oreo Keep Releasing New Flavors?" *New York Times*, December 16, 2020, https://www.nytimes.com/2020/12/16/style/oreo-flavors.html.

Oreo gained earned media because they regularly give people something to talk about. Wait. *Wasabi* Oreos? That might make you pause in the cookie aisle, and it might prompt you to grab a package out of curiosity. Or it might prompt you to grab a package of the traditional version of this iconic cookie. Either way, the Oreo brand wins, and its micro novel innovations are a key element of that success. Wasabi Oreos might not sound great, but people will talk and write about them, and that will get people excited over and over again about bringing more Oreos home from the store.

## A PAPARAZZI MOMENT

*Figure 7C. Cameron Diaz Carrying Health-Ade Kombucha*

In an interview, Diana Trout, Co-founder and CEO of Health-Ade Kombucha, explained how much trouble she had getting her brand established. She maxed out her credit cards and drained all her bank accounts. She tapped relatives for loans. She borrowed from "everyone on the family tree." Meanwhile, her neighbors complained about the odor of fermenting kombucha wafting from her apartment. Her landlord evicted her.

"We were scared as heck," she recalled. "But we had an unusual drive to work hard and achieve success. That got us through. We were so dedicated to it. Then Cameron Diaz was in a photo holding one of our kombuchas."[14]

The image appeared on E! News in April 2015 as the website reported, "Diaz was seen dressed in head-to-toe workout attire (a gray sweatshirt, matching leggings and bright neon sneakers), was carrying a bottle of Health-Ade Kombucha and smiled as she made her way into her car."

---

14   White, "Kombucha CEO."

So, what was so special about this single image? Diaz is known for her roles in such films as *Gangs of New York*, *Bad Teacher*, and my personal favorite, *Charlie's Angels*. But she's also the author of best-selling health books (*The Body Book* and *The Longevity Book*) in which she extols the benefits of kombucha. Now, with that photo, Diaz fans could associate her love of kombucha with a brand: Health-Ade Kombucha. Soon, Health-Ade Kombucha was known far and wide, and brand representatives found it easier to get retailers to carry the product.

The best part about the media was that it was seemingly random. The brand didn't do anything extra to earn the media. They didn't hire the paparazzi or pay E! to write the story. They simply kept ensuring their product was top of the line, and eventually, they were rewarded for their effort.

## CREATING A CONVERSATION

While earned media played an important contributing role in the growth of many of our study's winning brands, perhaps none executed better in this department than Dove.

Dove's success with earned media stems from a study the brand conducted to understand women's self-perceptions. Specifically, Dove asked, "Which *one* of the following words, if any, would you be most comfortable using to describe the way you look?"

A surprising insight was that only 2 percent of women described themselves as beautiful. The survey became the genesis for Dove's "Real Beauty" campaign, which emphasized the gaps between how women were portrayed in advertising versus how real women looked and felt about their bodies.

The campaign included imagery featuring regular, full-bodied women (instead of Photoshopped models) who appear comfortable in their own skin. Another ad featured everyday girls alongside messages like "thinks she's ugly," "hates her freckles," and "afraid she's fat," followed by an invitation: "Let's change their minds...because every girl deserves to feel good about herself and see how beautiful she really is." It was a powerful message that triggered conversations about how beauty was portrayed in media and advertising.

Figure 7D.
Women's Self-
Descriptors for
How They Look

Which ONE of the following words, if any, would you be most comfortable using to describe the way you look?

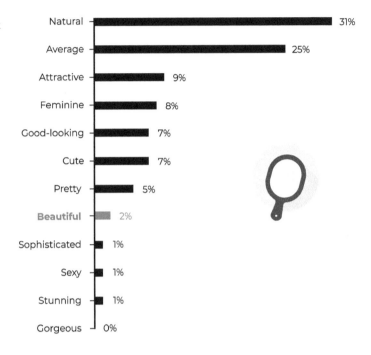

| | |
|---|---|
| Natural | 31% |
| Average | 25% |
| Attractive | 9% |
| Feminine | 8% |
| Good-looking | 7% |
| Cute | 7% |
| Pretty | 5% |
| **Beautiful** | 2% |
| Sophisticated | 1% |
| Sexy | 1% |
| Stunning | 1% |
| Gorgeous | 0% |

Figure 7E.
Screenshot
from Dove's
Video Ad:
Every Girl
Deserves to
Feel Beautiful

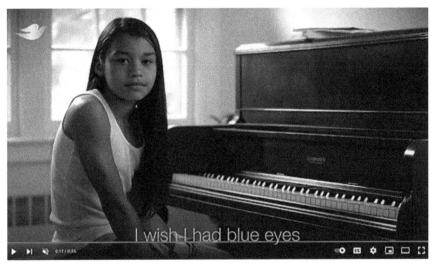

I wish I had blue eyes

While offline conversations can be hard to quantify, the sharing of content via social media and the resulting view counts are easy to measure. For example, Dove's three-minute YouTube video, which contrasted forensic sketches of how women described themselves versus how complete strangers described them, has garnered nearly 70 million views.

*Figure 7F.*
Dove's
Real Beauty
Sketches Video

While "Real Beauty" advertisements and videos are typically launched via paid media, the magnitude of their impact has come from creating content that earns media. "Real Beauty" has earned Dove's videos over 163 million views along with 4.6 billion PR and blogger impressions.[15] In 2015, *Ad Age* called it the best ad campaign of the century—and its effects continue to this day.

### EARNED MEDIA VALUE

It would be tempting to simply quantify the earned media value (EMV) or advertising value equivalent (AVE) by estimating how much

---

15    Google, "Case Study, Dove: Authentic Expression of Real Beauty Catapults Dove to 163 Million Global Views on YouTube," 2012, https://www.thinkwithgoogle.com/_qs/documents/4262/dove-real-beauty-sketches_case-studies_dciNDDN.pdf.

it would have cost to buy the same number of impressions via paid media. But there's a major flaw in this thinking. Would a *paid* YouTube ad that's three minutes long be nearly as effective?

Having consumers voluntarily engage with the earned media content is more effective at shifting consumers' probability of purchasing in favor of the brand. Earned media like this has a profound impact on a brand's value. It's no surprise that Dove was a major winner in our study, with incredible growth across its entire product portfolio, not just women's deodorant. Other brands have tried to build a conversation in this way but failed. One of our losing brands, Gillette, tried to do this with a campaign they launched in January 2019 in which they raised the issue of toxic masculinity. Ultimately there were calls for boycotts because the brand was simply jumping on the "Me too" bandwagon, and the campaign was seen as a divisively liberal political move.

Pepsi similarly tried to use an ad with Kendall Jenner addressing racial injustices.[16] It showed Jenner on a modeling photo shoot as a city street full of protesters marched past in an apparent Black Lives Matter–esque demonstration. Jenner is compelled to join them, dramatically pulling off her blond wig (and handing it to a Black woman standing nearby) and striding into the sea of humanity. In the cringeworthy culminating scene, she works her way to the front of the marchers and hands a policeman a can of Pepsi. He takes a deep drink. Protesters cheer, presumably because our common love of Pepsi is enough to dissolve centuries of discrimination and racial inequity.

Pepsi said it was trying to "project a global message of unity, peace, and understanding." The problem was that the ad was done in such a cheesy way that it lost all credibility. Bernice King, Martin Luther King Jr.'s daughter, mocked the ad, tweeting, "If only Daddy had known about the power of #Pepsi." Other critics pointed out that there

---

16   "Full Pepsi Commercial Starring Kendall Jenner," Yash Yadav, April 6, 2017, YouTube video, 2:48, https://www.youtube.com/watch?v=uwvAgDCOdU4.

was no credible link between the ad, the brand, and the fundamental issue of racial injustice. Once the ad campaign's earned media turned negative, the campaign was promptly yanked from the airwaves.

Earned media is a two-edged sword, and trying to wield it by force can be risky. But if you can create that conversation genuinely and organically, you might just find yourself holding King Arthur's fabled sword as you ride your way to victory.

## USER-GENERATED CONTENT AND INFLUENCERS

As the story of White Claw and comedian Trevor Wallace demonstrated, social validation doesn't just come through word of mouth, online reviews, or more traditional earned media. Sometimes, your customers will create the best advertisements for you. In the case of White Claw, the brand largely stayed silent while its fans created slogans and memes and branded stud earrings on Etsy. They stepped aside and let their fans—even those like Wallace, who at times mocked the beverage—create catchphrases and paint the brand's image in broad, often comical strokes.

"We want to let consumers have the conversation they want to have," said White Claw's marketing leader, Sanjiv Gajiwala. "I'm not interested in forcing myself into a conversation they're already having about me. I'm grateful they're having that conversation."[17]

This UGC, or user-generated content, can act as a social validation megaphone. And as long as that megaphone blares your praises, there's little need to spend money on paid advertising.

While White Claw stepped back and watched UGC explode, BodyArmor and Bang, both winning brands, purposefully assembled their user-generated content, doing a much better job than the corresponding losers in their categories. In the accompanying image,

---

17    Juntae DeLane, "White Claw Summer: How Does a Brand Become a Phenomenon?" *Digital Branding Institute* (blog), accessed August 31, 2022, https://digitalbrandinginstitute.com/white-claw-summer/.

you can see how BodyArmor's Instagram page used UGC to propel its brand with images of basketball legend Kobe Bryant drinking the product and athletes from other sports demonstrating that the beverage is "more than a sports drink." You see it featured at big sporting events. An athlete is being interviewed about it. It's all on brand and all connected to the people using the product. Meanwhile, Gatorade, the losing brand in this category, is all over the place: you see a car, then a guy making a funny face, somebody's shoes, then a "family edition" Gatorade flavor, which doesn't exactly feel "on brand."

The social feeds illustrate how some losing brands are not curating their UGC and paid influencers well. The losers are sloppy. They are all over the map. They seem to have fallen asleep at the wheel. The winners are sharper and carefully use UGC to cultivate the brand's favored image. This keen attention to image and message was common among many winners in our study; winners ensure high-quality user-generated content, whether paid or unpaid, appears prominently.

*Figure 7G.*
User-Generated
Content on
Instagram for
BodyArmor
and Gatorade

Brand managers can further promote their UGC content so that it is more prominent and gets more screen time. The first strategy is to make sure that what is posted is shared and liked a lot. By doing so, people will see the post first when the brand is searched. You also need to be sure that what you post is consistent and on brand. Finally, you can "boost" a post that's doing well with a small budget to get even more eyes on it—without fully raising consumers' alarm bells that they're being advertised to.

Social validation doesn't necessarily come from unbiased or unpaid sources. Paid influencers on social media are growing because they've shown that they can help boost a brand by bringing in more new customers and ongoing followers. By one measure, every dollar a brand spends on influencer marketing should return six to ten times in revenue for consumer packaged goods.[18]

Ten years ago, there was a raging debate about paying influencers. Their value stems from their followers believing that the influencer's recommendation is objective and trustworthy. But won't that trust erode when the influencer is paid for their endorsement? Good question. Some contend that trust in influencers is falling.[19] At the same time, many argue that influencers should be compensated for the hard work they do testing and evaluating the products and services they use and recommend.

One study concluded that influencers should be thought of as entrepreneurs and not as hobbyists or paid spokespeople. Influencers put long hours into their blogs and websites, writing articles, attending events, and posting photos. Rather than paid shills, they see themselves as an "advertising gateway to their cultivated communities." They protect their credibility because it directly affects their

18    Kristina Libby, "Why We Must Pay Social Media Influencers," *Business in Greater Gainesville*, May 2017, https://businessmagazinegainesville.com/why-we-must-pay-social-media-influencers/.

19    Peter Suciu, "Can We Trust Social Media Influencers?" *Forbes*, December 20, 2019, https://www.forbes.com/sites/petersuciu/2019/12/20/can-we-trust-social-media-influencers/?sh=4f3c841a63e8.

livelihood. Their followers expect them to do their due diligence before touting a product or service.[20] Influencing, the argument goes, is hard, honest work that should be rewarded. The successful "influencer-preneuers" will be those who make money promoting brands while maintaining their credibility with their audience. In other words, their posts will have value because they won't feel like advertisements.

The use of paid influencers isn't a new phenomenon. Celebrity endorsements have been around for decades and aren't going anywhere. Associating your brand with a well-known and highly regarded figure creates an instant "halo effect"—a powerful form of subconscious cognitive bias.

It works something like this: I like James Harden. James Harden likes BodyArmor. Therefore, I, too, like BodyArmor.

*Figure 7H.*
BodyArmor Ad with a Celebrity for Social Validation

But there's even more to the halo effect: the brand will be endowed with the celebrity's character traits. Consumers are more likely to notice and pay attention to James Harden than someone they are not

20    Suciu, "Can We Trust Social Media Influencers?"

as familiar with. And finally, if it's good enough for James Harden, I'm sure it's good enough for me.

When Scott Yacovino, Senior Brand Director for Nicorette, was planning the launch of Nicorette's new flavor-coated lozenges, he felt it was important to have a spokesperson with whom people would identify. "Quitting smoking isn't easy, but at Nicorette, we're committed to demonstrating our understanding and empathy for people on this difficult journey to quitting," said Yacovino. The brand eventually partnered with Dale Earnhardt Jr., who had also struggled to quit smoking.

"We love and admire Dale's authenticity," Yacovino explained. "His story and struggles to quit are similar to many smokers we've heard from, and we believe he can be a great coach for others who are starting their quit journey."[21]

"While I didn't talk about the fact that I was a smoker, the truth is, it was a part of my life," Dale Jr. said in a *Forbes* article. "Like many smokers, I tried many things and failed countless times. No longer relying on smoking or being at the mercy of my cravings feels great, and now I want to help others break free from the habit."[22]

Nicorette is a major brand, but influencers are especially important for challenger brands. Influencers can give a bigger microphone and lend greater credibility to smaller brands, thus spreading the word more effectively than they could on their own. It's no longer the case that consumers will only notice big brands that can afford costly ad campaigns. Tectonic shifts in how people consume media, particularly social media, have leveled the playing field.

---

21  Andy Frye, "Dale Earnhardt Jr. Talks about His Struggle to Quit Smoking," *Forbes*, May 21, 2019, https://www.forbes.com/sites/andyfrye/2019/05/21/dale-earnhardt-jr-talks-about-his-struggle-to-quit-smoking/?sh=3bc4fd9d3b8a.
22  GSK Consumer Healthcare, "Nicorette and Dale Earnhardt Jr. Launch New Nicorette Coated Ice Mint Lozenges to Help Smokers Succeed on Their Quest to Quit," PRNewswire, press release, May 21, 2019, https://www.prnewswire.com/news-releases/nicorette-and-dale-earnhardt-jr-launch-new-nicorette-coated-ice-mint-lozenges-to-help-smokers-succeed-on-their-quest-to-quit-300853562.html.

## KEY TAKEAWAYS

- A stamp of approval from another person is better than an ad. It's one of the best endorsements a product or service can get. When someone we trust extols the virtues of a product, we can be profoundly influenced. If they love it, it must be worth checking out.

- Customers acquired through word-of-mouth endorsements are more valuable and dependable than customers acquired through advertising. Word-of-mouth marketing delivers five times more sales than a paid media impression.

- Online ratings and reviews have become crucial. Even modest improvements in a star rating can trigger exponential increases in sales. The number of reviews—including negative reviews, which increase the reviews' overall credibility—can also boost sales.

- So-called "earned media"—unpaid, third-party stories describing your product and why it stands out—are worth their weight in gold. Earned media influences consumers far more than a paid sales pitch. Dove created its "Real Beauty" videos but they were posted as free content. Dove did not buy advertising time to get those videos in front of consumers. The resulting views came from people interested in the ideas and the content. Dove earned those views.

- Brands can create a public conversation through powerful campaigns like Dove's "Real Beauty" project. But this approach can backfire when the message is perceived as contrived or manipulative, such as Pepsi's offensive Kendall Jenner ad promoting the "power of Pepsi.

- Celebrity endorsements have been around for decades, and that's because they work. Consumers are more likely to notice and pay attention to James Harden than someone with whom they are unfamiliar. Famous figures also lend the credibility of their personal attributes to the brands they endorse, creating equity-building mental associations in the process.

# 8

# MEDIA AND ADVERTISING

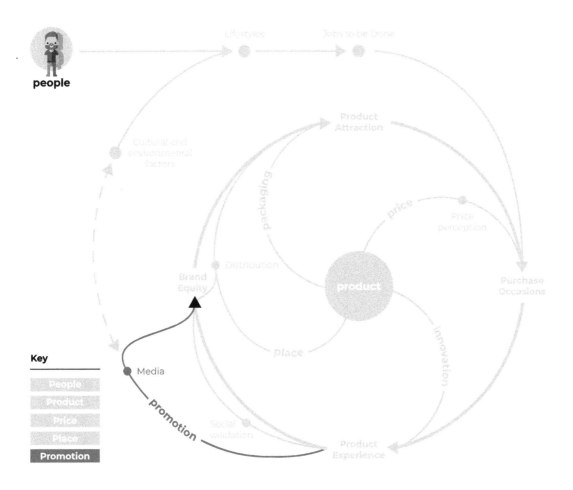

**Key**

People

Product

Price

Place

**Promotion**

Media

Promotion

wo women are recruited off a city street to take a blind "smell test." They are blindfolded and taken to what seems to be a dank cellar featuring a ratty couch covered in stains and animal hair. A couple of dogs sleeping on the couch are shooed away. Soiled blankets are draped over the back of the couch, and the plywood floors are filthy. Before the blindfolded women are led in, the couch gets sprayed with something. How do the women describe what they smell?

This isn't some random riddle. It is the story of how our winning brand in the air fresheners category set itself apart from the competition and fundamentally changed its sales trajectory and market share.

"Floral," says one.

"Maybe citrus," says the other. "Fresh laundry. Wispy white curtains."

"Yeah, beachy," her friend says. "Sitting outside. Fresh lawn being cut."

The women are invited to remove their blindfolds. Instead of finding themselves in a breezy coastal bungalow, they find themselves in a squalid basement with a couple of dogs prowling around. "Oh my God," says one woman. "Oh my *God*," says her friend.

*Figure 8A.*
Febreze's
Blindfold Ad
Campaign

This was the first commercial in a series of blindfold tests where unwitting everyday consumers found themselves in filthy rooms smelling clean and fresh thanks to Febreze. Within ten weeks of the first ad running, Febreze's sales jumped 18 percent, and within a year, it was one of P&G's more successful brands, racking up $1 billion in sales annually. That success continued in the following years as Febreze emerged from our study as the winning brand in the air freshener category.

Not bad for a product that in the 1990s was nearly discontinued due to poor sales.[1] Although the product was good at its job—its active ingredient is a molecule that neutralizes other molecules carrying

---

1    Adriana Estefania, "When Failure Leads to Success," *Medium*, May 4, 2019, https://medium.com/@adrianagurd/when-failure-leads-to-success-f77672153b4e.

unpleasant odors—people would use it a couple of times and then for-get they had it.[2]

Prior to the start of our study period, consumers viewing ads for Febreze, Air Wick, and Glade (the corresponding losing brand) were more likely to associate these brands' ads with a competitor than with the actual brand being advertised. The brands also lacked dif-ferentiation concerning the category's primary attribute: odor elimi-nation. The category's three leading brands were at parity with each other in consumers' minds according to a survey that asked, "When you think of odor elimination, which brand comes to mind?"

To address the brand's declining sales and lack of equity, the Febreze team conducted extensive research to diagnose the strug-gling brand's problems and gather insights into what could be done about it. This included focus groups, in-home interviews, shop-alongs, and brand equity deep dives.[3]

P&G sought to understand how Febreze consumers—especially their most loyal, heaviest consumers—would respond if deprived of their product. What pain points would emerge? What would consum-ers miss most and why? In addition, P&G put loyal buyers of Febreze, Glade, and Air Wick in a room to debate which brand was best and why.

The core insight that emerged was that a home can only be as clean as it smells and that a nice-smelling home will seem cleaner than it is. This led the brand team to take the position that "Febreze makes even the filthiest places smell nice, no matter what they look like."

Armed with this insight and refined positioning, the brand devel-oped a thoughtful brief that empowered their creative agency (Grey Group) to help Febreze "reclaim single ownership of odor elimination"

2    Jerry McLaughlin, "New Febreze Advertising Stands Out in a Crowded Market—Yours Can Too," *Forbes*, July 11, 2012, https://www.forbes.com/sites/jerrymclaughlin/2012/07/11/new-febreze-advertising-stands-out-in-a-crowded-market-yours-can-too/?sh=6c0af66c5609.

3    Mark Ritson, "Mark Ritson on the Effectiveness of Febreze's Award-Winning Ad," *Marketing Week*, June 10, 2019, YouTube video, 9:59, https://www.youtube.com/watch?v=OrmJQtPABXE.

as a brand equity attribute. This, of course, meant that viewers of the ads would have to correctly associate the message with Febreze instead of Glade or Air Wick.

After exploring several concepts and revising the creative's execution through pretesting, Febreze launched its "blindfold" campaign. In each test, people were blindfolded and led into locker rooms, public bathrooms, nasty restaurant kitchens, and abandoned fish lockers. They blindly smelled armpits, urinals, filthy boots, and sinks full of dirty dishes. And in the face of such squalor, they said they were reminded of spring, breakfast, caramel, forests, gardens, and a cool summer day next to a lake.

In addition, Febreze posted YouTube videos with behind-the-scenes footage from the ads' filming as further evidence of its credibility (including proof that the participants weren't professional actors).

The ads worked. After the campaign, 84 percent of consumers who saw ads for these brands associated Febreze with the category's primary benefit: odor elimination. Meanwhile, Glade and Air Wick languished far behind.

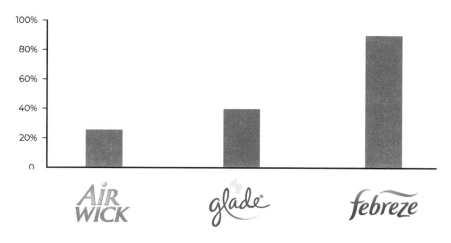

Figure 8B. Percentage of Consumers Correctly Associating the Brand with Odor Elimination

In addition, the Febreze team masterfully used trade promotions as an opportunity to drive activation at the point of purchase by linking the brand's advertising to their products in store via displays and merchandising.

*Figure 8C:*
*Febreze's In-Store*
*Displays Linked*
*Directly to Their*
*Nationwide*
*Advertising*

WALMART ENDCAP          NATIONAL FREESTANDING DISPLAY

The result was an immediate and ongoing rebound in Febreze's sales trajectory that continued throughout the study period.

While the greatest benefit of brand advertising comes from increasing the brand's momentum over the long term, this increase in long-term momentum cannot occur without an immediate short-term acceleration of sales. The difficulty is often to measure the signal of small increases in short-term sales resulting from brand advertising, which is often drowned out by a sea of market noise. Although the short-term sales boost delivered by this particular Febreze campaign was clear and compelling, it pales in comparison to the brand's ten-year gains.

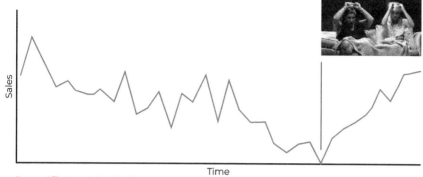

Source: Effie Awards Case Study

*Figure 8D.*
Febreze's
Media-
Driven Sales
Turnaround

Febreze's subsequent ads over the last ten years have built upon the foundation laid during this 2011 campaign. The brand still uses the "Breathe Happy" slogan, now reinforced with a jingle. The imagery of fluffy white clouds on blue sky backgrounds is as distinctive and consistent now as it was back then.

Moreover, Febreze's ads are effective because they address a real problem to be solved. *People can easily understand why they need the product.* The ads also show the actual product. *So you'll recognize it when you see it.* They also depict *how it is used.* Finally, they depict the *benefits of using it.* They masterfully associate all of this with the brand by reinforcing Febreze's distinctive assets: logos, colors, imagery, slogan, and jingle. This is a winning formula.

## PROBLEMS WITH ADVERTISING

Febreze's advertising success belies what we found in our study tying every ad campaign for every brand in our study to its retail sales performance. Despite the air freshener's triumph, advertising is rarely the panacea it's often made out to be. Advertising has its place, but it's not the magical elixir everyone thinks it is.

First, advertising and distribution go hand in hand. Some brands may find they have to commit to advertising to convince retailers to carry their product, but that advertising does little for the brand unless it is already widely carried by key retailers. This can be a bit of a chicken-and-egg conundrum. If you're advertising without distribution, you'll create frustrated customers who can't find your products. Once you have gained distribution, however, you have to avoid the trap of relying too much on advertising to drive your brand's flywheel. That overreliance on advertising is a mistake most brands make.

Advertising can increase sales, but the size of that increase is much less than most people think. While many expect advertising to drive 80 percent of sales growth for a brand, our study found that changes in advertising spending year over year bring much smaller returns. Even that smaller amount can be called into question because it represents a correlation and not causation. For example, if a brand is launching a major product innovation, it would be normal to expect a significant increase in both the advertising budget and retail sales. But that does not mean that the increased advertising caused the increased sales. It's often the innovation that is the primary driver of sales growth.

And while it may not always be true that more advertising drives increased sales, it *is* true that increased sales drive more advertising. That's because it's standard practice for brands to spend more on advertising as sales grow. The practice is based on the assumption that you need ads to sustain your sales momentum.

However, several scientific studies have shown the fallibility of that assumption. Even many industry leaders have mocked this *modus operandi*.

*Figure 8E.* Does Sales Cause Advertising?

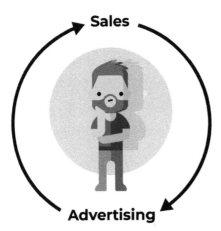

"You think that advertising causes sales?" General Mills' legendary research lead Larry Gibson used to ask. "Well, I know for a fact that sales cause advertising—because that's how we budget."

It's time to change this habit.

In a study by the University of Chicago and Northwestern University, researchers looked at "ad elasticity," which measures the percent change in quantity sales resulting from a given change in advertising. For example, if a 10 percent increase in advertising spend yields a 1 percent increase in sales, your advertising elasticity is 0.1 (1 percent divided by 10 percent).

When the academics examined sales and TV advertising data from 288 of the top 500 CPG brands from 2010 to 2014, they found an ad elasticity of .01. Whoa. In other words, if those brands increased advertising by 10 percent, they would increase sales by merely one-tenth of 1 percent (0.1 percent). That finding indicated that most TV advertising is about fifteen to twenty times less effective than most in the industry believe.

So why are so many brands continuing to pour money into advertising? Good question. We'll explore some of the reasons later in this chapter, but according to one of the researchers—Anna Tuchman of Northwestern University—one overarching reason is that marketers see billions of dollars spent on TV advertising every year and can't believe it isn't all that effective. The bias in favor of advertising is so strong that Tuchman told the *Freakonomics* podcast in 2020 that she worried her research would not be taken seriously.

"If you decide you want to take on this battle and publish your results (about advertising's ineffectiveness), you may face resistance in the review process at academic journals or skepticism from others who say, 'Hey, this isn't what we would expect if we see these firms spending millions of dollars on ads. It must be profitable. So there must be something wrong in your analysis.'"[4]

---

4   Stephen J. Dubner, "Does Advertising Actually Work? (Part 1: TV)," November 18, 2020, in *Freakonomics Radio*, produced by Daphne Chen, podcast, 38:12, https://freakonomics.com/podcast/does-advertising-actually-work-part-1-tv-ep-440/.

In our study, we were careful not to assume that advertising grows sales. We wanted to see the actual numbers before we drew any conclusions. We began by measuring annual advertising spend by brand for twenty-two different types of media: TV, radio, print, digital, etc. We then connected this data to retail sales for each brand year over year. Sure enough, retail sales did grow for each brand as advertising spend grew. However, although there was a correlation, there wasn't necessarily causation. Overall, we could not clearly attribute increases in our winning brands' sales directly to advertising, nor could we explain declines in our losing brands' sales by reductions in advertising. In her study, Tuchman found that "almost all brands... are earning a negative ROI from advertising."

In line with these and other long-term studies of advertising effects, we also found reason to believe that most brands are overadvertising.[5] Certainly, some ads can break through the noise and significantly increase sales—as they did in the Febreze campaign—but the real results of most advertising efforts year over year are bleak at best. Some brands, including some of our winners, showed that you don't need advertising. Rao's didn't advertise but continued growing year over year because they had an outstanding product and kept winning distribution at more and more retailers. Caulipower and Health-Ade Kombucha grew without significant advertising. Tesla wasn't part of our study, but it's another good example: even though most car brands have massive advertising budgets, Tesla doesn't advertise at all, and in early 2022 it reported a 70 percent sales increase while sales for other brands were declining.[6]

---

5    Greg Allenby and Dominique Hanssens, "Advertising Response," *Marketing Science Institute: Special Report*, no. 05–200 (2005), https://www.msi.org/wp-content/uploads/2020/06/MSI_SR_05-200a.pdf; Dubner, "Does Advertising Actually Work?"

6    Jack Ewing, "Tesla's Sales Jumped in the First Quarter, Bucking Industry Trend Again," *New York Times*, April 2, 2022, https://www.nytimes.com/2022/04/02/business/tesla-sales-electric-vehicles.html.

I don't want to suggest that brands should simply stop advertising, but that they should redeploy some of their advertising spending to more effective marketing activities.

No amount of advertising can overcome a bad product experience. At the same time, advertising can work as a source of news when there's something new to share and can help remind people of how much they love your product. Advertising can also shape the customer experience and embed it with added meaning.

The best ads can enhance consumers' experience when consuming your product. Consider the way Corona promotes its beer in TV ads. In each commercial, we see someone relaxing at a beach or enjoying a Corona outside their hectic schedule. The beer is, in essence, delivering a mini vacation, and this message is delivered consistently. If you see people on TV enjoying the sun and breeze as they drink, there's extra anticipation added. The message shapes the experience of drinking the beer and embeds it with added meaning. Still, if Corona weren't pleasant to drink, no amount of advertising would matter.

Tesla and Rao's can avoid the expense of advertising because consumers love the product. This product-led growth means that word of mouth and earned media (forms of social validation) do the brand-building work. A great ad campaign, such as the one for Febreze and Dove's "Real Beauty," also generates opportunities for earned media and word of mouth. Still, as our flywheel demonstrates, media and advertising are outside the flywheel and have a weaker impact on brand momentum than other factors.

Think of it this way. Say you turn your bicycle over so it rests upside down on its seat and handlebars. Now slap the front wheel so it spins freely. Continue to slap it to make it spin faster and faster. Eventually, you get the wheel spinning so fast that any additional slapping fails to help it spin faster. That's how advertising works. Applied effectively, it can help your flywheel spin faster—to a point. Spending beyond that point becomes less and less effective.

If growth through advertising is unreliable, what can you do as a brand manager to change your approach? First, stay away from the traditional budgeting model, which says that you must increase the advertising budget in proportion to your revenue growth. Instead, invest more heavily in advertising your new product innovations. As UCLA marketing expert Dominique Hanssens notes from his review of dozens of advertising effectiveness studies, it's a winning strategy to advertise your innovations; it helps make the innovation successful, and it increases your brand's overall equity.[7] Hanssens's conclusion is backed up by other scientific studies showing that advertising elasticities are two to five times greater for new products than for existing ones.[8]

These findings should convince you to change your approach. Rather than using the traditional budgeting model, strategically link advertising to innovations. If you're selling the same old laundry detergent, there's little point in using even more of your budget to

---

[7] Allenby and Hanssens (2005) reviewed advertising-response research of the last twenty-five years and found that short-run advertising elasticities for established products are very small, about .01. A recent meta-analysis by Sethuraman et al. (2011) finds a mean long-term elasticity across 402 observations of .24, with 40 percent of these elasticities between 0 and .1. Srinivasan, Vanhuele, and Pauwels (2010) report an average long-term advertising elasticity of .036 across 74 brands in four CPG categories. Sethuraman et al. (2011) also finds that advertising elasticity is lower in more recent studies, which suggests that advertising elasticity declines over time. This is "because of increased competition, ad clutter, the advent of the Internet as an alternate...ability to opt-out of advertising." [See Raj Sethuraman, Gerard J. Tellis, and Richard A. Briesch, "How Well Does Advertising Work? Generalizations from Meta-analysis of Brand Advertising Elasticities," *Journal of Public Policy & Marketing* 48, no. 3 (June 1, 2011): 457–71, https://doi.org/10.1509%2Fjmkr.48.3.457; Shuba Srinivasan, Marc Vanhuele, and Koen Pauwels, "Mind-Set Metrics in Market Response Models: An Integrative Approach," *Journal of Marketing Research* 47, no. 4 (August 1, 2010): 672–84, https://doi.org/10.1509%2Fjmkr.47.4.672.]

[8] Gert Assmus, John U. Farley, and Donald R. Lehmann, "How Advertising Affects Sales: Meta-Analysis of Econometric Results," *Journal of Marketing Research* 21, no. 1 (February 1984): 65–74, https://doi.org/10.2307/3151793; Leonard M. Lodish et al., "How T.V. Advertising Works: A Meta-Analysis of 389 Real World Split Cable T.V. Advertising Experiments," *Journal of Marketing Research* 32, no. 2 (May 1, 1995): 125–39, https://doi.org/10.1177%2F002224379503200201.

advertise it more heavily. However, if you've got a fancy new detergent coming out, tell the world about it and see the return for your money. You'll have short-term gains because humans are hardwired to pay attention to "new" information and long-term gains because consumers will associate your brand with being innovative—one of the qualities that separate our winning brands from their losing competitors.

## REASONS BRANDS OVERADVERTISE

Despite all the evidence that advertising is not as effective as it's often made out to be, why do most brands continuously overinvest in it? As I see it, there are three primary reasons:

1. The Fox and the Henhouse
2. Nuclear Proliferation
3. Missing Ghosts

Let's consider each of these.

### *The Fox and the Henhouse*

The agencies who create and place the ads are the same ones who measure the ads' effectiveness. These agencies have a built-in bias to make the ads appear more effective than they are. Even third-party firms that are hired to measure the ads are biased toward touting the effectiveness of the ads because they want to win repeat business for showing great results. If they don't, a different measurement vendor will be chosen the next time.

This is like asking the fox to guard the henhouse. These agencies and third-party firms are not incentivized to look out for your best interest. In economics, this is known as "the principal-agent problem."

Moreover, as Tuchman of Northwestern argues, the manager in charge of setting the television advertising spending and working with the advertising agency may have different goals than the firm. The firm wants to maximize profits, but the firm's ad manager doesn't want to put himself out of a job by revealing that, "Oh, it turns out our TV ads are unprofitable."[9]

**What's the solution?** Stop letting your brand marketers and agency partners grade their own homework. Use independent third-party measurement services overseen by your company's own market research team instead of by members of the brand or agency team.

In addition, never allow media platforms, marketing technology companies, and agency partners to dupe you into believing tricks like this one that Twitter previously employed to win ever greater shares of advertising spend.

Here's how the scam worked:

- Twitter matched its users with consumers' retailer loyalty card data.
- Twitter monitored those matched users to see which ones engaged with the brand's tweets.
- Twitter *then* compared the purchase behaviors of those users who engaged with the brand's tweets with those users who did not engage.

Surprise, surprise! Twitter could show huge differences in spending between consumers who engaged with the brand on Twitter versus those who did not. In doing so, they would suggest that advertising on Twitter had a large impact on brand sales. But that's nonsense. A brand's most loyal consumers, who already spend the most on the brand, are most likely to engage with the brand via social media. Those consumers already buy the brand because they love its products. This is why they followed the brand on social media.

Twitter's narrative flipped causation on its head by implying that because consumers follow the brand on social media, they buy more.

---

9    Dubner, "Does Advertising Actually Work?"

In truth, they follow the brand on social media because they already buy more.[10]

### Nuclear Proliferation

The reality of nuclear proliferation hit me as an undergrad. I was entertaining a career in politics and took a course on post–World War II global political dynamics. I remember distinctly when the professor said, "I've got $100 here awaiting the highest bidder. Who will give me a $1 bid for this $100 prize?" There was just one catch, the professor explained. Once you bid, the only way to get your bid money back is to be the highest bidder.

The bids poured in until at one point the bids began exceeding the amount being offered. Why? Think about it. If you bid $98 and the gal next to you bid $99, you stood to lose your $98. But if you bid $100 to get ahead of the $99 bidder, you had a chance to break even. Of course, when you bid $100, your predecessor now stood to lose her $99. This compelled them to bid more than the prize was worth. I think bids got up to about $120 before the professor ended the exercise and released us from our obligations in this terrible game of escalation.

This is precisely how nuclear proliferation works. It's also how advertising can work.

A brand that increases its advertising spending such that its "share of voice" exceeds its "share of sales" will typically grow its market share.[11] Since market share is a zero-sum game, their competitors will lose market share. The competitors don't want to do that, so in response, they increase their advertising spending to claw back their market share. Before long, brands going head-to-head like this are spending more and more on advertising to hold on to the same

---

10    Bart de Langhe and Stefano Puntoni, "Leading with Decision-Driven Data Analytics," *MIT Sloan Management Review*, December 7, 2020, https://sloanreview. mit.edu/article/leading-with-decision-driven-data-analytics/.

11    Les Binet and Peter Field, The Long and the Short of It: Balancing Short and Long-Term Marketing Strategies (London: IPA, 2013).

market share. Very quickly, all this spending stops making sense, and brands are spending just to keep from losing. This is nuclear proliferation. The race to maintain market share forces brands to spend past the point of optimal returns.

**What's the solution?** Recognize that winning the share-of-voice game via greater advertising spend is a fools' errand. You may grow sales this way (for a while), but not profit. You're simply playing into the rat race of nuclear proliferation. It can make sense to invest more in advertising ahead of sales with new product launches, but the goal should be to win the broader share of the voice game via more creative ads, word of mouth, and earned media. Remember Dove's "Real Beauty" campaign? They grew sales not by running more ads but by creatively building off of the effectiveness of a single campaign in a way that drove word of mouth and earned media.

### Ghost Ads

The final reason brands spend too much on advertising is because they do not properly measure the effectiveness of their ads by using ghost ads. Ghost ads placed within randomized control trials (RCTs) are the most scientific way of seeing if ads are driving incremental sales.

Let's say you're Modelo running a campaign on Facebook targeting consumers ages twenty-one to twenty-four with incomes at a certain range. Rather than sending out ads to everyone in that category, you send out ads to just 60 percent of the group. The remaining 40 percent of your target sees a different ad (a ghost ad) from a different brand and category. For instance, instead of seeing a Modelo ad, they see an ad for laundry detergent.

Then, after the ads run, you track the spending habits of everyone who was originally targeted. If the people who saw the Modelo ad go out and buy Modelo, great; that's what you want. But if the people who saw the ghost ads—the laundry detergent ads—go out to buy Modelo at the same rate as those exposed to the Modelo ad, you have to question whether your ads were effective.

What's the solution? There is no better way to measure advertising effectiveness than randomized control trials (RCT).

If you're a brand manager, you should partner with publishers and platforms capable of randomly delivering ghost ads to a statistically sufficient number of consumers who otherwise would have received your ad. You measure everything else in your business; why not this aspect? It's not difficult to do, either; digital and social media already provide powerful analytics about the effect of ads, and as more consumers transition to streaming content, it should become easier to measure TV ads as well.

As Rick Bruner, the CEO of Central Control and the genius behind the Wonks community of leading market researchers (of which I am a proud member), puts it, "In pharmaceuticals, people die if they don't [measure via randomized control trials]. In advertising, nobody dies, but people lose market share and their jobs." What we need in marketing is more scientific measurement.

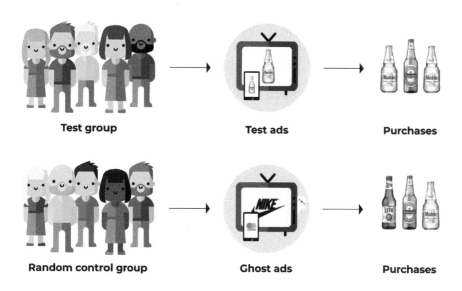

*Figure 8F.* Randomized Controlled Trial via Ghost Ads

**Test group**     **Test ads**     **Purchases**

**Random control group**     **Ghost ads**     **Purchases**

It's not enough to attribute the sales lift of beer during the summer to increased advertising without controlling for the natural seasonal uptick in summertime demand for beer. That doesn't mean that beer companies shouldn't advertise more during periods of higher demand—they typically should. It just means that simple lift-and-conversion models aren't enough to explain whether sales growth comes from advertising versus other effects. You need a more precise analysis of advertising's effect to measure the signal from the noise.

## THE BIGGER STRATEGY

To be clear, I'm not arguing that advertising is a waste of money. I'm also not claiming that you shouldn't advertise. What I'm saying is to be careful of overadvertising and to instead use it at the right time, in the right way, and then measure its effectiveness correctly.

While advertising has an important role to play, it should play that role within the context of an overall media strategy that invests strategically across owned, earned, and paid media channels. Even within paid media, advertising is just one way to play. There are other creative ways to bring attention to your products, such as product placements in movies, shows, and video games.

To understand a bigger media strategy, let's take a step back and consider why advertising works in the first place. Advertising works because consumers do not have strong brand preferences or loyalties in most of the product categories they buy. In fact, consumers switch brands from one purchase occasion to the next at least half of the time. That's right: consumers are at least as likely to switch brands as they are to repeat purchase the same brand they bought last time.

With most consumers not showing a strong preference for one brand over another, it only takes a little nudge to tilt the scales in favor of a particular brand via any form of media. Although my contemporaries may argue that "advertising can turn brand triers into loyal buyers and it can rebuild loyalty that was lost," I would argue that all it can do is load the dice a little more in your favor. It can improve the odds for you, making it a good investment—provided it isn't overused. So, how can you do that effectively?

First, you can understand what actually matters in advertising. To guide our exploration, we're going to leverage an NCSolutions study of nearly five hundred campaigns across all media platforms in 2016 and 2017 during the heart of this book's research period. The NCSolutions study relied upon the relatively straightforward and benchmarkable metric of sales productivity, which measures the incremental sales per shopping trip within the category for shoppers exposed to a brand's advertisement versus those not exposed.[12]

But what was it about the ad that had the most influence on these consumers? This is where the study offered some particularly valuable insights. Check out the accompanying graphic measuring the relative impact of such things as the ad's creative content, reach, recency, context, and targeting.[13]

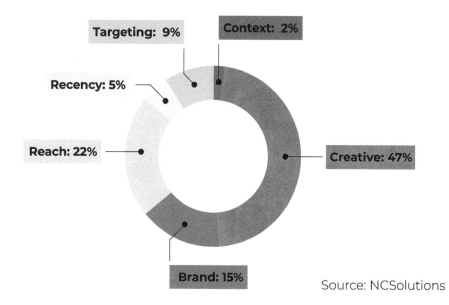

Targeting: 9%  Context: 2%

Recency: 5%

Reach: 22%

Creative: 47%

Brand: 15%

Source: NCSolutions

*Figure 8G.*
Drivers of Ad
Effectiveness

According to this study, by far the biggest lever is the quality of the ad's creative content, which accounted for 47 percent of its

---

12   NCS and Nielsen, *Five Keys to Advertising Effectiveness*, 2019.
13   Note that 'Brand' effects serve as a catch-all for other factors unique to the brand and/or its category such as the relative price of the products.

effectiveness. Since creative, reach, brand effects, context, and targeting are the most significant levers to which brand managers can apply direct pressure, let's take a closer look at each.

## CREATIVE

It was the best of ads. It was the worst of ads. It was Procter & Gamble's first foray into Olympic advertising with its heartwarming, tear-jerking, and award-winning "Thank you, Mom" campaign. Launched shortly ahead of the London Olympics in 2012, it was to be Procter & Gamble's largest campaign in the company's 174-year history and was projected to deliver $500 million of incremental sales.[14]

The campaign won P&G a Gold Effie and the 2013 Ogilvy Award. There was just one problem. The TV and digital video ads did not mention or depict any of Procter & Gamble's brands, such as Tide, Venus, Puffs, and Dawn, until their logos appeared at the very last second.

I had a hunch that no matter how incredibly emotive the ads were, they would do little to affect the sales of P&G products. Right after the Olympics, in the very first bit of market research ever performed by Numerator (known as InfoScout back then), I surveyed a representative sample

*Figure 8H. Procter & Gamble's "Thank You, Mom" Campaign*

---

14    MSL Canada, "Procter & Gamble Launches Global 'Thank You Mom' Campaign in Celebration of 100 Days to Go Until the London 2012 Olympic Games," Business Wire, April 17, 2012, https://www.businesswire.com/news/home/20120417006777/en/Procter-Gamble-Launches-Global-Thank-You-Mom-Campaign-in-Celebration-of-100-days-to-go-until-the-London-2012-Olympic-Games.

of one thousand consumers who had regularly been taking pictures of their shopping receipts with our Receipt Hog and Shoparoo apps. Only 18 percent of these consumers could both recall the ad campaign *and* credit it to Procter & Gamble (as opposed to other Olympic advertisers, such as Visa).

Among those who recalled seeing the ads, they were at least as likely to think the ads had been promoting competing brands.

### Soap and cleaning brands (select all that apply)

33% Dove

29% **Dawn**

26% I have no idea

17% Dial

*Figure 81.*
Consumers
Recalled the
Ads, but Not the
Brands Being
Advertised

Across nearly a dozen product categories it became clear that consumers' likelihood of associating these "Thank you, Mom" ads with any given brand correlated with the brand's market share in the category. This study showed that measuring "ad effectiveness" without accounting for the brands' existing market share or the direct measurement of incremental sales must be completely inaccurate. If consumers aren't associating an ad with your brand, the best you can hope for is that you're just advertising the category as a whole.

### FIRST IMPRESSIONS

As important as the final scene may be to make a lasting impression, there may be even more truth than we thought behind the adage, "You never get a second chance to make a first impression."

In a recent study of how the human brain responds to ads, researchers found that people see and register two-thirds of all ads in four-tenths of a second.[15] People then form a positive or negative impression of an ad in less than half a second. What's more, they reject ads much faster than they accept them. These findings were especially true of video ads, perhaps because they have been shown to generate a stronger emotional response and do so more quickly.

According to ad executive Greg Stuart, the CEO of MMA Global and the former CEO of the Internet Advertising Bureau, the study measured the brain activity of nearly one thousand consumers, tracking their attention and cognition at twenty-millisecond intervals as they watched a selection of ads. The selection included ads that had previously been shown (through other measurement methods) to be either effective or ineffective.

What researchers found was that weak ads started alienating viewers "well before the first second had elapsed."

"It turns out that thousands of years of human evolution have created a number of predictable shortcuts in the human brain and as a result, a common response to certain stimuli," Stuart said in 2021. "For example, we react to colors and shapes before we register an image (a person, animal, or object) as a concept...(and) images of people—faces, body parts, or icons shaped like bodies—get our attention immediately. Even incomplete faces pique our instinctive curiosity. Our brains have developed the ability to detect eyes more easily, a mechanism that scientists call the eye direction detector (EDD)."

According to the Mobile Marketing Association, the study reveals the need for brand marketers to have "a clear 'first-second' strategy" in their ads.[16] "Although brands have been trained to develop fifteen- or thirty-second creative and media strategies, or even six- or

15   Greg Stuart, "Advertising's Mis-understanding of Time: Brands Need a First-Second Strategy," *Man Saves Dog* (blog), March 21, 2021, https://mansavesdog.wordpress.com/2021/03/21/advertisings-mis-understanding-of-time-brands-need-a-first-second-strategy/.

16   Mobile Marketing Association, "Mobile Marketing Association Reveals Brands Need a First Second Strategy," March 6, 2019, https://www.mmaglobal.com/news/mobile-marketing-association-reveal-brands-need-first-second-strategy.

seven-second strategies, marketers should now develop plans and strategies that address the first one second."

With this in mind, watch a few ads for Reese's (our winning brand of chocolate) and Snickers (the corresponding losing brand). The accompanying images show the opening shot of an ad for each.

With Reese's, you'll notice that their video ads immediately convey the brand's iconic color and shape assets within the first second.[17]

*Figure 8J.*
The Opening
Scene for
a Reese's
Video Ad

*Figure 8K.*
The Opening
Scene for
a Snickers
Video Ad

17   "Reese's Minis Commercial 'In the Palm of Your Hand,'" Charles Morrison, March 31, 2016, YouTube video, 0:15, https://www.youtube.com/watch?v=w3QODu07_AA.

This is a stark contrast to Snickers' ads, which typically wait fifteen to twenty seconds before introducing the brand—often quite randomly. The brand's 2015 Super Bowl commercial featuring the fearsome Danny Trejo as Marsha Brady is a prime example.[18]

## STOP TALKING

One way to make your creative more effective is to talk less and show more. There is a strong negative correlation between the number of statements made during a commercial and consumers' willingness to pay attention.[19]

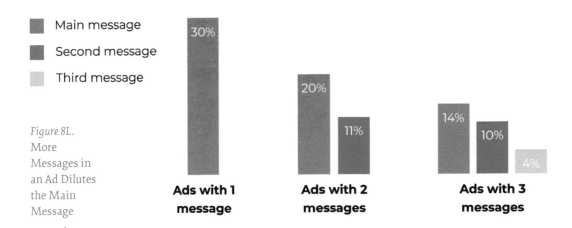

Main message

Second message

Third message

*Figure 8L.* More Messages in an Ad Dilutes the Main Message

30%

20%

11%

14%

10%

4%

**Ads with 1 message**

**Ads with 2 messages**

**Ads with 3 messages**

Studies have shown that the more messages an ad attempts to communicate, the less likely consumers are to recall even a single message. An important global study by Kantar Millward Brown demonstrates how more messages dilute your main message. The study found that, on average, 30 percent of people are able to play back the main message from a TV ad spontaneously (after watching it twice) if it attempts to communicate one message. This

---

18 "Super Bowl 2015: Snickers Ad," *Wall Street Journal*, January 29, 2015, YouTube video, 0:32, https://www.youtube.com/watch?v=3UO2A2p-19A.

19 Charles Young, "The Gift of Sound and Vision," *Quirk's*, accessed August 31, 2022, https://bluetoad.com/publication/?i=728186&article_id=4157207&view=articleBrowser&ver=html5.

percentage drops considerably for ads attempting to communicate multiple messages.[20]

This isn't a new idea. It's just one we seem to need to relearn over and over again.

We have to recognize that while the ads we create are important to us, there is very little reason for consumers to pay attention to our ad over every other ad vying for their attention. The per-adult consumption of advertising in America is nearly $1,000 a year.[21] A $10 million ad campaign will account for just 0.00004 percent (four one-thousandths of 1 percent) of all the advertising your consumers are bombarded with each year. So, how can you break through all the noise? Being louder is not the answer. Follow the advice of marketing legends Al Ries and Jack Trout: "The best approach to take in our over-communicated society is the oversimplified message."[22]

## A CULTURAL INFLUENCE

We all know media is irrelevant without culture, but when your brand's media is so relevant that it actually influences culture, you know you've accomplished the extraordinary. Just ask two of our winning brands, White Claw and Old Spice.

Both brands are effectively influencing culture. They're adding to the everyday conversation in the real world, regardless of whether people use the product. "Ain't no laws when you're drinking Claws" has become an everyday saying. And there are now countless memes that have been created based on the ads for Old Spice with Isaiah Mustafa and Terry Crews. The humor creates a buzz, and the images pass around and stay in people's minds.

---

20   "Advertising: Make a Lasting Impression," Kantar Millward Brown, 2017, https://www.millwardbrown.ru/library/Kantar_MillwardBrown_Make_a_Meaningful_Impression.pdf

21   Over $240 billion in advertising spending to reach roughly 240 million adults in America.

22   Al Ries and Jack Trout, *Positioning: The Battle for Your Mind*, (New York: McGraw Hill, 2001), 7.

Figure 8M.
Examples
of Winning
Brands
Influencing
Pop Culture

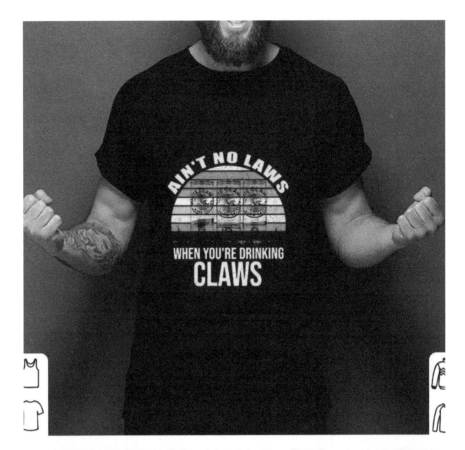

Less talking and more visual storytelling are key to getting consumers to pay attention. One technique to achieve this is to apply the "Spielberg Variables." The method is inspired by famed Hollywood director Steven Spielberg.

John Kastenholz, Vice President of Consumer Insights at Unilever, shared that each ad his company produces employs the same style and storytelling techniques used in feature films. Good movies win viewers' attention, propel the audience forward emotionally, and convey meaning, he said, and Unilever wants their ads to do the same.

"If we determine that we have a big idea hobbled by flawed execution, we put 'the Spielberg variables' to work," Kastenholz wrote in *Harvard Business Review*. "That is, we ensure that each of our ads employs the same style and storytelling techniques used in feature films. Good movies are often born in the editing room. We believe the same is true of good ads, so our goal is to diagnose problems and then fix them with a new director's cut, as it were."

Sixty ads from Unilever's health and beauty products units were approved for airing. Twenty-five of them started out as average performers but were recut using feature-film qualities and came out in the superior range. "This ability to optimize our advertising helps Unilever maximize ROI," Kastenholz said.[23]

Similarly, you can let a song do the telling for you. While a lot of talking heads in our industry babble about the concept of "brand voice," very few sing the praises of "brand sound." Do you know what your brand sounds like? What should it sound like?

If music triggers emotions and emotional arousal increases receptivity, then doesn't it logically follow that the proper use of music in ads should improve their effectiveness? Fortunately, we

---

23   John Kastenholz, "The Spielberg Variables," *Harvard Business Review*, April 2005, https://hbr.org/2005/04/the-spielberg-variables.

don't have to rely solely on an appeal to logic. A study of the use of music within ads from the IPA Databank found that ad campaigns that use music achieve better results across a wide range of success metrics, including sales.

Not only do consumers explicitly rate the likability of music-infused ads higher, but EEG tests of beta-gamma brain wave activation have also quantified greater implicit response. Finally, the research also shows that the specific music used within an ad "conveys strong rational and emotional associations for brands."[24]

So, at a minimum, you might consider bringing back a little jingle. At the other end of the spectrum, you could be like Apple, which has launched several musicians into stardom by using their songs as the creative basis for an advertisement. It's happened so many times that the music industry has literally dubbed it "The Apple Effect." A perfect example is the use of "Are You Gonna Be My Girl" by Jet to promote the iPod.

*Figure 8N.*
Imagery
from Apple's
iPod Launch
Campaign

---

24   Radiocentre, *Strike a Chord: How Music Enhances Communication* (London: 2015), https://www.radiocentre.org/research-projects/strike-chord/.

Finally, it's critical to understand that advertisements work via mental priming.

Priming is when we expose someone to something that influences their behavior later on—without that individual being aware that the exposure guided their behavior.[25] Recall the story of Pavlov's dogs who started to salivate whenever their dinner bell rang.

Priming is using a stimulus like a word, image, sound, or action to change someone's behavior. For example, research has found that we can prime someone to walk more slowly just by having them read words like *cautious* or *leisurely*. Or we can prime someone to be less rude by having them read words like *patient*, *polite*, and *respectful*.

In *The Long and the Short of It*, renowned ad effectiveness experts Les Binet and Peter Field explain that "another intriguing effect of emotional priming is that it makes people tend to believe positive rational messages about the brand, whether or not they are presented with any evidence."

The authors go on to show how emotionally focused campaigns generate stronger effects despite saying less. Emotional priming makes consumers more receptive to rational messages, which "unlocks the short-term sales potential of the brand." What's more, the cumulative effects of emotional priming grow over time and decay slowly.[26]

## REACH

It goes without saying that great creative that doesn't reach anyone won't make much of an impact. An ad campaign without reach falls

25  Vanessa Van Edwards, "Priming Psychology: How to Get People to Do What You Want," Science of People, accessed August 31, 2022, https://www.scienceofpeople.com/priming-psychology/.

26  Les Binet and Peter Field, *The Long and the Short of It: Balancing Short and Long-Term Marketing Strategies* (London: IPA, 2013).

like a tree in the forest. If no one is around to hear it, does it even make a sound?

Reach would not be worth our time to discuss if its effects were linear. But, as it turns out, the effects of reaching ever-larger audiences do not follow a simple, linear equation. Reach effectiveness follows an S-curve known as the Advertising Response Function. As outlined in *Harvard Business Review*'s classic article "Ad Spending: Growing Market Share," "The productivity of ad dollars rises as budgets grow from zero to a meaningful level, and then the law of diminishing returns sets in. Piling on more dollars becomes less and less productive."[27]

*Figure 80.*
The Advertising
Response
Function

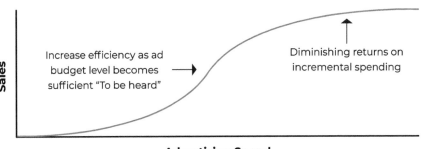

When it comes to achieving the greatest reach, TV still reigns supreme. Very few digital campaigns have been able to match the reach of a TV campaign with the same number of impressions.[28] Even in cross-platform campaigns, studies have shown that television remains the key to reaching a large number of consumers.

It's not just that TV remains central to reaching consumers; its influence on building brand equity and driving sales also played a central role during our study. It was the only medium for which there

---

27    James C. Schroer, "Ad Spending: Growing Market Share," *Harvard Business Review*, January–February 1990, https://hbr.org/1990/01/ad-spending-growing-market-share.

28    It typically takes more impressions via digital to achieve an equivalent level of reach obtained by TV because the digital campaigns serve more impressions to the same consumers.

was a clear positive correlation between increased ad spending and year-over-year sales growth.

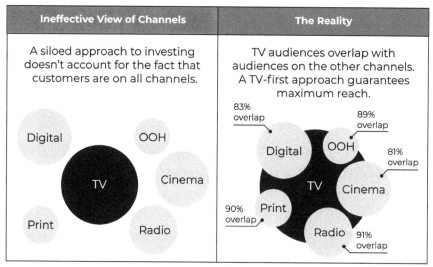

*Figure 8P.*
TV-First
Approach
Guarantees
Maximum
Reach and
Minimum
Duplication

Source: GroupM LivePanel September 2016

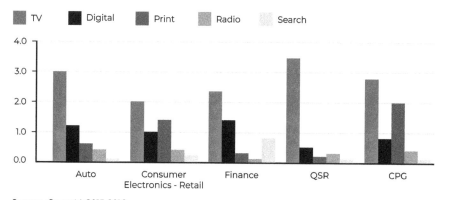

*Figure 8Q.*
TV Has the
Highest Lift
Factor on
Outcomes

Source: GroupM, 2015-2016

Every pundit has an opinion on why increased reach results in exponentially increasing returns until the point of diminishing returns sets in. But they're not here to weigh in, so here's my quick take. Most of the S-curve effects of greater returns from increasing reach come from TV advertising being more effective (especially on a per-impression basis, but even on a spend basis) than digital, radio, print, and other media. Is it any surprise that a video ad would be more effective than a single image or audio-only impression? Moreover, the fact that your brand is being advertised on TV conveys to consumers a sense that it must be a popular and successful brand of high quality. After all, only a strong brand could afford to advertise on TV, right? All of these subconsciously add to the brand's equity in a way that other media cannot yet match.

Fortunately, the rise of connected TVs has led the advertising industrial complex to develop capabilities for brands to run TV ads at a much smaller scale. In fact, advertisers can now target TV ads to specific households based upon all of the selection criteria that had previously been the differentiating hallmark of digital media platforms. This can help brands gain many of TV's benefits without busting the budget.

## TARGETING

NYU's Scott Galloway recently popularized the concept that advertising is a tax on the poor and technologically illiterate because they lack the resources to access ad-free media. I think there's growing truth to his argument, but I have a different perspective on advertising as a tax.

For example, let's look at consumers who buy chocolate. Imagine the amount of chocolate each consumer buys per year as their annual income. Some buy a lot of chocolate and represent those with high incomes, while some buy little (low income) and some buy none at all (unemployed). How shall we tax these buyers of chocolate with advertising? Should they be taxed with equal amounts of ad exposure, regardless of how much chocolate they buy? Or should heavy buyers of chocolate (those who are rich in chocolate) bear a heavier burden of being advertised to even more? Let's look at the options.

Option 1—Tax all chocolate buyers equally (e.g., two ad exposures per person per month). This is what we call a "regressive tax" because light buyers (lower incomes) end up paying a greater proportion of their income (chocolate spend) on taxes (advertising) than heavier consumers. Regressive tax regimes fail and collapse because they are unjust and are not sustainable. The same is true of regressive advertising schemes that target all category buyers equally.

Disciples of Byron Sharp and the Ehrenberg-Bass Institute often argue that this is the best targeting approach, but it flies in the face of empirical evidence and common sense. For example, heavier category buyers are always closer in time to their next purchase, so any advertising exposure to them is more likely to have a greater influence on their next purchase than an ad exposure to a lighter category buyer who is further away (in time) to their next purchase. In addition, heavier category buyers are more likely to notice and pay attention to an ad than a lighter category buyer for whom the ad is less relevant.

Option 2—Tax all chocolate buyers with a flat tax. In this scenario, we might say that for every five dollars a consumer spends on chocolate, they should be taxed with exposure to one advertisement. Each consumer, therefore, is exposed to ads proportionally to their chocolate spend. I am generally in favor of this flat tax advertising regime. First, light and nonbuyers of a category (or even a brand) are the least likely to respond to advertising and will deliver the lowest return on ad spend (ROAS). Heavier buyers are more likely to notice and recall advertising for the category and the brand because the product being advertised is more relevant and familiar to them. In addition, heavier category buyers are more likely to have a near-term upcoming category purchase occasion than light or nonbuyers, and an ad is most effective when its impression is made shortly before a purchase decision. This is called the "recency effect." As we noted earlier, recency accounts for 5 percent of an ad's effectiveness in the NCSolutions study.

Option 3—Tax chocolate buyers with a progressive tax. Under this option, very light buyers of chocolate would get little exposure to advertisements for chocolate. Heavy buyers of chocolate, however, would carry a disproportionate burden of the advertising tax. This might be the most profitable approach in the short run, but I question its long-term efficacy because medium and light buyers still account for a large portion of overall chocolate sales.

As Rory Sutherland, ad industry luminary and vice chair of Ogilvy & Mather, puts it, "If advertising is to work, it's a reasonable request of advertising that the advertising I see should be reasonably proportionate and commensurate with where the contents of my wallet end up."[29]

Disciples of the Ehrenberg-Bass Institute are likely gnashing their teeth (again) because they believe:

1. In the real world, it's not feasible to accurately target heavy category buyers.
2. Even if you could target them, what good would it do? According to Ehrenberg-Bass disciples, today's light buyers are tomorrow's heavy buyers and vice versa.

Let me dispel that second misconception first since it's the most erroneous. While heavy *brand* buyers do come and go from one period to the next, heavy *category* buyers remain heavy category buyers from year to year. Meanwhile, light category buyers remain light category buyers year after year. Ehrenberg-Bass aficionados like to think heavies go light and lights go heavy, but our data from a billion shopping trips proves otherwise.

Here's an example from when we tracked fifty thousand-plus chocolate buyers during 2017 and 2018. These consumers were ranked based upon their total category spend in each year and given a designation of heavy, medium, or light, with each segment containing an equal number of buyers. For example, there were seventeen thousand heavy buyers (ranked among the top third in spend) in 2017, and there

29   Rory Sutherland, "The Future of Advertising: A Conversation with Rory Sutherland," Web Wide Open, July 11, 2022, https://webwideopen.com/the-future-of-advertising-a-conversation-with-rory-sutherland/.

were seventeen thousand heavy buyers in 2018. And what we found was that 74 percent of the heavy buyers in 2017 remained heavy buyers (among the top third in spend) in 2018.

**Category level buyer segments**

*Figure 8R.* Chocolate Category Buyer Segments

| 2017 \ 2018 | Heavy (Top 33%) | Medium (Mid 33%) | Light (Bottom 33%) | Non-buyers |
|---|---|---|---|---|
| Heavy (Top 33%) | 74% | 22% | 4% | 0% |
| Medium (Mid 33%) | 22% | 53% | 25% | 0% |
| Light (Bottom 33%) | 3% | 25% | 70% | 1% |
| **Total** | **33%** | **33%** | **33%** | **1%** |

What's particularly interesting about the accompanying table is that only 4 percent of heavies became lights and only 3 percent of the lights became heavies from one year to the next. Moreover, nonbuyers of chocolate in 2017 did not emerge as significant buyers of chocolate in 2018. This phenomenon isn't specific to chocolate either.

But what about the brand-level purchase behaviors that we are trying to influence?

Keeping the category buyers in the heavy/medium/light segments, let's look at how much each segment spent on Reese's (one of our winning brands) in 2018. Heavy chocolate buyers in 2017 spent 7.5 times as much on Reese's one year later than those consumers designated as light chocolate buyers in 2017.

*Figure 8S.* 2017 Chocolate Buyer Segments Spending on Reese's in 2018

| 2017 Chocolate Buyers | 2018 Reese's Spend | |
|---|---|---|
| Heavy (Top 33%) | $ 27.71 | |
| Medium (Mid 33%) | $ 9.12 | 7.5x |
| Light (Bottom 33%) | $ 3.69 | |

Simply put, it's quite easy to predict one year in advance which consumers will spend more on your category and even your brand. This is not the rapidly moving target others may lead you to believe it is. And we're not targeting a small niche group. In the case of heavies, we're talking about the 33 percent of category buyers who account for 67 percent of category spend. If you include heavies and mediums, you're up to 66 percent of the population accounting for 92 percent to 93 percent of category spend. Why wouldn't you want to target these frequent and enthusiastic buyers?

Now let's explore that first objection—that targeting heavy buyers isn't feasible. Even though heavy category buyers are a stable segment to target, some brand managers have been falsely convinced that they're not targetable. Rather than try, they spray their advertising budget across all potential buyers and pray that enough of them will convert.

In truth, there are multiple ways to target heavy buyers. One is to use loyalty card data. There are numerous retailers, platforms, and agencies that have proven capabilities for leveraging this data to target ads (even TV ads) to consumers based upon what (and how much) they buy in the store. It's not that hard.

## FIVE TARGETING PRIORITIES

When it comes to most effectively targeting audiences with your advertising, here are five priorities (in rank order) to consider:

1. Target category buyers as close as possible to their next category purchase occasion (recency and relevance). This is where in-store media shines.

2. Target heavy buyers of the category because they're most likely to buy the category next (it may be a while before medium or light buyers buy the category again), and if heavy buyers choose your brand, the expected value of their repeat purchases is worth much more than lighter buyers.

3. Target preexisting buyers of your brand—they need to be reminded to buy your products.

4. When the above approaches are not feasible or do not generate enough reach, target people who are most likely to have the same kinds of lifestyles and jobs to be done as the people who buy your brand.

5. In the absence of any of the above, only then should you resort to demographic targeting (and only if doing so helps your brand reach likely category buyers more effectively).

Along with these five, a brand-new approach has emerged: targeting the "moveable middle." This approach was developed in 2021 by Joel Rubinson, the former Chief Research Officer of the Advertising Research Foundation and President of Rubinson Partners, in partnership with the MMA and Numerator. This methodology identifies buyers of the category with a 20 percent to 80 percent chance of buying your brand on their next purchase occasion. There's a clever mathematical trick used to figure out which consumers fall into that moveable middle versus which ones are at the extreme ends of the equation (already highly loyal to your brand or not interested in your brand). By focusing ads on the consumers who are most likely to waver in their brand choice, a brand can increase its return on ad spend by 50 percent.[30]

## BRAND EFFECTS

Remember the NCSolutions study we discussed earlier in this chapter? The study revealed that if someone was exposed to an ad within twenty-eight days of a shopping trip, they would spend 14 percent

30  Mobile Marketing Association, "Outcome-Based Marketing v2.0: Profitable Growth by Targeting Consumers in the Movable Middle," January 2021, https://www.mmaglobal.com/outcome-based-marketing.

more than those who were not exposed to an ad.[31] Dr. Leslie Wood, Chief Research Officer of NCSolutions, informed me that the role of "brand" in this benchmarking study had to do with the differences in the brands' existing sales volumes (e.g, market share, purchase frequency, household penetration, and price). Simply put, "brand effects" favor larger brands that require less spending to achieve the same results as smaller brands.

My first instinct was to exclude discussion of these brand effects in this book because such factors seem outside the control of marketers planning and executing advertising campaigns. However, a conversation with Joel Rubinson changed my mind.

Many years ago, Joel realized that higher-market-share brands achieved higher levels of profitability than their smaller-market-share competitors. You might think that's due to economies of scale in terms of manufacturing, logistics, or overhead costs, but Joel found that higher-market-share brands' profitability stemmed more from lower marketing costs. But why should this be the case? His answer goes something like this:

1. Higher-market-share brands have greater retail distribution—they are more likely to be carried everywhere that consumers shop for that category of product. Smaller-market-share brands' ads are more likely to reach consumers who do not shop at a retailer that carries their products. In this respect, distribution acts as an advertising force multiplier. (Not to mention the fact that market-share-leading brands win better merchandising and shelf placement within those retailers.)

2. Larger, more established brands are expected by their parent companies to deliver greater profits than smaller brands.

---

31  NCSolutions, "Five Keys to Advertising Effectiveness," The Nielson Company, 2017, https://ncsolutions.com/case-studies/five-keys-advertising-effectiveness.

But in bigger companies, the financials can be under greater scrutiny and budgets can be squeezed.

3. Bigger brands have a bigger "moveable middle" that will deliver a higher return on ad spend than the smaller "moveable middle" audiences reachable by smaller brands.

This means that within the same audience of consumers, our market-share-leading brand will reach twice as many influenceable consumers. It's no wonder that a market-share-leading brand can achieve a $4 return on ad spend from a campaign that, if run by a smaller challenger brand, might only achieve $2.50. That's because the job to be done by advertising is fundamentally different for well-established market-share-leading brands than smaller challenger brands.

*Figure 8T. Advertising's Job to Be Done Differs for Market Leaders versus Emerging Challengers*

| Market share leading brand | | Smaller challenger brand |
|---|---|---|
| Repeat buyers | **Primary audience** | New trialists |
| Remind them to buy | **Primary objective** | Convince them to try |
| Reinforce associations | **Approach** | Create new associations |
| Less critical | **Creative's importance** | Very critical |
| Short-term ROAS | **ROI measurement** | Long-term CAC to LTV |

Sadly for smaller brands, numerous studies dating as far back as 1971 have shown that advertising is much better at reinforcing existing preferences and repeat purchases than it is at winning new buyers.[32] Brand effects are real and they favor bigger brands. The excep-

---

32   Demetrios Vakratsas and Tim Ambler, "How Advertising Works: What Do We Really Know?" *Journal of Marketing* 63, no. 1 (January 1, 1999): 26–43, https://doi.org/10.1177%2F002224299906300103.

tion, of course, is when the advertising presents the consumer with entirely new information such as the introduction of a new product. New product innovations are the great equalizer.

## CONTEXT

The final factor influencing advertising effectiveness according to the five-hundred-campaign study was the context within which the ad was placed.

According to *Ad Age*, eighty-nine of the top one hundred biggest TV audiences in 2018 were for live sporting events.[33] Live sports on TV can deliver reach like no other medium. It's rich in natural drama, strategy, and athletic theatrics. Viewers are immersed—either because they are rooting for their favorite team or have a wager on another. Brands that are part of the experience gain all kinds of benefits, but brands whose messages fuel the viewers' pitched emotions will gain even more. In fact, ads that deliver a strong emotional response deliver 2.4 times more impact than more mundane messages. In one 2017 study, Peter Field and Les Binet concluded that "emotional campaigns are significantly more effective, and in particular, more profitable, than rational campaigns."[34]

A study in the *Journal of Advertising Research* that analyzed fifty-two academic papers on the effectiveness of advertising found that media content involvement, content likeability, and ad congruency are the most effective at improving an ad's impact[35]. This is why advertising food products during culinary programs makes sense

---

33  Anthony Crupi, "Broadcast Autopsy: 6 Things We Learned from Digging in the Guts of the 2018–2019 TV Season," *Ad Age*, May 31, 2019, https://adage.com/ article/media/broadcast-autopsy-6-things-we-learned-digging-guts-2018-19-tv-season/2174686.

34  Les Binet and Peter Field, Media in Focus: Marketing Effectiveness in the Digital Era (London: IPA, 2017).

35  Eun Sook Kwon, et al., "Impact of Media Context On Advertising Memory," *Journal of Advertising Research* 55, no. 1 (March 2019): 99–128, https://doi.org/10.2501/ JAR-2018-016

but it's also why funny or uplifting ads work best during comedy or entertainment programs. Another study by the Advertising Research Foundation reinforced this idea when it found that matching ad content to programming content delivers more than 20 percent sales lift, which measures increases in sales when businesses run promotional campaigns during a specific time period.[36] When consumers are immersed in a program, such as a live sports event, they pay more attention to the ads.

And at the bottom level of memory are our networked memories—the human "cloud." These are memories that we share with others, and they bind us to a common culture. Advertising exists in a context, such as the cultural context in which it's placed. Understanding how a brand fits within the cultural memories associated with specific media, such as popular TV shows, can help media companies more effectively place advertising.[37]

*Figure 8U.*
Relationship
between
Program
Attention and
Commercial
Attention

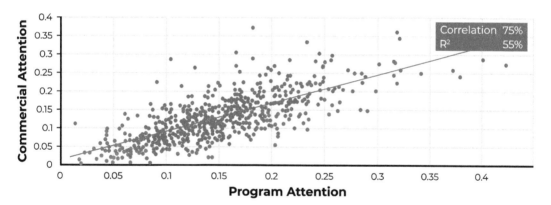

Source: TVision, 2017

36  Bill Harvey and Howard Shimmel, *Quantifying the ROI Impact of DriverTag Context Resonance: Final Full Report of First ARF* "How Advertising Works" Context ROI Case Study, Research Measurement Technologies, October 2, 2017, https://www.rmt.solutions/sales-lift.html.

37  Chuck Young, Eldaa Daly, and Russ Turpin, "Mapping Brand Memories," Ameritest, accessed August 31, 2022, https://ameritest.com/wp-content/uploads/2021/03/Mapping-Brand-Memories.pdf.

# KEY TAKEAWAYS

- Most brands overadvertise. There is a built-in bias to exaggerate the benefits of ads because the agencies that create the ads and platforms that deliver them also get paid to measure their effectiveness. To optimize your ad spend, apply unbiased, scientific methods (e.g., Ghost Ads via RCT) to measure ad effectiveness and put your market research team in charge of measurement.

- Advertising is not the panacea everyone thinks it is. It can increase sales, but not as much as most brand managers think it will. Most of a brand's growth comes from other factors, such as better distribution, innovation, and product experience.

- Ads for new product innovations have demonstrated twice to five times the impact on sales (elasticity) than advertisements for existing products. These ads in support of new product launches also have a halo effect on the entire brand by endowing it with greater perceptions of innovation and quality that drive superior brand equity for years to come.

- When it comes to advertising, the "creative" is the product. If the creative doesn't resonate with the consumer, no amount of media spending on that creative will deliver a positive return on ad spend. As the agency-world legend David Abbott used to say, "Shit that arrives at the speed of light is still shit."

- Winning brands tend to employ creative that demonstrates a real problem to be solved and masterfully associate the ad back to the brand by reinforcing its distinctive assets: logos, colors, imagery, slogan, and jingle. Losing brands fail to do this.

- Talk less and show more in your ads. The more statements you make, the less likely a consumer will pay attention and be able to recall even a single message.

- Target heavy category buyers. You can predict how buyers will behave given what they did last year, so use loyalty card data, lifestyle look-alikes, or any other available behavioral data to target heavier buyers of your product's category. Experiment with efforts to target the "moveable middle" who are most likely to be persuaded by your ads.

# 9

# TRADE VERSUS BRAND PROMOTION

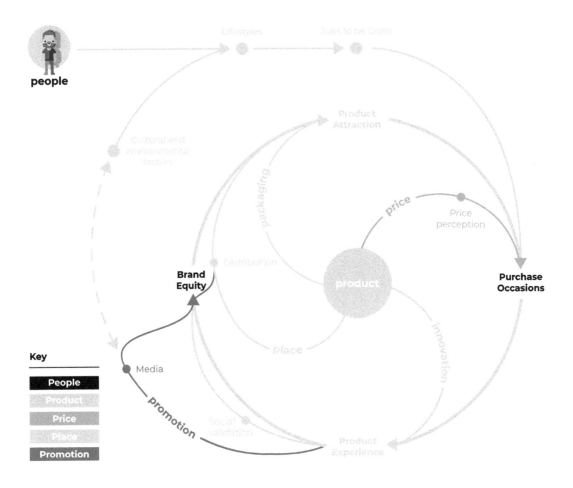

people

Key

People
Product
Price
Place
Promotion

magine yourself watching the Winter Olympic Games. As a figure skater goes to finish her routine, she enters the final spin. At first, she keeps her hands outstretched as wide as possible. Then, as she pulls her hands in closer to her body, almost magically she begins spinning faster and faster.

Viewers watch in mild astonishment. They've seen this before but it never fails to amaze. How can she possibly be speeding up like that?

Physics—in particular, Newton's Second Law of Motion—helps explain what's happening. The figure skater theoretically has the same momentum whether she's spinning with her arms out wide or if her arms are held tight to her body. When she had her arms out, her mass was extended from the center and she revolved more slowly. As she pulls her arms in, she spins ever more furiously. But that dizzying whirl lasts only for a short time because her skates are rapidly drilling a hole in the ice—this additional friction is actually depleting her momentum.

What's any of this have to do with trade promotions? Stay with me.

Now, imagine that our figure skater represents a brand. Her outstretched hands represent a brand's regular (full) price. Then, she pulls her hands tight to her body; this represents a temporary price reduction (TPR). When brands reduce (pull in) their prices, sales velocity jumps for a short time. It's like an illusion. But those fast-spinning transactions come at the expense of the brand's momentum because they increase friction during shoppers' subsequent purchase cycles.

As we'll learn in this chapter, TPRs and other forms of trade promotions have the greatest impact on a brand's month-to-month sales changes. As a result, these promotions have earned an inordinate amount of measurement focus and financial investment. Retailers push for them because they drive sales while locking in their profits via trade funds from brands. Brands agree to them because it helps them get (and keep) shelf space from the retailer. Brand sales managers love them because they result in sharp revenue increases—which are key to their bonus plans. Shoppers, of course, love them most of all because they can get a great deal and stock the pantry for the future. Is it a win, win, win, win. Right?

Not really.

## THE TRADE PROMOTION TRAP

Trade promotions make consumers think your regular price is too high and, according to our study, result in a 10 percent increase in switching to competitors on the very next occasion.

When we look at the bigger picture, trade promotions fail to demonstrate any long-term positive effects on brand sales and share growth. Sure, trade promotions will boost a brand's sales volume from one month to the next, but those numbers subtly drop when the promotion ends and it can be a struggle to get them back up again. Trade promotions make consumers think your regular price is too high and, according to our study, result in a 10 percent increase in switching to competitors on the very next occasion. Slashing prices to drive a successful promotion only devalues your brand equity and hurts long-term sales. It is a trap that brands frequently find themselves snared in.

In our study, losing brands relied more on promotions to generate sales than their corresponding winners. In other words, winners were less likely to fall into that trap. While we can't say that excess use of trade promotions caused brands to become losers, we did find that increases in trade promotion activity did *not* correspond to brand growth among the brands we studied.

Ours is not the first study to discredit trade promotions as a lever for brand growth. Several long-term empirical studies have reached the same conclusion, yet retailers keep asking for them and brands keep agreeing to them. Brands need to stop and realize that the money going to trade promotions is better spent elsewhere—in a way that has lasting benefits and doesn't sap your brand's momentum.

## THE $100 BILLION PROBLEM

Trade promotions represent a $100billion dollar problem for our industry—and that's just in America. We know this because it's the amount of marketing spend that has shifted from traditional brand advertising to funding retail trade promotions since Nielsen started providing brands the ability to measure retail sales via syndicated point-of-sale (POS) data in the 1980s.

The shift has occurred in large part because brands have become so caught up in instant and easily measurable results. The signal is clear, after all; when the price goes down, sales go up. It's only natural that brands would want to shift their money from difficult-to-measure advertising via TV, radio, and print to instantly gratifying trade promotions.

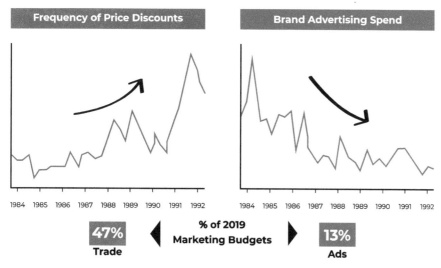

Source: The Long Term Impact of Promotion and Advertising: Cadent Consulting Group, 2020 Marketing Spend Study

*Figure 9A.*
The $100B Shift in Advertising Budgets to Trade Promotions

When a brand agrees to subsidize a retailer's price drop to boost short-term sales, watching sales surge is like the short-lived high of an addictive drug. Unfortunately, the highs are ephemeral and the negative effects are long-lasting. The promotional price tells consumers that this is what your product is truly worth and they become reluctant to pay full price when the promotion is over. Your brand's value, in their mind, becomes anchored at the lower price. In addition, there's a further setback caused by "pantry stuffing" by loyal consumers, which actually steals future sales that would have occurred at your higher regular price.

Unfortunately, these follow-on effects are not so easily measured. Syndicated POS data from retailers can't measure the behaviors of consumers who bought on promotion versus those who did not. Instead, temporary increases in aggregated weekly sales data are assumed to be incremental—the result of your promotion efforts—while ever-so-slight decreases in sales during the weeks that follow are often—and wrongly—ignored. These decreases are hard to see. They continue to appear over several weeks, but it's hard to discern them amid the noise of natural variability in sales. This is why it's so critical to track individual consumers from one purchase occasion to the next; only then is the noise reduced and the true impact of your trade promotion becomes clear. Your trade promotion helped you briefly but the damage it caused continued for a long time after.

Sadly, "we deem important what's measurable rather than measuring what's important" as Rory Sutherland recently put it.[1] Overcoming this addiction requires a longer-term and more granular measure of consumer behavior—a perspective that wasn't available from the smaller, legacy consumer panels.

### DANGERS OF TRADE PROMOTION

In David Aaker's book *Managing Brand Equity*, he outlines the risks of trade promotions on a grand scale.

The first pitfall is the effect trade promotions can have on perceptions of product quality. When a brand uses trade promotions, price plays a central role in the consumer's decision-making process. And as price becomes more and more important, Aaker notes, the brand is under increasing pressure to keep prices low. To achieve that, brands may be tempted to "reduce the quality, features, and service offered" to help keep the price low.

Furthermore, price promotions lead to a short-term approach to business that is not sustainable. This promotion cycle is in fact maintained by the short-term orientation of many marketing organizations. Brand managers are rotated frequently and assessed on short-term sales and profitability.

If we zoom out, we can see that brand managers taking a short-term focus are often trying to please executive leadership and their

---

1    Sutherland, "The Future of Advertising."

shareholders. Stockholders, Aaker notes, are "inordinately influenced by quarterly earnings" and believe "future returns will be related to current performance." Other brand-building efforts may pay off in the long run but "have little visible impact upon sales in the short run."

How can brand-building activities be justified in a world with extreme pressures for delivering short-term performance? Aaker argues that "we need to find measures of long-term performance to supplement or replace short-term financial measures that will be convincing enough to satisfy shareholders."[2]

I believe a suitable measure of long-term performance is how often a consumer returns to the store to buy the same product on their very next shopping trip for the category. We call this the consecutive repeat rate[3] and we talk more about this in Chapter 11 and the Appendix. The key point Is that the metric is not fooled by short-term changes in sales velocity, but is instead core to measuring the brand's ongoing momentum.

Aaker is not the only one who has pointed out the dangers of relying on trade promotions. In "The Long-Term Impact of Promotions & Advertising on Consumer Brand Choice" in the *Journal of Marketing Research*, the authors identified the same risks from trade promotions, finding:

- In the long run, price promotions make both loyal and unloyal consumers more sensitive to price. Trade promotions train them to look for deals in the marketplace, and the effect is four times greater for unloyal consumers than for relatively loyal consumers.

---

2    David A. Acker, *Managing Brand Equity: Capitalizing on the Value of a Brand Name* (New York: The Free Press, 1991), 12.

3    Consecutive repeat rate, as we mentioned in Chapter 1, differs from the traditional repeat rate metric in that it focuses on whether consumers repeat buy the brand on their very next category purchase occasion. The traditional repeat rate metric measures whether they purchase it again anytime in the next year.

- In contrast, advertising helps a brand in the long run by making consumers (especially unloyal ones) less price-sensitive as well as by reducing the size of the unloyal segment.[4]

In a study done at the Harvard Business School, two professors ran tests to see how marketing budgets should be allocated. In one test, they sent brochures with price promotions to one group of established customers and sent brochures without price promotions to the other. They found that the overall future revenue per customer was sharply lower among customers who had bought a product because of a trade promotion. In other words, the promotion had a negative long-term effect among established customers.[5]

Dominique Hanssens of UCLA gives the warning succinctly: "Be careful about sales promotions. They're wonderful in the short term. And if you have unsold inventory that you need to get rid of, fine. But if you turn that into a habit, then you really erode the value of the brand."[6]

## TRADE PROMOTIONS ARE LIKE SIMPLE A/B TESTS

Susan Athey, former Chief Economist at Microsoft and a board director at many large companies such as Lending Club and Expedia, saw first-hand the false promise of A/B tests during her time working with Microsoft's Bing search engine team. Many of the ads showing up during a user's search were not related to the term they were searching. *Why is Bing putting up so many irrelevant ads?* she wondered.

---

4   Carl F. Mela, Sunil Gupta, and Donald R. Lehmann, "The Long-Term Impact of Promotion and Advertising on Consumer Brand Choice," *Journal of Marketing Research* 34, no. 2 (May 1997): 248–61, https://doi.org/10.2307/3151862.

5   Sunil Gupta and Thomas J. Steenburgh, "Allocating Marketing Resources," *HBS Working Paper Series*, January 28, 2008, https://www.hbs.edu/faculty/Publication percent20Files/08-069_17a7715d-c34b-4d9e-92fa-2ea2834a0cbe.pdf.

6   Dominique Hanssens, "Q. Looking at all the things most marketers (still) do today, what is the one thing you recommend people stop immediately?" MMA, Q&A, September 22, 2020, https://www.mmaglobal.com/question/looking-all-things-most-marketers-still-do-today-what-one-thing-you-recommend-people-stop.

As she looked more closely, she realized that even the irrelevant ads were still attracting clicks and therefore bringing in revenue for the search engine—at least according to the A/B tests.[7] But was this result the best thing for Bing's users? Were the irrelevant ads affecting consumers' faith in Bing's ability to deliver relevant content? It had to. But Microsoft's A/B tests weren't measuring the longer-term usage effect of these irrelevant ads. All Microsoft apparently could see was that the irrelevant ads were generating clicks and making money, so the company assumed everything was working as it should. The company didn't bother to replace the irrelevant ads with more appropriate ones to determine if revenue increased with a more relevant ad, let alone measure its effects on ongoing usage of Bing by consumers.

"That kind of insight was an aha moment," Athey said. "It's not just that this is a little bit of a mistake, but that the entire system is constructed to not get the right answer."

When she spoke with colleagues at other marketing tech firms, she found that all of them were experiencing the same problem of A/B testing driving them to short-term optimums that are actually bad for business in the long run. People might click on the irrelevant ad and Microsoft might make money, but how many Bing users were looking at these unhelpful results and asking themselves, *Why am I using a search engine that delivers irrelevant content? I need to find a better search engine!*

"If you optimize for a short-term objective, you are going to head in the wrong direction," Athey concluded.[8]

Similarly, brands have been basing their budgets and plans on the short-term optimums offered by trade promotions. Without the perspective offered by a massive omnichannel consumer purchase panel

<hr />

7    A/B testing—also called split testing or bucket testing—compares the performance of two versions of content to see which one appeals more to visitors/viewers.
8    Susan Athey, "Susan Athey: Tech Economists, Machine Learning, and Causation," interview by Auren Hoffman, *World of DaaS*, SafeGraph, July 29, 2021, audio, https://www.safegraph.com/podcasts/susan-athey-tech-economists-machine-learning-and-causation.

(such as Numerator's), brand managers have lacked the ability to see that TPRs actually hurt repeat purchases and long-term sales.

The following graph helps illustrate the effects of brand-building advertising compared to the effects of trade promotions—especially those reliant upon temporary price reductions.

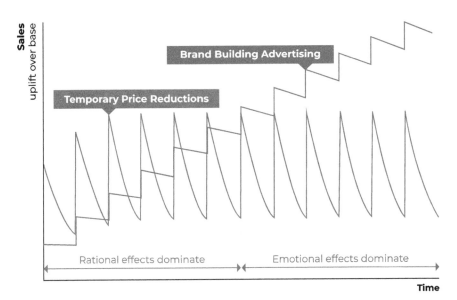

Source: The Long and the Short of It by Les Binet and Peter Field

In the short run, rational effects dominate and the incremental sales lift from TPRs drastically outperforms any measurable effects from longer-term brand-building activities. But, as we've previously discussed, there are no positive lasting effects from these promotions (except for during the launch of new products). In contrast, every bit of brand-building advertising—especially those with emotionally primed creative—increases consumers' ongoing probability of purchasing your products. Sure, there is a small increase in sales during the advertising campaign, but the real benefit is the ongoing lift the brand experiences once the campaign is over. That is the massive difference that allows cumulative momentum to build.

It's a bit like the fable of the tortoise and the hare. If you only watch the first part of the race, it's obvious that the hare will outperform the tortoise with ease. But growing a brand is a long-distance race. There isn't a competitive distance runner in the world who sprints-rests-sprints-rests and then sprints their way to victory. It's a losing strategy. You can sprint a bit at the very start to get into the lead and avoid being boxed in by competitors, but in order to win, you must maintain your momentum by exerting energy at a relatively constant rate. Short bursts of speed midrace aren't sustainable and the extra energy lost typically has a negative effect on the runner's ability to keep the pace from that point forward.

## CAN TRADE PROMOTIONS EVER WORK?

Trade promotions can be helpful when you're introducing a new product. The extra merchandising and discounted price can be just enough to convince risk-averse consumers to try your product for the very first time. If they like it enough (i.e., have a great product experience), they'll buy it again at the regular price.

Additional ways in which trade promotions can be beneficial are

*Figure 9C.* Multibrand Deodorant Display by Unilever at Walgreens

when they are used to cross-promote products and/or help better inform consumer choice. Consider this in-store display by Unilever for its Dove and Degree deodorants. It achieved both of these objectives.

The idea behind this display was to turn confused deodorant users into reengaged, educated shoppers while elevating the benefits of Unilever products in the process.

The display highlighted a price discount but also helped consumers choose a product capable of delivering a better usage experience. A better experience should improve the odds of that consumer buying the product again. Unilever also used a "Buy one, get one 50 percent off" tactic that prevents the anchoring of a particular price in the shoppers' minds.[9] The next time around, they wouldn't necessarily remember anything about the price, but they would remember the product.

## GREAT SHOPPER MARKETING BEATS TRADE PROMOTIONS

A great alternative to traditional trade wpromotions involving price reductions is advertising through the retailer (also known as shopper marketing) to reach customers as they are about to buy. Shopper marketing can take many forms. Some brands offer free samples to whet a customer's appetite while they're buying food. Beer and chip makers construct elaborate display ads inside stores during football season. One United Kingdom dairy whose slogan was "Tastes so good, the cows want it back" displayed ads around the store that looked like ransom notes.

Several studies have shown that when we are in the act of shopping, we are more attentive to relevant marketing, more receptive to a suggestive nudge, and less likely to forget the message before making a purchase decision. "Advertising" that is placed in front of someone just about to buy from the category is really "physical availability"—it's like buying shelf space. Those aren't my words—that's a direct quote from Byron Sharp that I find to be a particularly relevant take on how to think about shopper marketing. In fact, it's almost impossible to deny when you look at these sponsored results for BodyArmor above Gatorade on Amazon's digital shelf. Ask yourself, is this "shopper marketing" or "physical availability"? I think the answer is, "Yes."

---

9    "Axe, Dove Men+Care, Degree for Men, Degree for Women, Dove Female; Walgreens 'Do Deo Better,'" Effie, 2017, https://www.effie.org/case_database/case/SME_2017_E-135-743.

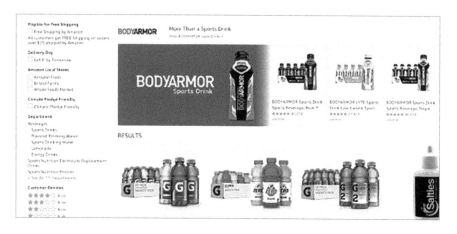

*Figure 9D.*
Amazon's
Digital Shelf for
Sports Drinks

Another great example is this 2017 Effie Gold Medal–winning shopper marketing campaign from Dove through Target. There was no temporary price reduction, only incremental value offered in the form of a bonus gift: a simple decal. The real brilliance of this campaign, however, was the cross-promotion of Dove products across categories.

*Figure 9E.*
Dove's Award-
Winning
Shopper
Marketing
Campaign
through Target

As a megabrand, 54 percent of households already bought Dove products, but only 24 percent were giving Dove deodorant a try. If those consumers already preferred other Dove products, why not try Dove deodorant too?

## THE BRAND MANAGER'S RESPONSE

Since it's clear promotions only surge sales and share in the short run (month over month), but have a negative impact in the long run (year over year), how should brand managers respond?

The answer lies not in measuring a brand's sales velocity, but in measuring its underlying momentum. In order for brand managers to deliver on the promise of a strong image and a powerful brand franchise, they need to be given long-term targets and be empowered to invest budgets in brand-building advertising rather than price-cutting sales promotions.

On an organizational level, this means reassessing the performance targets given to brand managers and addressing the pricing issues that have led retailers to demand trade funds to fuel temporary price reductions.

*Figure 9F.*
Braun's
Merchandising
Fixture as a
Better Use of
Trade Funds

So, what if these changes could be made? How could brand managers use that $100 billion more effectively, beyond putting some of it back into advertising? For one, they could invest more in sales activities to increase distribution. They could also spend money to maximize merchandising effectiveness (in-store displays, for example). This Braun razor display is the perfect example of money being spent through the retailer to effectively stand out from (or even completely box out) the competition.

Most importantly, brand managers could focus more on continued innovation—on research and development. Today, most CPG brands spend only 2 percent of their budget on innovation. This should move up to at least 5–10 percent. More highly valued tech companies know the importance of innovation and allocate 20 percent of their budget to it, on average. While CPG brands function differently than tech companies, there's no denying the importance of innovation in this world as well—a topic we'll dive deeper into in the following chapter.

## KEY TAKEAWAYS

- Retail trade promotions via temporary price reductions increase sales velocity for a time but actually hurt long-term momentum. Losing brands are more reliant upon selling through trade promotions than their corresponding winners.

- Lowering your price tells consumers that this is what your product is truly worth. This damages your brand equity and increases the likelihood that consumers will switch to another product next time they shop.

- Research shows that promotions have a negative long-term effect among established customers and increase a brand's reliance on nonloyal switchers. This is exactly what we independently discovered as a core difference between the winning and losing brands in our study. (See Chapter 6: Brand Equity.)

- Trade promotions can be beneficial when they are used to cross-promote products and convince people to initially try a product.

- Instead of solely measuring a product's sales velocity, brand managers should also measure its underlying momentum, starting with its consecutive repeat rate.

- Brand managers should be given long-term targets and be empowered to invest budgets in brand-building advertising rather than price-cutting sales promotions. They should reinvest trade budgets into sales activities to increase distribution and make investments that maximize merchandising effectiveness.

- Brand managers should focus on research, development, and continued innovation. Most CPG brands spend just 2 percent of their budget on innovation, which should be more than doubled—even if it simply results in gimmicks such as Oreo's outlandish yet PR-worthy flavors.

# 10

# PRODUCT EXPERIENCE AND INNOVATION

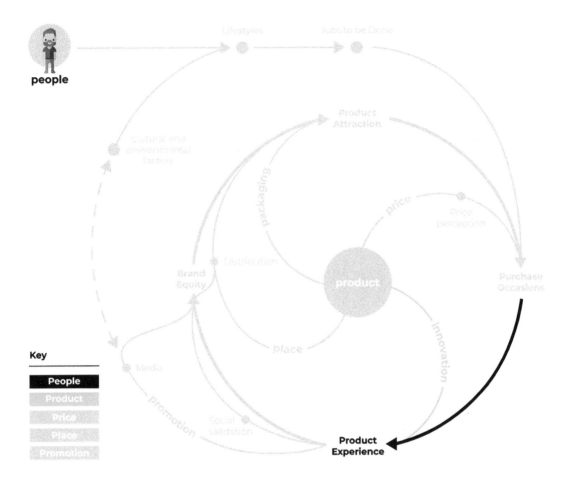

**people**

**Key**

| People |
| Product |
| Price |
| Place |
| Promotion |

O lly co-founder Eric Ryan was shopping in Target one day when another customer, thinking Eric was a Target employee, asked him for some help finding a supplement to help a specific problem the customer was having. Ryan quickly saw that products in the supplement aisle were failing to do a specific job: making it clear what benefits their products provided.[1]

Thus, the idea for Olly was born, a line of vitamins and supplements that make it easier for customers to navigate the supplement aisle. Olly's product names make it clear how their supplements will help.

---

1    Rebecca Norris, "Olly: Brand Review and Our Favorite Products," *Byrdie*, last modified March 8, 2022, https://www.byrdie.com/olly-nutrition-5190495.

From their top-selling SLEEP gummies (melatonin with L-theanine and a botanical blend of chamomile, passion flower, and lemon balm) to their BEAUTY, IMMUNITY, ENERGY, and SKIN products, each is named for the primary benefit it delivers, not for their ingredients.

When it comes to innovation, Olly did many things right: the company leaders were guided by their own personal experiences, they failed fast and failed cheap, and they considered why consumers stick with products and made sure their products delivered usage experiences that would encourage that.

While Ryan's shopping in Target was pivotal, Olly CEO Brad Harrington gained valuable insights about his product by examining his own preferences. Harrington hates taking pills, which led Olly to develop tasty gummies rather than capsules, pills, or tablets.

"I gag on pills, and here I was working on this company where the whole form of nutrition was larger pills," Harrington said. "And it got to the point where it became difficult for me to take my own product. Meanwhile, we wanted to develop something that people would want to ingest every day.

"Things came together as we were going through development, and we launched twenty different products last year, including sixteen in gummy form and four others that were swallowable soft gels. And when the numbers started to come in, we watched the soft gels fall to the bottom, so now we [produce only] gummies."

From the start, Olly wanted to create products that consumers would look forward to using regularly. The gummy format helped, but so did the two grams of sugar the brand adds to its products to make them as much a tasty treat as they are a health benefit.

"If we made a chewable without sugar, that probably wouldn't be such a great experience either," Harrington said. "We're looking to establish good habits, and if you have to put a bit of sugar to create those habits, I don't see anything wrong with that."[2]

---

2    Loizos, "Olly Has Built a Breakout Brand."

## THE VALUE OF INNOVATION

A sizable number of our winning brands—Biofreeze, Caulipower, Harry's, Hillshire, Olly, Similac, SkinnyPop, and White Claw—appeared on Nielsen's list of Breakthrough Innovations during the study period.[3] Among the losing brands in our study, only Gillette and Glade scored a breakthrough innovation during this period. So, if you're keeping score at home, that's Winners–8 and Losers–2.

Of the more than twenty thousand new products evaluated in Nielsen's annual Breakthrough Innovation reports from 2012 to 2016, only ninety-two had sales of more than $50 million in their first year and sustained those sales in year two. That's less than one-half of 1 percent.

According to the report, every one of the ninety-two successful new products targeted a specific job to be done and provided a product experience superior to preexisting options. This is product differentiation at its finest.

Reese's achieved breakout success by following the same formula. Its researchers were curious about when and why Reese's Peanut Butter Cup enthusiasts chose alternatives. They discovered that their large-format peanut butter cup was too big and messy for consumers in an array of situations—driving the car, standing in a crowded subway, or playing a video game. Even smaller, individually wrapped cups were too much hassle because opening their wrappers required two hands. In addition, the accumulation of foil wrappers created a guilt-inducing consumption tally. *I had that many?*

So, the company began focusing on the job that smaller versions of Reese's were hired to do. After some trial and error, Reese's Minis were introduced. Reese's Minis come in a resealable flat-bottom bag that you can easily dip a single hand into, and there's no foil wrapping to hassle with—or to tally the guilt. Reducing friction in the usage

---

3    "Nielsen Reveals Its 2019 Breakthrough Innovation List," *The Shelby Report*, December 4, 2019, https://www.theshelbyreport.com/2019/12/04/nielsen-breakthrough-innovation-list-2019/.

experience led to increased consumption. The results were astounding: $235 million in sales in the first two years and the birth of a breakthrough category extension.

**Before**

**After**

*Figure 10A.*
Reese's
Massively
Successful
Packaging
Change

What we should learn from these case studies is that innovation can be far more predictable—and far more profitable—if you start by identifying the jobs that customers are struggling to get done. Without that lens, it's a hit-or-miss proposition when it comes to innovation and product experience.[4]

Bridgette Heller, the former President of Danone, agreed, telling me, "What marketing should be doing is delivering value by figuring out a customer problem and solving it. Have the courage to challenge your own perceptions of the category and its boundaries." From her experience, the best way to do that is by asking the consumer.

"One successful approach is to focus on the dissatisfiers in the category," Heller said. "Ask consumers, *What do you hate about it?* The key

---

4    Clayton M. Christensen et al., "Know Your Customers' 'Jobs to Be Done,'" *Harvard Business Review*, September 2016, https://hbr.org/2016/09/know-your-customers-jobs-to-be-done.

to long-term success is to make sure this exercise isn't limited to your own products or those of specific competitors. Customer issues need to be understood from a category (or broader) perspective."

The key, Heller said, is to focus less on the category and more on the consumer's problem.

"I'm often reminded of the story of what happened to the lettuce industry. Every producer was focused on how to deliver fresher lettuce while ignoring that consumers who used lettuce to make salads still had to clean it, shred it, and dress it up. Then came packaged salads and salad kits, which completely reshaped the market for lettuce."

As we've seen, winning brands win purchase occasions, but to do this, they must go a step further. Winning brands deliver product experiences that provide superior value and exceed the consumer's expectations. If consumers of your brand have an initial reaction of "Wow!" you will fundamentally shift the consumers' probability of buying your product again and reap the reward of ongoing repeat purchases. If the initial experience is subpar, research shows that consumers are unlikely to purchase the product a second time. This is true in every industry, not just consumer packaged goods.

## START WITH THE EXPERIENCE

When people buy a product, they expect it to perform a certain way. When a product exceeds their expectation, an extra dose of dopamine is released. It's no wonder satisfied consumers are willing to pay even more for their favorite products than they already do. They get more value than what they pay for. That's a clear signal that you're delivering a great product experience.

But what do we mean by *product experience*? In short, it's the *effect* of consuming or using the product.

Start by considering the functional aspects of a product—the elements that affect our senses. If the product is a jacket, does it feel comfortable to wear? Does it keep you warm enough when you head outside? When thinking about your product's experience, start with all five senses: sight, sound, taste, touch, and smell. Then move to the higher-order emotional factors. Do the jacket's color and style match the rest of your outfit? Will others compliment your sense of style? What does the jacket say about you and your personality? Does wearing it make you feel more confident? Even the most mundane of products (e.g., glue) can deliver emotional benefits (unleashing your creativity, for example, or being confident your kid's art project won't fall apart and embarrass them). You have to dive deep to understand the fullness of the product experience and what it means to the consumer. Will their life be improved in some way by using your product?

As we'll see, innovation only matters when it improves the product experience. Too many brands focus on "innovations" that don't affect the overall usage experience. A slight change to packaging, for example, won't get you very far. Sure, attractive packaging might lure first-time customers, but it won't keep them returning for more. If, however, you develop a new flavor and a consumer finds it delicious, they'll remember that experience and want to have it again and again. These are the kinds of innovations that matter because they directly impact the experience.

Nicorette certainly found this to be true. When the brand evaluated the entire category of smoking-cessation products, they found that competing private-label products "just didn't taste good," former Nicorette Brand Manager Scott Yacovino said. So Nicorette introduced its tasty coated lozenge and the innovation made the brand a winner.

"You have to focus on the innovations that can really be different and incremental to the brand and the category," Yacovino said. "Just because you can do it doesn't mean you should. Launching a mint-flavored product when one already exists doesn't help. A coated lozenge that tastes good was a real innovation."

One of the most interesting findings of our study was the major causal link between improved product experience and brand equity. The marketing industry often thinks of brand equity as a function of advertising. The truth is that you can advertise all you want, but if someone buys a product that doesn't fulfill the job to be done, ads can't make up for that. Consumers will always trust their firsthand experiences over the biased claims of a self-interested third party when they go to make their next purchase.

## EXCEEDING CONSUMER EXPECTATIONS

Winning brands don't just meet consumer expectations; they exceed them.

How do you do this? You must first pay attention to how consumers respond to your products versus competing alternatives.

Years ago, I helped a popular yogurt brand gather critical data about a subbrand of products they recently launched. Typically, strawberry is the top seller in this category, but their new strawberry yogurt was not selling as well as expected relative to the other newly launched flavors. They wanted to know why. We found that consumers would try the flavor on their first occasion, but they wouldn't buy it the second time around. This data led the brand to adjust the strawberry flavor to deliver a better taste experience for consumers. Sure enough, after a flavor adjustment was made, the reformulated strawberry yogurt began to sell at a much higher rate. The brand listened effectively to its customers and made the necessary changes.

I learned from this experience just how important it is to understand what consumers expect and how important consecutive repeat purchase rates can be in measuring performance against expectations. Make sure that what you're claiming about your brand is consistent with the actual usage or consumption experience. If it isn't, there will be a disconnect for consumers, and they'll lose trust in the brand.

Even before the recent decades of advancements in neuroscience and psychology, marketing trailblazer Philip Kotler understood how important it was for the brand experience to match the brand image marketers create. He wrote, "Much of a brand manager's work is to build the brand image. But the brand manager's work must not stop there. The brand manager must ensure that the brand experience matches the brand image."[5] This is where too many marketers fall short in their job; they act as if the brand experience is someone else's responsibility. If you want to be a great marketer, step up and take responsibility for improving product and brand experience so that they align with the brand story you want to tell.

Remember that when consumers decide at the moment of purchase, the marketer's work has just begun: the postpurchase experience shapes the consumer's opinion for every subsequent decision in the category, so the journey is an ongoing cycle.

### IMPROVING EXPERIENCE

As part of a marketing debate series sponsored by the MMA in 2020, I asked my copanelist, Dr. Hanssens, about the role of product experience as it relates to brand equity. He replied that the quality of product experience delivered "is not only a driver of brand equity and customer equity, but it is the dominant driver. And that is because once the purchase is made, whether or not there is an additional purchase depends primarily on the experience of that first purchase."

Clearly, you must have a good product experience to build momentum in the flywheel. So, how can you improve the product experience? To answer this question, consider how Toyota and Honda built brand equity over time.

While American auto companies like Chrysler and GM relied heavily on sales and promotions to push their vehicles, Toyota and Honda bolstered their brand equity by building more reliable vehicles. The American companies might have gained new customers through their promotions and deals, but they were fighting the wrong battle for long-term success.

These import brands have always focused on how their automobiles perform. In this way, the companies built strong reputations,

---

5    Philip Kotler, *Kotler on Marketing*.

and therefore strong brands, over time. Consider, for example, how reliable Toyotas and Hondas are. Not only do they last much longer than most cars and have very few warranty recalls, but they rarely need repairs.[6] When they do need work done, the repairs are usually easy and cost-effective. In the end, the consumer has a much better usage experience.

Of course, there's a reason why many brands choose the promotions route. After all, it's not easy maintaining status as the best product. However, when a brand overlooks product experience and innovation in favor of sales and marketing, there is always a price to pay down the road.

A good example is when Intel lost its lead in the computer central processing unit (CPU) industry. In 2000, when I started my first job after college at Intel, the company was growing rapidly and had become the world's most valuable company. It had the fastest CPUs, ahead of its longtime rival AMD. As long as it had the best-performing CPU, it would win in the market and be the prime choice for most customers.

AMD struggled for survival until the company, under the guidance of new CEO Lisa Su, launched a new brand of processors in 2016 that finally outperformed Intel's to become customers' top choice—even at a premium price higher than Intel's. The market capitalization of AMD grew from $1.7 billion to over $108 billion in five years from the beginning of 2016 to the end of 2020. Focusing on delivering the best possible product made AMD one of the world's best-performing stocks in the last decade.

### BECOMING A WINNER OF PRODUCT EXPERIENCE

Sometimes, it's easy to spot why certain brands win through product experience. If you compare Energizer to Duracell rechargeable batteries, you will find that the two are almost identical. They even have

---

6   Jerry Hirsch, "Asian Brands Score High in Consumer Reports Reliability Ratings," *Forbes Wheels*, last modified November 20, 2020, https://www.forbes.com/wheels/news/asian-brands-score-high-consumer-reports-reliability-rankings/.

the same price. The big difference is that Energizer's batteries can be recharged up to four times more than Duracell's—making the choice easier for consumers.[7]

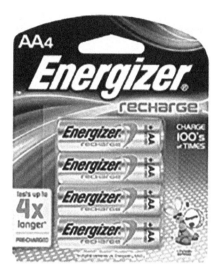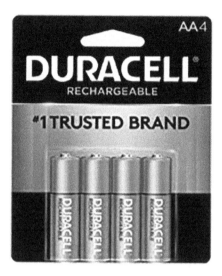

*Figure 10B.*
Energizer
Out-recharges
Duracell

In other cases, brands need to be much more attuned to the nuances of consumer experience to come out on top.

The winner of the *Good Housekeeping* Tasters' Pick Award for barbecue sauce in 2013 was Sweet Baby Ray's. It was a big hit among tasters who loved this sauce's "sweet and smoky" taste. A few noted a "peppery aftertaste" while others enjoyed that "nice level of spice." Many tasters were also fans of this sauce's "good consistency." The brand had captured just the right formula to delight consumers.

On the other hand, one of the budget options on your grocer's shelves, KC Masterpiece, did not fare so well. This was our loser in the barbecue sauce category, and there are good reasons. In a 2019 *Mashed* article titled "Grocery Store Barbecue Sauces, Ranked Worst to First," critics didn't mince words in describing the sauce.

---

7    Daniel Walker, "Battle of the Battery Giants: Comparing Duracell vs. Energizer," *HBPlus Battery Specialists* (blog), September 8, 2021, https://batteryspecialists.com.au/blogs/news/duracell-vs-energizer.

"This stuff is absolutely awful. KC Masterpiece attempts to use hickory smoke flavor to balance its sickly sweetness, resulting in an overpowering taste of mediocrity. If you make the mistake of adding it to meat of any kind, this sauce is all you will taste...Additionally, KC Masterpiece Original BBQ sauce has a chemical aftertaste, which is not the taste you want in your mouth after an evening spent slaving over a hot grill."[8]

## INNOVATION CHALLENGES

A recent McKinsey poll found that 84 percent of global executives said innovation was extremely important for business growth, yet 94 percent were dissatisfied with their own innovation performance.

Why do so many innovation initiatives fall flat?

In his theory of disruptive innovation, Clayton Christensen says executives often fail because they study the wrong product and customer data, which leads them to design innovation processes that "churn out mediocrity."

According to Christensen, widely regarded as one of the world's top experts on innovation, **good innovations solve problems that formerly had only inadequate solutions—or no solution.** And the result of good innovation is more customers buying more of your products.

The secret to winning the innovation game lies in understanding what causes customers to make choices that help them achieve progress on something they are struggling with in their lives. To get to the right answers, Christensen says, executives should be asking: *What job would consumers want to hire a product to do?*

"Your customers not only need a job fulfilled, but they often need work-arounds. They need better answers than the ones they have right now. They need you to be the answer to their frustrations.

---

8    Kori Ellis, "Grocery Store Barbecue Sauces, Ranked Worst to First," Mashed, last modified January 11, 2021, https://www.mashed.com/168769/grocery-store-barbecue-sauces-ranked-worst-to-first/.

Product developers often spend a lot of time building complicated customer profiles to consider what those profiles typically buy. Most customer data is structured to show correlations: this customer looks like that, or 68 percent of customers say they prefer version A to version B. These approaches to data fail because innovations don't play by the same rules. Innovations work when you can anticipate what a customer is trying to get done. Then you can design products, experiences, and processes that make the customer's life better, not the same.[9]

## RESPONDING TO RISKS

Because innovations take a lot of time to pay off, choosing investments in innovation is the equivalent of choosing to lower profits in the short run in hopes of greater revenues and profits in the long run. In many cases, the process takes so long that most initial contributors to the innovation will never reap the reward down the road. So, there's naturally a disincentive for larger companies and brands to innovate. This is especially true of brand managers whose investments in innovation may only lead to results long after they've been transitioned into a new role working on a different brand.

Still, if you understand why innovations fail in the first place, you can fail faster and get to the right innovations faster. Looking across thousands of product launches, Nielsen observed three common causes of innovation failure that often don't get the attention they deserve:

1. Neglecting to address a broad consumer need (too niche)
2. Failing to provide a good product experience
3. Providing insufficient marketing support[10]

---

9   Christensen et al., "Know Your Customers.'"
10  "Setting the Record Straight on Innovation Failure," The Nielson Company, accessed September 26, 2022, https://www.nielsen.com/wp-content/uploads/sites/3/2019/04/setting-the-record-straight-common-causes-of-innovation-failure-1.pdf

Many brands also overestimate consumer demand for particular innovations and misjudge trade-offs. For example, Cheetos came out with a low-calorie option, and it flopped. The brand clearly misjudged the importance of health considerations relative to taste for its target customer. Brands often make these kinds of mistakes because they're looking at overall trends rather than listening to what customers want from their products.

Smaller brands have an innovative advantage over larger brands because there is less risk involved if their innovation fails. In fact, if they want to succeed, they have no choice but to innovate and risk failing.

On the other hand, Nielsen BASES noted in its 2018 report, *Setting the Record Straight on Innovation Failure*, larger brands have to worry about "sibling brands" competing for resources from the parent company and pressure from financial markets to show immediate return. Large, established brands often have to choose between spending money on innovation or spending money on media and advertising, distribution, or merchandising—actions that help drive their flywheel. Smaller brands, on the other hand, are often forced to innovate because they can't double down on existing success because they haven't had any yet. For larger brands, the choice between innovating and lubricating their flywheel can be best made by looking at their consecutive repeat rates. If your consecutive repeat rate drops relative to your desired market share, you may need to innovate. If your consecutive repeat rate justifies greater market share, invest more in distribution, merchandising, and advertising for growth.

Whether you're running a big or small brand, though, you must remember that minor enhancements—small tweaks to your packaging, ingredients, or flavor—aren't going to move the needle. If you truly want innovation that drives growth, you must invest in significantly improving the product experience.

With the world's largest product-testing database, BASES has observed that initiatives with strong product performance are fifteen times more likely to succeed in the market than those with poor performance. In the accompanying chart, you can see how a weak product will compare to a strong one. BASES' long-term study of new product launches showed that good products also have stronger repeat rates. The products start out from the same point, but as the number of repeat purchases increases, the number of households they reach is always higher for strong products. Moreover, BASES also found that those products deemed "not ready" on product-driven dimensions but launched anyway have an 80 percent failure rate in market.

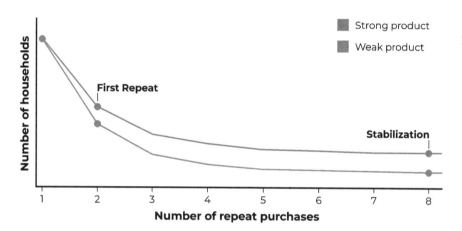

*Figure 10C.*
Buyer Attrition:
Repeat
Purchase
Patterns for
Strong versus
Weak Product
Innovations

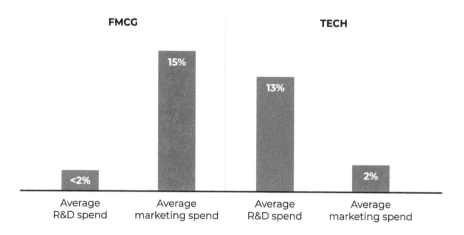

*Figure 10D.*
Fast Moving
Consumer
Goods Brands
Invest Very
Little in R&D

In a recent survey of more than 350 innovation professionals, Nielsen reported that testing and refining the product experience tends to suffer most compared to other stages of the innovation process when speed to market is a priority.[11]

In *Kotler on Marketing*, we find several helpful methods for identifying ways to improve product experience through the innovation process. Here are three helpful methods:

- **The Problem Detection Method**: Ask people who use the product if they have any disappointments or suggestions for improvement.

- **The Ideal Method**: Interview a set of consumers and ask them to imagine an ideal version of the product or service that they are consuming.

- **The Consumption Chain Method**: Interview consumers to chart their steps in acquiring, using, and disposing of a product.[12]

## HACKING INNOVATION

When it comes to winning through innovation, there are two key questions to ask:

- Will consumers buy my product (over existing alternatives)?
- Will they like it enough to buy it again?

The formula for innovation success is pretty simple on the surface. If you make a product that is physically attractive and delivers the satisfaction it promises, you win. However, there are actually major risks involved.

---

11   "Setting the Record Straight on Innovation Failure," The Nielson Company.
12   Kotler, *Kotler on Marketing*.

The effort that goes into creating a product that consumers will love requires massive investments with long lead times to results. And even after all of that investment, you still don't even know if consumers will buy (try) the product to begin with.

That said, you can hack the first question quickly and easily by borrowing a trick from Silicon Valley startups.

Entrepreneurs preparing to quit their jobs and invest their life's savings to pursue a risky startup idea have learned to master this invaluable trick. With a few hundred dollars of investment, they will create website landing pages for their product (or service) concept as if it already exists and is available to buy. They then test a few different ways of drawing attention to their product's landing page (via a Google Adwords or Facebook ad, or even a free Reddit post) to see how many people click through to the website and of those how many convert via a "Buy Now" button or even a simple email registration form.

Consumer goods companies can massively lower the risk of research and development (R&D) investments by taking a similar approach to evaluating the attractiveness of product variants, line extensions, and new category entries. You can do this in just a few weeks on a shoestring budget.

For example, a brand can add the envisioned item to their own e-commerce website or a third-party marketplace to see how often the product gets clicked on and added to carts—before informing the consumer that it's not currently available. Then, once convinced of a product concept's market viability, the heavy work can truly begin to create that product.

## KEY TAKEAWAYS

- Winners innovate and they do so by fundamentally improving the product experience for their consumers.

- The secret to winning the innovation game lies in understanding what causes customers to make choices that help them achieve progress on something they are struggling with in their lives. To get to the right answers, you should ask: *What job would consumers want to hire a product to do?*

- To find innovation opportunities, you should look at the frustrations faced and the work-arounds that your customers need to do to get the full benefit of your products in achieving their goals.

- Brands can significantly derisk the innovation process by test marketing and test merchandising products before they have even been developed.

# 11

# THE BRAND GROWTH FLYWHEEL

Jon Brelig,
InfoScout's
Co-founder,
accepts the
award for San
Francisco's
fastest-growing
company
in 2016.

A fter another year of incredible company growth in 2015, Numerator (then InfoScout) was named San Francisco's fastest-growing company in 2016.[1] This breakout performance by our team coincided with the rise of our local NBA team: the Golden State Warriors. In 2015–16, the Warriors won more games than any other NBA team in history and are widely acclaimed as the greatest NBA team of all time.[2]

But some disagree, arguing that Michael Jordan's 1995–96 Chicago Bulls were a better team because they excelled at both ends of the

---

1    Renée Frojo, "Because InfoScout Gives Retailers Data They Can't Get Otherwise, It's the Fastest Growing Company in the Bay Area," *San Francisco Business Times*, October 13, 2016, https://www.bizjournals.com/sanfrancisco/news/2016/10/13/fast-100-infoscout-jared-schrieber-retail-redbull.html.
2    Andy Bailey, "Ranking the 50 Best NBA Teams of All Time," Bleacher Report, July 24, 2020, https://bleacherreport.com/articles/2901057-ranking-the-50-best-nba-teams-of-all-time.

court. The Bulls not only led the league in scoring but also gave up the third-fewest points that season. However, the 2015–16 Warriors ranked just nineteenth out of thirty teams in points allowed.

On the surface, this seems like a compelling argument in favor of the Bulls. But it's flawed.

Here's why: the 2015–16 Warriors offense was so quick to shoot (and score) that their opponents ended up with far more possessions (and far more opportunities to score) than when they played other teams. If you "normalize" for this fact and compare the Warriors and Bulls for points surrendered per 100 possessions (also known as "defensive efficiency"), the Warriors had the fourth-best defense in the league. That's not weak; that's strong. Furthering the argument is the fact that the Warriors' opponents only made 43.5 percent of their field-goal attempts (ranking third in the league that year) while the Bulls' opponents made 44.8 percent of their shots (just eighth best in the NBA during their best season).

It's a fallacy to say the Warriors were soft defensively. It's the kind of logical error that comes from assigning too much weight and explanatory power to a single metric. It's a lesson that brand managers and marketers should take to heart. Although some measures—such as consecutive repeat rate—are more informative than other popular measures—such as promotional sales lift—complex system dynamics simply don't allow any single measure to explain overall performance. Just as the 2015–16 Warriors' strength came from creating and converting on more scoring opportunities while allowing their opponents to convert on fewer of their scoring opportunities, winning brands create and convert on more purchase occasions than their competition. Simply put, "Winning brands win occasions."

This central finding was not on our radar screen when we first set out to understand how winning brands win and why losing brands lose. We simply set out to find a significant sample of exceptional brands whose sales growth far exceeded their category competitors and then to understand what set them apart. We sought to test every claim we could find among industry thought leaders and highly accomplished practitioners in hopes of finding marketing's fundamental truths while debunking the myths that have led us all astray.

In the process, we developed a new framework, the Brand Growth Flywheel. The flywheel revealed that we should be activating marketing levers within the context of their complex interrelationships instead of thinking about each lever independently. It incorporates all the factors we've been discussing—new buyers, jobs to be done, purchase occasions, product experience, brand equity, social validation, advertising, trade promotion, and product attraction. Building a great brand, we realized, is like synchronizing the various instruments of an orchestra into a harmonious composition. Everything should work together to create momentum that builds.

*Figure 11A.*
The Brand
Growth
Flywheel

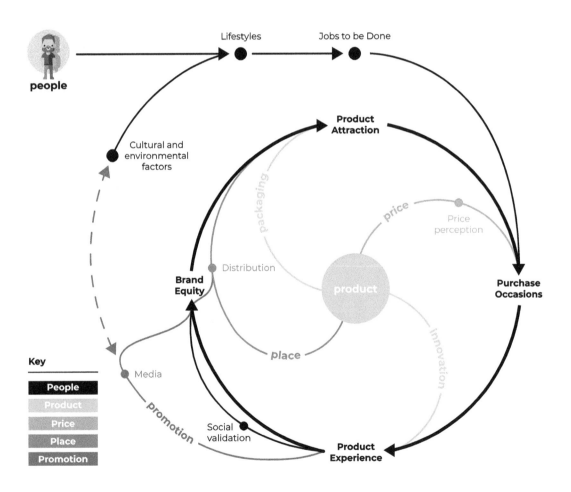

We could have taken the easy route and argued that building great brands, like creating great music, is more art than science. But doing that would ignore the overwhelming evidence that marketing is a science and that it deserves the same treatment that social scientists in fields such as sociology, psychology, and economics are giving to their disciplines. In those fields, researchers use causal graphs to explain and test causal relationships. Why not do the same for marketing? Why do we continue to rely on expert opinions rather than empirical evidence? When we converted the empirical findings from our study (along with those from dozens of independent, peer-reviewed studies) into a unified causal graph, the Brand Growth Flywheel emerged. In the Brand Growth Flywheel, every arrow represents a causal relationship that matches real-world data. For the first time, we could see how marketing levers worked together to drive brand growth. Understanding these relationships can help practitioners manage their brands as a systemic whole. The causal graph behind the flywheel can be tested by practitioners and academics alike, and in that way, it can be further refined into a living model for brand management.

Along the path of the Brand Growth Flywheel, there are many leverage points where you can increase your brand's momentum. You can leverage data-driven sales techniques to convince more retailers to carry your products, thus improving their distribution and availability (e.g., Rao's and Health-Ade Kombucha). By incorporating your products' packaging into your marketing communications, you will enhance the noticeability and attractiveness of your products in store (e.g., Febreze and Harry's). Furthermore, you can position your brand and package your products to win specific types of purchase occasions based upon their distinctive choice hierarchies (e.g., Jimmy Dean's and Liquid I.V.).

## A COMPLEX SYSTEM

As humans, we like simple answers. But there is no simple answer for how to best grow a brand. Too many factors can affect the process, and the only way to accurately show how they interact with each other is to treat brand management and marketing as a science.

My journey to apply science to the question of brand growth goes back to my systems engineering studies at MIT. There, I focused on the nature of complex systems and how to manage them. These systems, with their confounding, time-delayed and nonlinear effects and reinforcing feedback loops, are full of second- and third-order effects that lead to unintended consequences. It's a challenge to envision them, let alone control them, and you need powerful data sets to model, test, and refine the system.

But when my work in marketing began to produce an unrivaled trove of data about what, how, why, and where people shop, I saw an opportunity to create a unique model for brand growth. In science, empirical data is the oracle. You can discern the future by asking the oracle the right questions. So we started asking our data a lot of questions, and the answers revealed an entirely new way to see and understand why some brands grow and some brands languish.

During this analysis, I had to resist the pull toward simple answers. For example, many experts in brand marketing like to claim that growing the number of new buyers is the key to brand growth. But our data suggested that while new buyers are important, they are hardly the only factor or even the most important factor. Calling them the answer is like claiming that the key to growing tomatoes in your garden is to consistently give them plenty of water. This advice ignores the critical importance of adequate sunlight, warm temperatures, rich soil, and support for the plant as it grows. You need water, of course, but water won't do you much good if you don't manage the other factors.

The breadth and depth of our data—culled from a billion shopping trips and supplemented with instant surveys and continuous monitors of advertising, brand equity, and trade promotions—gave us an unprecedented opportunity to see precisely how *all* the different marketing levers work in concert to influence each other. It allowed us to move away from the industry's simple depiction of this process—the marketing funnel, a simplified linear model focused on the process of acquiring new customers—and allowed us to develop a causal graph that depicted the actual interplay of these many factors.

Causal graphs have risen to prominence in many social sciences over the last decade due to their superior explanatory powers. Why were we so concerned about causality? Because they have predictive powers. For example, it's easy to determine if countries with higher minimum wages have less poverty. You just look at their wage level, compare it to their poverty level, and draw a conclusion. But that's correlation, *not* causation. If you want to know if *raising* the minimum wage *reduces* poverty, you need a causal graph that can explain the complex interrelationships between wages, employment, investment, spending, and poverty. And it must match the observed data for these variables.

Having completed much of the quantitative analyses for this brand growth study with my team, I worked to figure out what our findings were telling us. How did these puzzle pieces all fit together to form a coherent bigger picture? If the highly linear marketing funnel couldn't explain the phenomenon we were seeing, how could we apply systems thinking to create a unified causal graph that painted a clearer picture of the reality we measured? How did all the different marketing levers influence each other? Which factors were important? I knew the various levers driving brand growth weren't acting independently, but I also didn't understand how they affected each other.

It was a long process of finding the truth about these causal relationships. But after dozens of iterations to align the causal graph with what we saw in the data, a primary positive feedback loop started to appear, with the brand's products at the center. We didn't set off searching for this loop—it's where the data led us. And as it turned out, that loop helped us understand the primary importance of the repeat purchase journey (the Repeat Loop) as the central concept empowering brand growth.

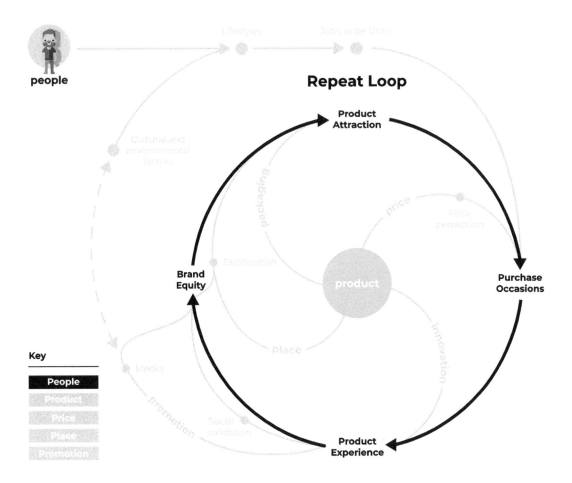

people

**Repeat Loop**

Product
Attraction

Brand
Equity

product

Purchase
Occasions

Product
Experience

Key

People

Product

Price

Place

Promotion

*Figure 11B.*
The Repeat
Loop Is Central
to the Brand
Growth
Flywheel

This Repeat Loop functions like a mechanical flywheel, where the different growth levers and market forces act upon each other to increase (or decrease) brand momentum.

This flywheel is presented here as a conceptual model but it's also the basis for a new mathematical model that can be used to quantify a brand's *momentum*—not just its sales velocity. We call it the Brand Growth Flywheel.

Jay Forrester, who invented the field of System Dynamics and guest-lectured in my class on the subject at MIT, used to say, "A goal without a method is cruel." The Brand Growth Flywheel gives brand managers a clear method to reach their goal of sustainable year-over-year growth. The flywheel helps a brand manager understand how all the pieces of the system fit together into a whole so that they can be managed effectively. Why is that so important? Well, as W. Edwards Deming, the great physicist turned management guru, put it, "If you can't describe what you are doing as a process, you don't know what you're doing." We wanted to help brand managers understand the process at work so they could manage it with greater skill, confidence, and success.

## HOW A FLYWHEEL WORKS

If you've read the book this far, you have a good idea of the nature of our Brand Growth Flywheel. However, it's worth taking a step back to better understand what a flywheel is and how it works.

Flywheels are typically heavy, round discs that store energy in the form of rotation. These spinning discs were the very first machines invented by humans and have been in use for over eight thousand years in the form of potter's wheels and spindles for producing thread. Flywheels were core to the Industrial Revolution and remain central to all industrial economies because they enable engines to transmit the power from a piston firing into the rotational energy that drives cars, trains, ships, planes, and even entire factories.

A single piston firing once generates a powerful but fleeting punch. However, if that piston's punch is correctly applied to a heavy round disc, that disc will slowly start to rotate. As the piston fires over and over again, each punch will drive the heavy disc to spin faster and faster. The heavier the disc and the faster it spins, the more energy it stores in the form of rotational momentum (a.k.a. angular momentum). And the momentum of an object is a measure of how difficult it is to change its speed and direction (a.k.a. velocity). That is, as an object builds greater and greater momentum, the more difficult it is to slow it down or change its course—just like a freight train barreling down the tracks.

If you're winning a higher percentage of consecutive repeat purchases, your brand's flywheel builds momentum faster and spins at a quicker clip. If somebody buys your brand but then moves on to a different brand or tries out several others before coming back to you, your flywheel is spinning much slower because your repeat cycle is happening much less frequently.

When you have repeat customers, they're going around the Repeat Loop. They've bought for a purchase occasion. They have a great product experience. This creates positive mental associations (brand equity) that increase product attraction, and they buy it again. While this finding seems simple at the surface level, it directly contrasts with more commonly adhered to mental models that emphasize new customer acquisition or equity through advertising.

## KEEP IT SPINNING

While the key to spinning the flywheel is repeat customers, brands cannot meaningfully grow without a healthy flow of new buyers. But those new buyers, however necessary, are not sufficient. They can never make up for the loss of existing, repeat buyers who will account for the lion's share of a brand's sales.

Tracking consumers across every shopping occasion over a four-year period revealed the significance of sales from repeat buyers versus those who buy once and never again. Winners earned 87 percent of their sales from repeat buyers, whereas losers earned just 81 percent. This may not seem like a big difference, but let's look at these numbers from a different angle. Our study's losing brands earned 19 percent of their sales from one-time buyers who didn't repeat. Our winning brands earned 13 percent of their sales from one-time buyers. This means that losing brands saw nearly 50 percent more sales from one-and-done buyers than winning brands. That's an enormous difference, and it spotlights why winning brands win and losing brands fail. Winning brands win repeat occasions—they win the Repeat Loop. Their flywheel builds momentum and propels their brand to grow.

Of course, to get repeat buyers, you need new buyers who actually like your product. We found over the four years we studied that winning brands converted slightly over half of the people who tried the brand into repeat buyers, while losers converted less than half, at 45 percent. This might not seem like a big difference, but it's a difference with compounding effects that accumulate over time.

Repeat buying is a central factor but only one of many that affect brand growth. If we zoom out, we see that the Repeat Loop is a reinforcing feedback loop where purchases that result in positive usage experiences breed greater levels of positive mental associations (brand equity) that lead to even more attraction to the brand's products in the future.

On an everyday level, this boils down to, "I just ran out of Downy fabric softener, and I need to restock because Downy does the job. I don't want to take a chance on a different brand that may not be as good." This happens predominantly in a reflexive manner versus a conscious and considered one, but the more times it happens, the more habitual it becomes, as long as nothing interrupts this cycle.

## FUNNEL VS. FLYWHEEL

The idea that companies can repeatedly take actions that generate accelerating momentum and deliver long-term business growth was popularized by Jim Collins in his best-selling book *Good to Great*. As I mentioned earlier, that book heavily inspired this one. Just as Jim and his research team uncovered the distinctive activities that build upon each other to separate long-term growth companies from their laggard industry peers, I along with the dynamic duo Jacob Grocholski and Paul Stanley discovered the underlying mechanics that explain how winning brands win while losing brands fail.

{JaredSchrieber_COLOR_Graphic114_R1_Lock}

As insightful and popular as *Good to Great* has been, the book and its research methods are not without their critics. For one, the flywheel described in *Good to Great* failed to provide a causal graph showing how particular actions build upon each other to generate momentum for the business. Instead, the book offered a set of individual principles that served more as foundational pillars upon which a strong structure could be built. It remained unclear how each of those pillars related to the others or if the set of pillars was collectively necessary or comprehensively sufficient to explain the long-term growth of some companies over others.[3]

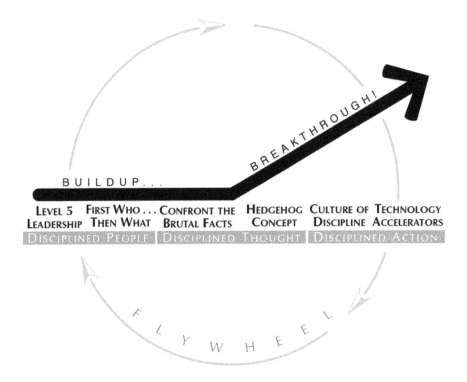

*Figure 11C.*
The Flywheel
Effect as
Depicted in
*Good to Great*

In our study, we identified and mapped the interdependencies of marketing's many "P's"—product, price, promotion, place, packaging, etc. Rather than treating each as a stand-alone pillar, we showed how they work in concert. Product innovation adds momentum

3    Jim Collins, *Good to Great: Why Some Companies Make the Leap...and Others Don't* (New York: HarperBusiness, 2001).

to promotion, making it more effective than it would otherwise be. Promotion's intersection with place is a critical point of leverage (it's no use promoting a product where it isn't available to buy). Packaging should align with place to maximize their joint effects on product attraction.

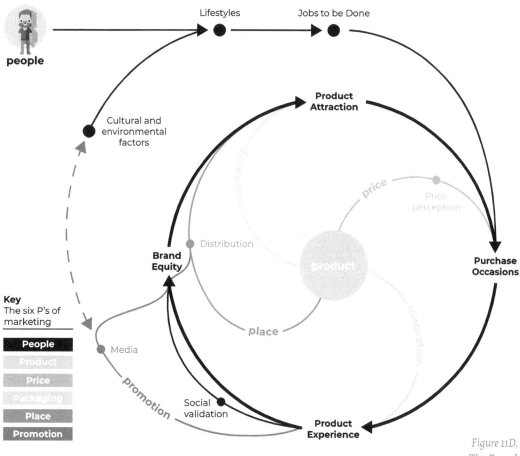

*Figure 11D. The Brand Growth Flywheel and the Six P's of Marketing*

Our approach also contrasts with the marketing funnel point of view, which has long dominated how we think about managing growth. The funnel's very design presupposes that marketing's only role in driving growth is to land new customers. How can that possibly be when nearly 90 percent of our winning brands' sales came from repeat buyers?

Awareness

Interest

Consideration

Intent

Evaluation

Purchase

Yeah!
New customers!

The marketing funnel serves a purpose, but our study shows that it's time to stop treating new customers as the destination and more like an important step along the brand growth journey. Although many versions of the marketing funnel added stages such as loyalty and advocacy, these are clearly force-fitted bolt-ons that don't actually follow the initial purchase in such a linear fashion. In contrast, our model continuously tracks customers throughout their ongoing experience with our brands. Only by reorienting ourselves from a linear funnel to a systemic flywheel can we properly manage the complex interrelationships among the leverage points in our marketing mix.

I'm not the only one arguing that it's time to rethink our reliance on the funnel as the primary framework by which we manage marketing activities and drive brand growth. As previously noted, a McKinsey team studied twenty thousand consumers across three continents as they made purchase decisions in various industries. A key outcome of that study was a realization of the marketing funnel's limitations and the need to incorporate feedback loops from product usage experiences into the "Consumer Decision Journey."

As they put it:

Marketers have been taught to "push" marketing toward consumers at each stage of the funnel process to influence their behavior. But our qualitative and quantitative research in the automobile, skin care, insurance, consumer electronics, and mobile-telecom industries shows that something quite different now occurs. Actually, the decision-making process is a more circular journey. After purchasing a product or service, the consumer builds expectations based on experience to inform the next decision journey.[4]

## A DIFFERENT PERSPECTIVE

Byron Sharp and the Ehrenberg-Bass Institute have popularized the concept of 'mental availability' and 'physical availability' as the keys to brand growth. In their terms, "A brand's mental availability refers to the probability that a buyer will notice, recognize and/or think of a brand in buying situations."[5]

### THE POWER OF POSITIVE EXPERIENCES

Our study concludes that while distinctive brand assets may play an important role as anchor points to which memories are attached in our brain, those memories and their influence on our future purchase decisions are strongest when they are based upon positive experiences using or consuming the brand's products.

---

4   Court et al., "The Consumer Decision Journey."
5   Byron Sharp, "Mental Availability Is Not Awareness, Brand Salience Is Not Awareness," *Marketing Science* (blog), March 26, 2011, https://byronsharp. wordpress.com/2011/03/26/mental-availability-is-not-awareness-brand-salience-is-not-awareness/.

Figure 11F.
Mental
Availability's
Relationship
to the Brand
Growth
Flywheel

If you think this definition of mental availability sounds a lot like "product attraction" in the context of the Brand Growth Flywheel, trust your instincts. The two concepts have significant overlap. In the Brand Growth Flywheel diagram, mental availability is best represented by the black arrow that links brand equity (what you remember) to product attraction (what you notice).

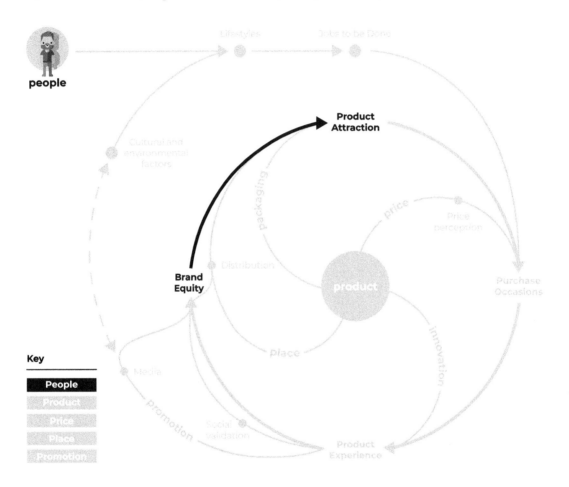

Byron Sharp and the Ehrenberg-Bass Institute claim that mental availability stems from creating memories in consumers' minds related to a brand's distinctive assets (e.g., colors, logos, slogans, tone, and characters). Our study concludes that while distinctive brand assets may play an important role as anchor points to which memories are attached in our brain, those memories and their influence on our future purchase decisions are strongest when they are based upon positive experiences using or consuming the brand's products. Brand equity isn't based on colors, slogans, and jingles. It's built mostly by experiences with the brand's products.

According to Sharp, "Physical Availability refers to a brand's presence during a buying situation."[6] How easy is it for category buyers to find and buy your brand? Physical availability is a function of the brand's presence (e.g., is the product on the shelf at this retailer?), prominence (e.g., does it have premium merchandising that gets noticed?), and relevance (e.g., is this the pack size I want right now?). These concepts align nicely with the Brand Growth Flywheel's arrows for place and packaging and their contribution to product attraction where product attraction represents the degree to which consumers both notice the brand when shopping and are drawn toward choosing it based on expectations of the value it will deliver.[7]

Simply put, there would be no flywheel allowing brands to build momentum without mental and physical availability. Without them, there would be no product attraction, no first dates, and certainly no repeat purchases. However, there are some important points of difference between Byron Sharp's worldview and the findings of our research. Here is a review of those key differences.

## NEW VS. REPEAT BUYERS

Byron Sharp and the Ehrenberg-Bass Institute argue that repeat purchase behaviors (and loyalty) are simply a function of acquiring ever-larger numbers of new brand buyers. Our study of winning and losing brands demonstrates that brand growth depends heavily on a brand's differences in repeat buying versus one-and-done trial purchases. In addition, our model demonstrates that just as repeat buyers are a

---

6    Sharp, "Mental Availability Is Not Awareness."
7    Byron Sharp and team also rightly emphasize the value of linking advertising and other brand marketing activities to what consumers should look for in the store.

function of new buyers, so are new buyers a function of repeat buyers. For example, delighted customers not only repeat buy the brand but also contribute to the social validation (e.g., reviews and word of mouth) that leads to greater new customer acquisition. This underlying virtuous cycle helps explain the Double Jeopardy Law of brand growth, which states that lower-market-share brands have fewer buyers (single jeopardy) and lower brand loyalty (double jeopardy). Could it be that greater brand loyalty (probability of purchase) among existing customers increases the odds that new customers will try your product? (See the Appendix for an explanation of the math behind this phenomenon.)

## PRODUCT EXPERIENCE AND DIFFERENTIATION

There is little to no room for product experience or brand differentiation to play a role in the Ehrenberg-Bass Institute's model of brand growth. I wonder how they could explain the success of Rao's Homemade pasta sauce, which charges a hefty price premium without advertising, premium merchandising, or truly distinctive packaging. Why are consumers willing to pay such a premium for a jar of Rao's marinara? Our model demonstrates that repeat purchase behaviors and overall brand growth depend heavily on the differences in product experience that each competing brand delivers. There is an underlying emotional connection that occurs when a product delights a consumer during a usage occasion. Fans of Rao's would no doubt agree because when they write reviews about the sauce they sound almost intoxicated with the generous amounts of olive oil and the well-balanced sweetness of its tomatoes, onions, and garlic.[8]

## LIGHT VS. HEAVY CATEGORY BUYERS

Byron Sharp and his team argue that reaching light category buyers via mass marketing is critical to brand growth. As quantified and

---

8    Alex Delany, "Rao's is the Best Jarred Pasta Sauce There Ever Was," *Bon Appétit*, May 1, 2018, https://www.bonappetit.com/story/rao-best-jarred-pasta-sauce#.

shown in this book, both winning and losing brands see relatively similar growth rates among light category buyers. The real difference in their performance is among heavier category buyers. Losing brands lose most among heavier category buyers while winning brands hold onto or even gain share among the heavies. Moreover, heavier category buyers continuously deliver more than seven times as much revenue as lighter category buyers. These differences also manifest themselves in how best to allocate limited marketing budgets. Rather than regressively taxing light category buyers with continuous advertising, we advocate a flat to slightly progressive marketing tax, which puts more emphasis (impressions) on heavier category buyers while still reaching all category buyers, as advocated by the Ehrenberg-Bass Institute.

## A BALANCED FLYWHEEL

Imagine the process of shaping pizza dough by hand. After working a mound of dough into something resembling a circular pie, the pizza maker begins to toss and spin the dough. The effect is to expand the size of the pie without tearing and use the centrifugal force to shape the pie into a more perfect circle—creating balanced harmony from the center point to its edges. This pizza dough analogy is a delicious recipe for building a more perfect brand. We want our brand flywheel to spin faster and faster, seamlessly expanding its coverage area, and creating symmetric balance around the entire wheel.

In their physical world applications, flywheels tend to be perfectly round and equally balanced to help reduce energy loss and maximize round-trip efficiency. In the same way, brands can benefit from a balanced, well-rounded approach to developing their flywheels. What does this approach look like?

Let's start with the balance between *product attraction* and *product experience*—which are on opposite ends of the Brand Growth Flywheel. If a consumer has high expectations for a product (high expected utility coming from product attraction) when they buy it, they will have high expectations when they go to consume it. If the consumers' expectations exceed the actual consumption experience, then this disappointment represents an imbalance in the flywheel, and "round-trip efficiency" (i.e., consecutive repeat rate) will be lost.

A similar balance is required between *purchase occasions* and *brand equity*. It's harmful to brand equity when premium brands are sold at a hefty discount because the price is in itself a signal of a brand's quality.

Reducing the price decreases the flywheel's radius and shrinks the entire flywheel. If you want a larger flywheel capable of generating greater momentum and holding that momentum, you need to be able to charge a higher price. Remember the figure skater analogy? The counterweight to reducing the price is greater *product experience* and non-price-oriented media and advertising, both of which have been proven to reduce consumers' price sensitivity by increasing *brand equity*.

Thinking of brand growth in terms of a flywheel also helps explain why trade promotions (e.g., temporary price reductions) rapidly accelerate sales in the short term without delivering any ongoing incremental sales as a result.

The flywheel concept explains how advertising and other brand-building activities can have significant long-term effects on sales without demonstrating immediately sizable sales increases. Once a flywheel is spinning, the firing of an additional piston will accelerate the flywheel's spin rate (rotational velocity) ever so slightly, but by adding to its overall momentum, subsequent rotations will continue to happen with greater inertia (making them more difficult to disrupt). This is a subtle effect that plays out over time, and brand managers need to trust these long-term effects if they want to see lasting momentum and growth.

## WHAT SLOWS THE FLYWHEEL

If we have a balanced flywheel, what can possibly slow it? Friction, wasted energy, and time.

*Friction*

There are two primary types of friction affecting your brand's flywheel. The first is the ease with which your flywheel rotates—that is, your brand's ability to convert consecutive repeat purchase opportunities. This can be held back by specific products that underdeliver, a lack of distribution across the retailers where your consumers shop, or even something as simple as poor merchandising. To help rapidly diagnose these issues, we offer the following metrics:[9]

- **Product Issues:** What is the same-store consecutive repeat rate for each SKU relative to its product-line peers and the brand's overall SKU portfolio? (Recall the strawberry-flavored yogurt example. The brand saw that sales for its strawberry yogurt were not what they should be so they tinkered with their recipe and got sales back on track.)

- **Distribution Issues:** When someone buys your brand but then shops the category at a different store on their next occasion, does your brand underperform against the competition? To measure this, contrast overall consecutive repeat rates by SKU to "different-store" consecutive repeat rates by SKU and check to see if your brand or any of its SKUs stand out as losing more than their fair share versus the competition.

- **Merchandising Issues:** Does your brand suffer lower consecutive repeat rates at particular retailers versus others? Did your brand's consecutive repeat rate drop after a recent planogram change by the retailer?

---

9   Since higher market share products and brands have higher consecutive repeat rates, some of these metrics will best be normalized to allow for useful comparisons.

The second type of friction slowing your flywheel is caused by competitor actions, which ultimately steal purchase occasions. This is one reason why every brand should understand how and why it wins and loses consecutive repeat occasions from competing brands relative to fair-share expectations. If a particular competing brand has a 10 percent market share, but that brand wins 20 percent of the time that your brand loses out on a consecutive repeat occasion, then you need to understand exactly why that brand is winning twice its fair share (20 percent versus 10 percent).

### Wasted Energy

Wasted energy happens when a piston fires without transferring its energy into the flywheel. In the case of your brand's flywheel, it's when a marketing action (such as an ad campaign or new product launch) misses the mark and fails to move the sales needle. Although immediate sales impacts can be hard to measure, they must exist if there is to be any momentum generated by marketing activity. Because at least half of all campaigns fail to generate incremental sales (above their cost), it becomes imperative to invest additional amounts in pretesting and in-market measurement (e.g., randomized control trials with ghost ads) to ensure the full spend on campaign activities contributes to growth.

### Time

Finally, in the absence of a perpetual motion machine (which would violate the laws of physics), we are always and everywhere fighting against time. As time passes, momentum declines. The probability of repeat purchasing a brand on the next trip drops significantly as the time between repeat purchase occasions, product usage experiences, and advertising exposures increases. One way to shrink the time between repeat purchase occasions is to remind consumers to use your product after they've bought it. For example, in product categories like dental floss and barbecue sauce, advertising serves to remind consumers to buy your brand as well as to use it once they've bought it. That way, when they've run out, your brand will be in the driver's seat to more rapidly capture a repeat purchase.

## RAO'S: AN IDEAL FLYWHEEL

Rao's provides an excellent example of a flywheel efficiently harnessing ever greater momentum. Why?

First of all, its product was so good that if a consumer tried it, they almost certainly had a great experience. "Best pasta sauce ever!" as one Amazon shopper titled their review. Delighted consumers were compelled to buy it again the next time they shopped, and this way many consumers became repeat buyers. That repeat buying helped drive greater distribution and social validation—both of which introduced new consumers to the brand. Rao's, as you may recall, didn't even have to spend money on advertising to grow. They had invaluable earned media from the likes of *Bon Appetit* magazine ("Rao's Is the Best Jarred Pasta Sauce There Ever Was") and *Cooking Light* ("Jarred Pasta Sauce That Tastes (Dare We Say It) Better than Homemade"). Their products and the consumers they delighted did the talking for them. This is the hallmark of product-led growth—a winning strategy in every industry.

## HOW WINNERS WIN

Let's take a look at a few of the most important factors that set winners' flywheels apart.

### CONSECUTIVE REPEATS

We weren't the first to report that 90 percent of all purchases for winning brands come from repeat buyers, but we did uncover the unrivaled explanatory power of *consecutive* repeat purchases. What are the odds that a consumer will repeat-buy the same brand the next time they shop in that category? This is a key question because the more consecutive repeat purchases a brand gets, the more it will increase its sales and market share. (For more on the math behind this, see the Appendix.)

In our study, winning brands had significantly higher consecutive repeat rates than losing brands relative to their market share. This metric makes sense, of course, but we haven't been aware of it because legacy panels *can't track this metric*. Their size and rate of participation were insufficient to measure this accurately and the computational horsepower required was too demanding—so it's been hidden from us for more than fifty years! It was not until we applied modern analytics techniques to consumer panel data that consecutive repeat rates became such a clear benchmark of success.

*Figure 11G.*
Comparison of
Consecutive
Repeat Rates
for Winner–
Loser Pairs

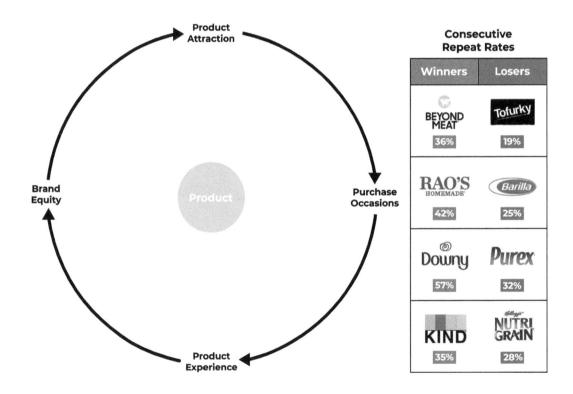

It's important to note that each category has its own distinctive dynamics as far as competition goes. Pasta sauce is a particularly competitive category, whereas fabric softener is less competitive.

Why? There are fewer brands of fabric softener and its buyers are less interested in variety versus sticking with a product that gets the job done. The usage experience for fabric softener also engages fewer senses than the consumption of pasta sauce. You can't taste the difference and you're a lot less likely to tell your friends how amazing it is. Still, whether you're working in a higher- or lower-competition category, consecutive repeat rates compared to other brands in the category matter a lot. They measure the degree of consumer preference for your brand and dictate your potential market share.

## MOMENTS OF TRUTH

Procter & Gamble's highly acclaimed chairman and former CEO, A.G. Lafley, introduced us to the moments of truth and their importance to growing brands. "The best brands consistently win two moments of truth," said Lafley back in 2005.

According to Lafley, the First Moment of Truth (FMOT) is the "moment a consumer chooses a product over the other competitors' offerings." This is the *purchase occasion*, which results in consumers choosing specific products over others.

The Second Moment of Truth (SMOT) occurs "when (the consumer) uses the brand—and is delighted, or isn't." This is the *product experience* and how well it lives up to the consumers' expectations.

Procter & Gamble later identified a Third Moment of Truth (TMOT) as "that powerful inflection point where the product experience catalyzes an emotion, curiosity, passion, or even anger to talk about the brand." If the product experience is sufficiently positive, this will lead to word-of-mouth endorsements, ratings, and reviews—the primary forms of *social validation*.[10]

More recently, Google popularized the idea of a Zero Moment of Truth (ZMOT) in a very self-serving piece of marketing brilliance. According to Google, ZMOT is "the precise moment when (consumers)

---

10    Kevin Roberts, *Lovemarks*, foreword by A. G. Lafley, (New York: powerHouse, 2005).

have a need, intent, or question they want to be answered online."[11] This may be the Zero Moment for a search engine, but by removing the last few words of Google's self-serving definition, we find ourselves with a universally valuable concept: ZMOT is the precise moment when consumers have a need and purchase intent is triggered. This manifests itself in the form of *jobs to be done*.

As Procter & Gamble has repeatedly shown (including with the dominant performance of their seven winning brands in this book's study), gains in each of these four moments of truth are among the most important factors contributing to long-term brand growth.

*Figure 11H.* How the Moments of Truth Relate to the Brand Growth Flywheel

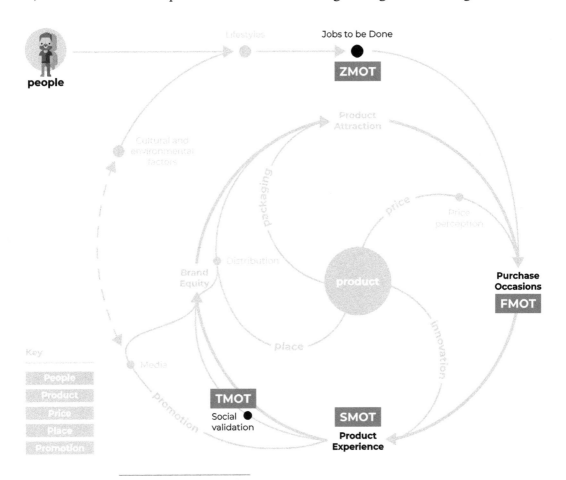

11    Jim Lecinski, "Winning the Zero Moment of Truth," *Google Inc.*, 2011, https://www.thinkwithgoogle.com/_qs/documents/673/2011-winning-zmot-ebook_research-studies.pdf

## LOYALTY

Remember the McKinsey model of the Consumer Decision Journey? It redefines the traditional marketing funnel as a circular system composed of a positively reinforcing feedback loop. Within this system, a Loyalty Loop is formed when a consumer bypasses the consideration of alternative brands and repeatedly purchases a particular preferred brand instead. McKinsey's finding is consistent with our own research.

As I have often shared with clients, "brand nirvana" is reached when ZMOT and FMOT converge. Think about that for a moment. What does this statement really mean? Take a closer look at our Brand Growth Flywheel below with a focus on the factors that influence brand choice at the First Moment of Truth (purchase occasions).

Three primary factors influence consumer choice at the point of purchase:

1. The consumer's criteria for the job to be done
2. Consumer expectations about different products' abilities to meet or exceed those criteria
3. The relative perceived price (cost) of each product being considered

How would the role of each of these factors change in light of ZMOT (job to be done) converging with FMOT (brand choice)? Very simply, the expectations of competing brands' products and the consideration of price would disappear. It's as if your brand were the only brand that could fulfill that consumer's want or need.

In brand nirvana, your consumers only have eyes for your brand; there are no other options considered. Your product can be out of stock or not among the assortment of products carried by the store where the consumer is shopping and you still won't lose the sale because your loyal consumer will shop for your product elsewhere. They don't even consider a substitution. You can charge (almost) as much as you want for your product and consumers will still buy it. Price sensitivity does not apply to a brand's most loyal customers.

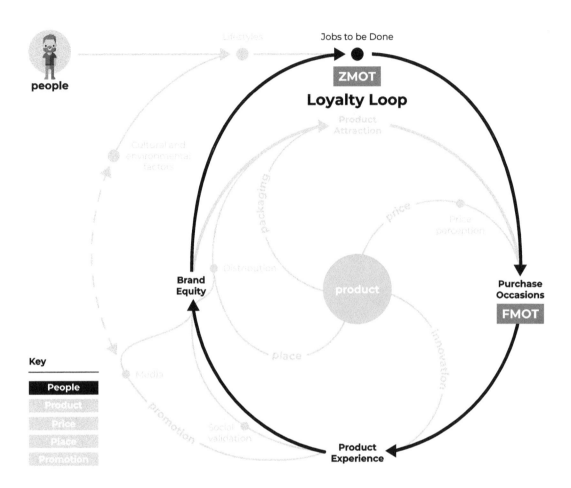

In brand nirvana, there is only certainty—the certainty that if the consumer experiences an urge to buy the category, they will only buy your brand. The consumer's mental model unifies your brand and the category as one. Your brand *is* the category, and the category is your brand.

True loyalty exists when there is no difference in time and space between the moment a need arises (job to be done) and the consumer's decision to buy your brand. It's when "I need a coffee" gets replaced with "I need Starbucks." When this happens, your consumer has entered the Loyalty Loop.

But can brand nirvana be achieved? It may be possible to achieve with a fraction of your most ardent consumers but profoundly difficult to achieve beyond that. Some of your fans will think of your brand *as the category*, but most will not. But that doesn't mean you shouldn't strive to help ever greater proportions of consumers to reach brand nirvana. If we can articulate what perfection looks like, and we can measure ourselves against that, then we can set goals and objectives that move us in the direction of that perfection and lead to ever greater performance.

## HACKING LOYALTY

Loyalty programs that subsidize the purchases of established brand buyers without increasing the share of spend they capture are worthless.

In contrast, signing customers up for automated and regular purchases of your brand via a subscription is a great way to hack into the Loyalty Loop. Subscriptions bypass consumers' propensities to buy other brands, their physical attraction to other brands, and even their price perception. Instead, these consumers just continue to buy the subscribed-to brand without even having to think about it.

Hint water (in which I am an early angel investor) has built a brilliant business, locking in continuous demand from its heaviest consumers via a direct-to-consumer delivery model that bypasses traditional retail. Most of their sales still occur in a retail setting, but because Hint isn't carried at every retailer where its consumers buy enhanced water products, the subscription model helps prevent losing purchase occasions to competing brands with greater distribution. Subscribers always get the product they want without relying on the retailer to keep it in stock or having to carry tons of heavy water bottles home from the store. No discounting is necessary.

The best subscription programs are the ones that consumers are willing to pay for. And the most valuable subscription program that's emerged this century is Amazon Prime—a loyalty program that consumers actually pay to be a part of. Before Amazon launched this loyalty program in 2007, its retail sales growth had begun to slow. Jeff Bezos realized that Amazon was struggling to win shopping occasions because the delivery lag time created an inconvenience and the shipping cost made the perceived price too expensive. Prime solved this with free delivery, guaranteed two-day shipping, and a "sunk cost" anchor for paid members to make Amazon their first choice for online shopping.[12]

## A SELF CRITIQUE

The Brand Growth Flywheel is not perfect. It pains me to say that, but my goal in presenting the flywheel is to correct so many of the misconceptions that have plagued our industry for decades. Marketing relies heavily upon folklore, guesswork, and instinct because we've known so little about our consumers' habits and inclinations. We now have enough data to employ science in our decision-making, and the Brand Growth Flywheel is an effort to wrestle that data into a representative model. Over time, as our data set increases and our understanding of it sharpens, I expect modifications to the flywheel. I also expect it to generate a healthy debate. I look forward to the insights that the debate will generate. By putting this model to the test against empirical observations and refining it accordingly, I'm confident we will overcome the dark art of marketing mythology and become enlightened by the true science of marketing.

So let's get that debate going. To join, visit the Brand Growth Flywheel community forum at *www.BrandGrowthFlywheel.com/forum*

---

12   Colin Bryar and Bill Carr, *Working Backwards: Insights, Stories, and Secrets from inside Amazon* (New York: St. Martin's Press, 2021).

# 12

# FROM INSIGHTS
# TO ACTION

No doubt some of what you've read in this book was either counterintuitive or contradicted what you've been told previously. You're not alone. Our research team had the same experience. As we reconciled what we were seeing in the data with prevailing marketing wisdom, several new truths emerged. When we found other peer-reviewed studies of real-world brand performance backing our findings, we became confident enough to publish our results and make firm recommendations to brand managers and marketers seeking to lead their own Breakout Brand.

In this chapter, I'll describe action steps you can take based on our findings and the rationale behind those actions. Use these to guide or influence your future brand decisions.

## ACTION STEPS

1. **It's not enough to either acquire more customers or earn greater loyalty. You have to do both.**

Rationale: Every winning brand gained new customers *and* increased its share of category spending. Losing brands lost customers and their share of spend captured from retained customers. Greater loyalty doesn't simply come from winning more customers as others claim. Instead, winning more customers comes from actions that also win greater loyalty. Delighted customers generate new customers for a brand via word of mouth and other forms of social validation, such as online reviews and earned media. In some cases, that social validation plays out by convincing a retailer to carry a brand based on the repeat purchase rate and share of spend your brand captures at competing retailers. The added distribution (thanks to the purchases of "loyal" customers at retailers who already carry your product) helps your brand land new customers more effectively than any other known method.

As you work to add new customers and gain greater loyalty from your existing ones, explore the following questions.

Action Steps:

- Are you capturing your fair share of new category buyers? Which is higher: your brand's market share or the percentage of time new category buyers choose your brand versus competitors?

- Is your consecutive repeat rate high or low relative to your brand's market share? If it's high, then focus on maximizing distribution by closing PCV gaps.[1] If it's low or on par, then focus on improving the product experience through innovation.

- When customers switch to a competitor, use purchase-triggered surveys to figure out why.

- What percent of customers score your products a perfect ten in NPS surveys or give it five stars in online reviews?

- What are the primary reasons customers don't give your product a perfect review?

2. **Focus more on heavy category buyers.**

Rationale: Despite what some experts say, growing among light category buyers is *not* what distinguishes growing brands from those in decline. Both winning brands and losing brands show similar levels of year-over-year sales growth among light category buyers. But winning brands retain and increase demand among heavy category buyers while losers hemorrhage sales from heavy category buyers. Keep in mind that light category buyers follow the behaviors of heavy category buyers, not the other way around. Where the heavy category buyers go, the entire category will follow.

---

1    PCV represents product category volume, which is superior to all commodity volume (ACV) when prioritizing sales efforts to close distribution gaps for a particular brand or product.

Remember, too, that the notion that today's heavy buyers are tomorrow's light buyers (and vice versa) is patently false. There is some migration, but it's small—our study found that less than 5 percent of the top one-third of category spenders drop into the bottom third of light buyers annually.

Action Steps:

- Which brands win more than their fair share of purchases from the category's heaviest buyers? Why?

- When heavy category buyers switch away from your products from one occasion to the next, which competing products are they choosing? Use trigger surveys to start figuring out why.

- Is your advertising reaching heavy category buyers proportionate to how much they spend on the category? If not, improve your targeting.

- What needs of these heavy category buyers remain underserved? Why do they switch brands from one occasion to the next? Understand their jobs to be done and the resulting criteria in fine detail.

- What do they hate most about buying and using products in the category?

- Are your marketing efforts reaching heavy category buyers proportionately to their importance or are you overtaxing the poor light buyers of the category?

3.  If your brand has greater appeal among certain demographic groups, don't double down on them; instead, address your brand's affinity gaps.

Rationale: Demographic differences between your customers and the category as a whole are not strengths but weaknesses. Focusing on distinctive demographic affinities reduces growth and alienates many would-be customers. Winning brands focus on closing their affinity gaps so that their consumers look more like the consumers of the category as a whole. Having the broadest possible appeal within your category is a proven way to win.

Action Steps:
- Find out which demographic segments you are failing to capture your fair share from. Do you understand why?

- Which brands in the category overperform among those demographics? Figure out why and course correct.

- Extend these analyses and gap-closing initiatives to include life stages, lifestyles, and psychographics.

4.  Segment the context, motivations, and prevalence of different usage occasions (jobs to be done). Understand how your product can better deliver on key occasions and design your marketing and innovation behind it.

Rationale: Most brands focus too much on segmenting consumers and not enough on occasions. Winning brands win occasions that grow categories because they meet needs existing competitors fail to satisfy. If you're going to build a Breakout Brand, chances are you will win a disproportionate amount of your sales from smaller brands; the category's largest brands already satisfy most needs. Consumers try their luck with niche brands when these large competitors don't fully serve their needs.

Action Steps:
- Attitudes and usage (A&U) studies done well (e.g., strong methodology tied to actual purchase behaviors) should establish the prevalence of key segments of usage occasions and their distinctive context and criteria for the "job to be done."

- Calculate your brand's market share by purchase occasion *and* by usage occasion. Position and deliver products that offer differentiated value propositions with respect to those occasions where your brand has the right to win.

5. **Minimize price-centric trade promotions that accelerate short-term sales velocity at the expense of long-term brand momentum.**

Rationale: In Chapter 9, we exposed why the CPG industry's affection for trade promotions is actually a $100 billion affliction. Calculating short-term sales velocity without also measuring brand momentum has led us all astray. Reducing prices shrinks the flywheel and steals brand momentum; as soon as prices go back up, consumers are more likely to switch to competing brands and are less likely to pay full price. Overreliance on trade promotions and temporary price reductions to drive sales is a telltale sign of a declining brand.

Action Steps:
- Measure consumer trial and switching behavior incrementally, not just point-of-sale sales lift.

- Minimize and/or mask the role of price in retailer promotions (e.g., bonus gifts or 'buy two, get one free') to prevent anchoring low prices (and perceived quality) in consumers' minds.

- Shift trade funds toward investments in improved merchandising and displays, rather than price subsidies alone.

- Add brand messaging to all trade-based communications—don't let trade promotions be just about price discounts.

- Remember that trade works best when it wins distribution and boosts trial for new products.

6. Measure what's important instead of deeming important what's easily measurable.

Rationale: Brand momentum and consecutive repeat rate are among the most important measures of brand performance, but they don't get measured because they haven't been measurable by legacy panels. Remember, the consecutive repeat rate differs from the traditional repeat rate metric in that it focuses on whether consumers repeat buy the brand *on their very next category purchase occasion.* As you'll learn in the Appendix, it's a proxy for momentum because it stems from consumers' probability of purchasing your brand without the noisy, short-term effects of promotions and competitor advertising.[2] Brands become winners when their consecutive repeat rate outpaces their competitors.

Billy Beane, the former general manager of the Oakland A's baseball team, enjoyed great success when he disregarded broad legacy performance metrics and examined more precise, insightful data about players, such as "wins above replacement" and "on-base percentage." Twenty years later, Beane's "Moneyball" metrics are now standard practice in professional baseball because they lead to better decisions and better outcomes. Brand management's "Moneyball" moment

---

2   Research is well underway to establish a more holistic measure of momentum that incorporates pricing, purchase cycles, and customer mass as variables into the physics of measuring a brand flywheel's momentum.

is now. Winning brands in the coming decade will take a different approach to performance measurement than their predecessors. One that measures what's important rather than deeming important what is easily measured.

Action Steps:
- Add consecutive repeat rate measures to your brand and product KPIs alongside sales, market share, and brand equity.

- Use the incrementality of consumer behavior to measure the effectiveness of trade promotions, not just immediate sales lift extracted from POS data.

- Establish the ability to measure CAC (customer acquisition costs) and LTV (lifetime value) to guide marketing investments.

- Consider a "wins above replacement" approach to SKU rationalization decision-making.

7.  Buck the trend of making brands distinctive (ala Byron Sharp) instead of differentiated (ala Philip Kotler); focus on being *both* innovative and unique.

Rationale: Our data shows that the biggest differences between winning and losing brands in the minds of consumers (across 144 brand attributes measured by BERA) are the extent to which they are seen as "innovative" (a.k.a. differentiated) and "unique" (a.k.a. distinctive). Reinforcing distinctive brand assets should be part of a winning strategy, but it is best paired with innovative products that deliver differentiated product experiences. Dove women's deodorant is a great example. Odor and wetness protection were table stakes in the category, but when Dove added skin care (addressing skin sensitivity and irritation) to the mix as a point of differentiation, its sales took off. Rao's branding isn't particularly distinctive and it had almost no media support, but it is incredibly differentiated in terms of the quality of its ingredients and the flavor it delivers.

Action Steps:
- Do your marketing communications and packaging crisply articulate differentiating benefits, preferably higher-order benefits (e.g., the "Elements of Value" pyramid)?

- How does your brand rank, and what is its trend relative to the competition in its perception as "innovative" and "unique"?

- Do your research and development efforts adequately prioritize truly innovative and unique innovations versus those that are incremental or copy-cat in nature?

8. **To drive brand equity, focus on product quality and the experience it delivers to consumers, not on advertising.**

Rationale: Too many marketers falsely believe advertising is the primary driver of brand equity. But we always believe our own experiences over the biased claims of those trying to sell us something. Additionally, we tend to believe the unbiased claims of others who speak from their own experiences. This is human nature, and it's a failure to ignore it.

Advertising's influence is greatest for new products—when consumers do not yet have their own experiences or the experiences of others to rely upon. After that, advertising primarily serves to remind consumers of those (hopefully pleasant) experiences so that they will be ever-so-slightly more likely to buy and consume the product more often in the face of alternatives.

Action Steps:

- Apply proven research approaches to innovation such as the Problem Detection Method, the Ideal Method, and the Consumption Chain Method to identify opportunities.

- Focus innovations around specific jobs to be done through a deep understanding of key types of usage occasions.

- Harness the treasure trove of insights into consumers' wants and needs stemming from online reviews, social media posts, and perfectly targeted trigger surveys.

- For a more lively discussion on these topics (and many more), you're encouraged to visit the Brand Growth Flywheel community forum at *www.BrandGrowthFlywheel.com/forum*.

## HOW TO HACK THE FLYWHEEL

In addition to these overarching action steps for managing your brand and gaining market share and sustainable sales growth, there are many other actions you can take to stimulate the Brand Growth Flywheel and accelerate your brand's momentum. While none of the following hacks are necessary—and many may only make sense to pursue for short periods under just the right circumstances—they each represent proven tools for invigorating brand growth. Let's examine a few options.

### DELIVERING PRODUCT EXPERIENCE WITHOUT A PURCHASE

Product sampling is a highly effective (though expensive) means of bypassing the *purchase occasion* to initiate *product experience*. I would never have considered buying Degree for Men deodorant if it hadn't been for the small sample I received at the finish line of a Tough Mudder race years ago. The product worked well, and I liked the mild smell and soothing feel. From then on, it was my preferred brand, and

I became a repeat buyer. As our research uncovered, sampling is a tactic that can work equally well for newer brands (such as Health-Ade Kombucha) and more established brands (like Modelo).

Sampling is often undervalued as a marketing tactic to attract new buyers. That might be because brands don't consider the lifetime value (LTV) of newly converted buyers who try the product, love it, and keep buying it. When you factor LTV into the ROI equation, sampling looks like a smart way to create a product experience that doesn't require the consumer to purchase your product first. If your product is great and the sampling experience nets new devotees, the piston will pump, and your flywheel will spin.

## SOCIAL VALIDATION AND BRAND EQUITY WITHOUT PRODUCT EXPERIENCE

Advertising with a celebrity spokesperson has repeatedly proven to be an effective way to build brand equity via social validation without the need for product experience to generate word of mouth. For example, the winning brand BodyArmor signed endorsement deals with professional athletes Mike Trout and Rob Gronkowski shortly after it launched in 2011. These endorsements lent the nascent brand credibility as a professional-grade sports drink. Then, they partnered with Kobe Bryant starting in 2014 to help level the playing field with Gatorade—and the brand's growth took off. Nicorette became a winning brand after hiring Dale Earnhardt Jr. as its celebrity spokesman (albeit to help launch a new product that truly delivered a better experience). Celebrity endorsements aren't the only way, however. Good ole public relations (e.g., Caulipower) and even paid influencers (e.g., Bang) can also boost social validation and brand equity.

## PRODUCT ATTRACTION WITHOUT BRAND EQUITY (OR DISTRIBUTION)

If you lack brand equity and distribution, there are still ways to gain product attraction. One way is to sell-in an eye-catching stand-alone display or shelf-hanger that doesn't require the retailer to change their existing shelf assortment. This is a low-risk way for the retailer to gauge demand for your product in their stores. Then, use the display's sell-through as validation for the retailer to carry your product as part of its standard assortment on an ongoing basis.

Another way to gain distribution is to pay slotting fees and a premium for prominent placement. The e-commerce equivalent is a sponsored ad on the retailer's website. When your product appears among the first options in the category and looks like it's already among the best-selling items in that category, it's more likely to win new triers. To convert browsers into buyers, you'll still want eye-catching and compelling packaging—there's no substitute. BodyArmor, Caulipower, and Olly are examples of winning brands that did this particularly well.

## WINNING PURCHASE OCCASIONS WITHOUT PRODUCT ATTRACTION

Coupons and trade promotions can help drive sales when initial *product attraction* lags. Coupons are expensive but worthwhile if they drive first-time trials that lead to ongoing repeat purchases. But coupons devastate margins (and sustainable growth) if they are used to incentivize ongoing repeat purchases. As Al Ries and Jack Trout wrote back in 1993, "Couponing is a drug. You continue to do it because the withdrawal symptoms are just too painful."[3] Unfortunately, nearly thirty years later, too many brands remain addicted.

So, while there are many proven ways to move or accelerate the flywheel, remember that most hacks are unsustainable by design. They can only contribute to a brand's long-term growth trajectory if they lead consumers into the Repeat Loop. For example, celebrity endorsements can't overcome a bad product experience. A poor trial experience will dominate the mental associations in consumers' minds and block all further repeat purchases.

---

3    Ries and Trout, *22 Immutable Laws of Marketing*, 64.

13

# CONCLUSION
## HINDSIGHT IS MORE
## THAN 2020

The COVID-19 pandemic disrupted people's lives in extraordinary ways. I'll spare you the details, but in my case, it's a primary reason this book is being published in 2022 instead of 2020. On the bright side, this extra time allowed my research team to look back at what happened in 2020 and 2021 and compare it to what we had seen during our study's core period: 2016–2019.

How did the winners and losers fare in 2020 and 2021? Would past results predict future performance? Would COVID completely disrupt the trends we'd seen? Did the growth of any winning brands suddenly reverse course? If so, why?

Were any losing brands able to turn things around? If so, how? Would any new evidence emerge that should call our prior findings into question? Or, did the Brand Growth Flywheel continue its momentum?

Here's what we found:

Overall, the winners kept winning, and the losers kept losing. The differences in these brands' flywheel momentum continued. Winners gained an average of 90 basis points (0.9 percent) of market share in 2020 and 2021, while the losing brands dropped another 70 basis points.

*Figure 13A.* The Winners Kept Winning, and the Losers Kept Losing (Market Share)

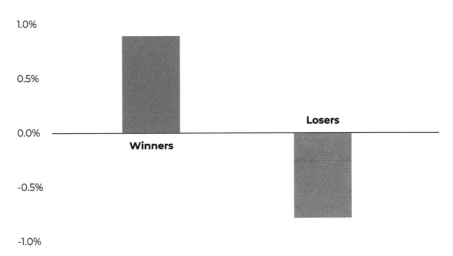

There were some exceptions to this macro trend, however. Much of this is expected due to the law of large numbers and its resulting reversions to the mean. Still, only three of the fifty-eight winning brands from our 2016–2019 study reversed course to become losing brands in 2020: Nicorette (stop smoking aids), Slimfast (weight loss), and Fisher (nuts). It's important to note that we would hardly expect any of our winning brands to continue to qualify as winners given how strict we set the threshold: growing market share by half a percent a year and revenue by $10 million. Remember that only fifty-eight out of twenty-five thousand brands qualified previously, so the odds of them continuing to qualify are very small. The fact that so many of our winners continued to win suggests that these standout brands maintained the momentum of their flywheel.

On the flip side, only four of our study's fifty-eight losing brands showed signs of a turnaround with cumulative share gains of over 1 percent from the end of our study in 2019 through 2021. Of those, two really stood out: Colgate toothpaste and Marie Callender's each gained nearly 3 percent in market share from 2020 to 2021. The other two were Degree women's deodorant at just a little over 1 percent and private-label stop-smoking aids.

The story behind Marie Callender's recovery has more to do with a COVID-induced shift in consumer lifestyles and resulting dessert-at-home occasions than any corrective actions the brand itself took to drive the turnaround. The data clearly show that throughout 2020, consumers—who could no longer dine out at restaurants—grew tired of making their pies from scratch or even with the help of a premade frozen pie crust. Instead, they gradually began to prefer the ease of Marie Callender's ready-made "Heat & Eat" products.

This consumer trend toward heat-and-eat products during the back half of 2020 and into 2021 was true across many food categories. Marie Callender's won share by delivering a more convenient, more premium solution than the pie-crust-only competitors it stole share from. Marie Callender's also benefited from new category entrants (consumers buying frozen pies for the first time) who had previously purchased Marie Callender's frozen food products in other categories. This demonstrated a brand equity halo effect across categories similar to what we saw with Dove and its women's deodorant. Most importantly, Marie Callender's delivered the delicious "pie for dessert" craving that restaurant-goers were missing during COVID lockdowns. When these consumers' lifestyles changed, Marie Callender's got the job done.

## THE FLYWHEEL IN ACTION

The biggest story to come out of 2020 was Colgate's "Renewal," a new subbrand marketed as a toothpaste that will "revitalize gums" and stop bleeding. By 2021, Colgate emerged as a near-perfect example of the flywheel in action.

This massive, long-established toothpaste brand not only got back on track but earned the title of Breakout Brand of the Year in 2021, growing US retail sales by nearly $250 million year over year with sales up more than 20 percent. How'd they do it?

Well, the brand did a lot of things right. It effectively used innovation and advertising together to build brand equity. It identified a job to be done that other products didn't solve and then sold its new product at a premium price. Finally, it gained great distribution by utilizing existing brand equity with retailers and by expanding its footprint online.

## THE IMPORTANCE OF INNOVATION

Colgate's turnaround starts at the top. In 2019, the Colgate-Palmolive board appointed a new CEO to lead the company: Noel Wallace. Wallace swiftly implemented a new growth strategy for the company centered around three key initiatives: "driving premium innovation in our core businesses, pursuing adjacent categories and high-growth segments, and expanding in faster-growing channels and markets."

According to Wallace, "We started with revamping our innovation process to focus on delivering transformative, disruptive innovation across our product portfolio and especially in our larger, core businesses...Our focus right now is on bringing real value to categories through premium innovation."[1] With more than 50 percent of Colgate toothpaste's breakout growth in 2021 coming from two premium innovations, it's fair to say that this strategic focus paid off.

## MEETING AN UNDERSERVED NEED

Colgate launched Renewal in early 2021 as a new premium product that met an underserved consumer need. The leading incumbent choice, Sensodyne (a winning brand in our original study), had been focusing more on helping consumers with tooth (and secondarily gum) sensitivity. Through gum-centric research and clinical studies, Colgate developed a toothpaste that could "prevent and repair early gum damage."

At the same time, Wallace also inherited the recently relaunched Colgate Total with an all-new formula that eliminated a highly controversial ingredient—triclosan, which had been holding sales back and damaging the brand's reputation. With the relaunch, the brand could legitimately position the product as both "better for you" and "better for the planet"—a combination of messaging that clearly resonates with consumers today.

Across the board, Colgate has shown its understanding of what America's rapidly aging and relatively well-off population needs. In particular, more consumers are facing health challenges with their gums, and Colgate answered that call.

## BRAND-BUILDING ADVERTISING

The innovative Colgate Renewal was brought to market in premium packaging more reminiscent of a high-end beauty product and at an

---

1    Colgate, "We Are Colgate: 2020 Annual Report," Colgate-Palmolive Company, 2021, https://investor.colgatepalmolive.com/static-files/1d8483af-a8b5-485f-9cff-992592a92b3b.

eight-dollar price point that is four times more expensive than Colgate's most basic toothpaste.

Rather than focusing on price promotions, Colgate strategically focused on brand-building advertising and social validation tactics to market the new product. Two celebrity endorsements—Brooke Shields and Ana de la Reguera, an actress with greater appeal among the Latino population—helped the brand reach the categories' consumers as a whole.[2]

Just as Nicorette had successfully done with its popular mint-flavored lozenge, Colgate boosted the launch of the product with social validation from these celebrities appearing in their commercials as the "ideal consumers." The marketing also nailed the combination of functional and emotional benefits: healthier gums and more beauty as you age.

## EXPANDED DISTRIBUTION AND GROWTH

The launch relied heavily on "equity advertising" as opposed to performance marketing—even via digital ads on retailers' e-commerce websites, where it would have been all too easy to offer price discounts to lure consumers into trying the product. Colgate was smart to advertise more heavily through select retailer websites since the new product wasn't yet carried by all the key retailers. This meant that if the ad was effective at building brand equity in the consumers' minds, the product was there to be found when those consumers went to buy (i.e., a necessary component of product attraction).

---

2    Lina Jordan, "Colgate Renewal Focused on Improving Gum Health Names Ana de la Reguera and Brooke Shields as Brand Ambassadors," *Hombre*, November 15, 2021, https://hombre1.com/colgate-renewal-focused-on-improving-gum-health-names-ana-de-la-reguera-and-brooke-shields-brand-ambassadors/.

Remember that the most effective advertising in the world is practically worthless if the consumers can't find the product when they go to buy it.

Alongside its new innovations, Colgate saw growth across its existing product portfolio as well. Renewal accounted for $92 million and Colgate Total accounted for another $64 million of the total of $250 million in growth the brand experienced in 2021. As Wallace put it, "Our choices to invest in innovation, digital transformation, and advertising are helping to deliver growth across our portfolio."[3]

*Figure 13C. Colgate Renewal Digital Ad Placed on Retailers' E-commerce Websites*

For Colgate, digital transformation involved creating more engaging digital media content and taking steps to win more than their fair share of sales online.

"Across all of our businesses we are developing more sophisticated digital content to draw attention, truly differentiate, and, importantly, earn loyalty for our brands going forward," Wallace said.

In a world full of distractions, it's harder than ever to truly "draw attention," but there's no doubt that the brands capable of garnering attention are better positioned to get their message across. Of course, true differentiation doesn't hurt either. While Byron Sharp emphasizes the role of distinction—or making it easy to recognize one brand from another—Colgate's turnaround demonstrates that differentiation matters, too. In this case, the product is innovative, premium,

---

3   Colgate-Palmolive Company, "Colgate Announces 4th Quarter 2020 Results," press release, January 29, 2021, https://investor.colgatepalmolive.com/news-releases/news-release-details/colgate-announces-4th-quarter-2020-results.

and clinically tested for gum revitalization—a differentiating factor versus the competition.

But can this "sophisticated digital content" do more than garner attention and truly "earn loyalty," as Wallace claims? If we define loyalty as the habit of repeatedly choosing a particular brand over competitors, then there is no doubt that effective advertising (of any kind) can play a supporting role by loading the dice (probability of purchase) in your favor. The focus on digital content and advertising was a key highlight reported by Wallace in the company's end-of-year earnings call. "Our digital transformation is paying off with e-commerce market shares growing in key markets and strong e-commerce sales growth across all of our categories," he said.[4] In reviewing the data, our team found that Colgate grew its online market share (including buy online and pick up at stores) from 21 percent to 33 percent from 2019 to 2021.

Colgate's turnaround provides an excellent example of how brands really grow, pulling so many of our findings together. The brand beautifully leveraged the key forces of brand growth to generate a powerful flywheel effect.

## WHAT DOES THE FUTURE HOLD?

If I were just a little smarter, I would have put down my pen and concluded the book before writing those five words directly above. I don't own a crystal ball, and my ability to predict what the stock market will do over the next twelve months could probably be bested by monkeys throwing darts. That said, I have the privilege of occupying a distinctive vantage point from which to observe many emerging trends that will influence our industry in the decade(s) to come.

For one, passive data collection at scale will lead us to look for insights from naturally occurring experiments rather than always

---

4    "Colgate-Palmolive Q4 2021 Earnings Call Transcript," MarketBeat, January 28, 2022, https://www.marketbeat.com/earnings/transcripts/68750/.

designing artificial research studies. (Hat tip to Kirti Singh, Chief Analytics and Insights Officer at Procter & Gamble, for his influence on my thinking about this topic.) As a result, we will be less and less fooled by consumers' misleading rationalizations and more attuned to the hidden motives that drive their real-world behaviors.

The internet search, click-stream, and completely traceable purchase behaviors stemming from e-commerce will fuel greater and greater learnings that will be transferred from digital to analog in the form of physical retail. The flow of learning has shifted from its origin of physical retail (Shelf 1.0) informing online best practices to a world where online retail has developed best practices that are fundamentally distinctive from how in-store retail operates (Shelf 2.0). What comes next is Shelf 3.0, whereby physical retail gets reengineered to apply best practices learned from e-commerce.

In teaching AI-powered machines how to make humanlike decisions, we'll learn more about how humans actually make decisions. These learnings will influence branding, packaging, and merchandising first, then advertising, communications, and finally product innovation.

The importance of research and development for new product development and enhancement of the product experience will receive greater boardroom attention and funding—which has dropped to an absurdly low 2 percent of revenues for large CPG companies. A new class of innovation-oriented CPGs will become growth stocks rather than cyclical stocks. In addition, artificial intelligence (AI) will be harnessed to automate the brainstorming and testing of new product formulations, ingredients, packaging, and label claims.

The prevalence of genetic predispositions toward flavors, scents, nutritional content, and allergens will play an increasing role in new product development and, subsequently, marketing (i.e., Did you know that 87 percent of Americans need more vitamin X based on their genetics than the FDA daily recommended amount?).

Categories will continue to evolve and fragment into new subcategories according to finer and finer distinctions (e.g., beer versus hard seltzer) as product experiences align to more tightly defined usage occasions and their corresponding jobs to be done. The evergreen challenge of defining a category and best positioning your brand within it will only get harder. However, avoiding standardized category definitions will provide differentiating perspectives that will lead to competitive advantages regarding products offered and their distinctive value propositions. Moreover, the brands that first establish those new categories will be the market leaders for decades.

Although the macrotrend of consolidated market share among each category's top three brands will continue, those national brands competing on a "value" basis (a.k.a. low cost) will continue to lose share to store brands and generic "nonbranded" entrants. The real winners will be those brands that establish themselves as the premium option within their categories (e.g., BodyArmor, Liquid I.V., Olly, Kodiak Cakes, Swiffer).

And finally, my most outrageous prediction: As the Many Worlds Interpretation of Quantum Mechanics gains further acceptance among physicists, so will the belief that we're all just living in enormous and incredibly realistic simulations. What could justify the massive amounts of energy invested into such simulations? Well, the answer probably lies somewhere between forty-two and a search for Wanamaker's half. ;)

# THE SCIENCE BEHIND CONSECUTIVE REPEAT RATES AND MARKET SHARE

*Coauthored by* Joel Rubinson *and* Jared Schrieber

The primary finding of this study, and the core of the Brand Growth Flywheel, is the central role of the Repeat Loop—that is, the frequency with which consumers repeat-purchase a brand dictates the brand's growth or decline. That repeat-purchase frequency improves when consumers become more likely to repeat-buy the brand on their very next occasion for that type of product (versus switching away for a few occasions and then coming back). The percentage of time that consumers repeat-buy the same brand on the very next occasion is called the consecutive repeat rate, or, among us math nerds, the Markov Repeat Rate. But what causes the consecutive repeat rate for a brand to increase?

Consecutive repeat rates increase when consumers' underlying probability of purchasing the brand increases. Let's start with the simple example of a single consumer (you) and a single brand (Ruby's BBQ sauce). Suppose you have a 20 percent probability of choosing Ruby's when you buy barbecue sauce. In that case, you have roughly a 4 percent probability (20 percent times 20 percent = 4 percent) of choosing Ruby's on two consecutive shopping occasions.[1] However, if you have a 50 percent probability of choosing Ruby's BBQ sauce, then the odds of two consecutive purchases being Ruby's will jump from 4 percent to 25 percent (50 percent times 50 percent). To capture 50 percent of your barbecue sauce purchases, Ruby's will have to get you to consecutively repeat 25 percent of the time. This is why brands with higher market shares have consecutive repeat rates significantly higher than their competitors.[2] And while we can't yet plug a Neuralink into consumers' brains to figure out their purchase probability for a given brand, modern consumer purchase panels allow us to measure their consecutive repeat rate as a mathematical proxy. Moreover, we can track this behavior across consumers and brands to understand what is driving changes in market share within a product category. This starts with a simple brand switching matrix (a.k.a. Markov Matrix) common to "Gained–Lost–Retained" analyses. Let's start with a very simple example where the barbecue sauce category is limited to just three competing brands with stable market shares.

In Figure A1, Morty's had 60,000 buyers on the first purchase occasion, of which 45,000 purchased Morty's again on the very next occasion (75 percent consecutive repeat rate). In addition, Morty's won 11,250 purchases from consumers who had purchased Ruby's on their first occasion and another 3,750 consumers who switched from

---

1   This oversimplified example assumes no influence of purchase probability from one occasion to the next. While we do not believe this to be entirely true, it remains a hotly debated topic among leading marketing scientists. Regardless, this "zero-order" assumption does not affect the mathematical certainty that brands with a higher probability of purchase must have a correspondingly higher consecutive repeat rate. If, in fact, a purchase occasion does influence the shopper's choice on the very next occasion, then the role of consecutive repeat rate in explaining market share changes is even greater than what we have outlined in these simple examples.
2   Consecutive repeat rate for a given brand is defined as the percent of consumers who repeat buy the exact same brand on their very next purchase occasion for the category.

Reggie's. This pattern is typical in categories where brand switching is balanced and market shares remain stable.

*Figure A1.*
Brand
Switching
Matrix with
Steady Market
Shares

|  | Second purchase occasion | | | Totals for first occasion | Market Shares for first occasion |
|---|---|---|---|---|---|
|  | Morty's BBQ sauce | Ruby's BBQ sauce | Reggie's BBQ sauce |  |  |
| Morty's BBQ sauce | 45,000 | 11,250 | 3,750 | 60,000 | 60% |
| Ruby's BBQ sauce | 11,250 | 16,880 | 1,870 | 30,000 | 30% |
| Reggie's BBQ sauce | 3,750 | 1,870 | 4,380 | 10,000 | 10% |
| Totals for second occasion | 60,000 | 30,000 | 10,000 | 100,000 |  |
| Market Shares for second occasion | 60% | 30% | 10% |  | 100% |

What if Morty's suddenly lost 8,000 MORE buyers to Ruby's? Its consecutive repeat rate would decline to 62 percent (37,000 repeats out of 60,000 opportunities to repeat) and its market share would decline to 52 percent (52,000 Morty's purchases out of 100,000 category purchases). This would indicate that the market is no longer in equilibrium and that market shares for each brand are moving toward a new balance of power.[3]

So, when a brand's consecutive repeat rate changes, the brand's market share will also be changing. This is an arithmetic certainty that will lead us to powerful conclusions about the nature of the underlying force that causes both metrics to move together. The bigger the brand's market share, the higher its consecutive repeat rate must be! We see this in real-world data across all product categories, just like in this example.

---

3    This new stabilized set of shares can be estimated via linear algebra using eigenvectors.

Figure A2.
Market
Shares and
Consecutive
Repeat Rates
Derived from
Figure A1

| | Market Share | Consecutive Repeat Rate |
|---|---|---|
| Morty's | 60% | 75% |
| Ruby's | 30% | 56% |
| Reggie's | 10% | 44% |

## BREAKING IT DOWN

The figures above represent aggregated data patterns, but what is the underlying process that generates this relationship between market share and consecutive repeat rate? By understanding the micro level, we will garner greater insights and intuitions about how brands win (and lose) market share at the macro level.

Let's bring back our very first hypothetical example of Ruby's BBQ sauce, where you have a 20 percent probability of purchasing the brand, and every other consumer has their own probability of purchase. Is there a process that explains how each consumer can have their own probability of purchase, yet the aggregate of those probabilities results in the kind of market shares and consecutive repeat rates we see in the real world?

There must be an underlying distribution of consumer purchase probabilities for each brand, going from 0 percent to 100 percent. The shape of each brand's probability distribution curve explains the market share and consecutive repeat rates measured for each brand in the category.

Fortunately, there is one type of probability distribution that best explains what we see in real-world data. It is called the beta distribution and it is widely used throughout all the sciences as a probability distribution of probabilities. In our industry, it demonstrates what percent of category buyers have close to a 0 percent chance of buying a given brand, versus a 30 percent chance, versus near 100 percent loyalty.

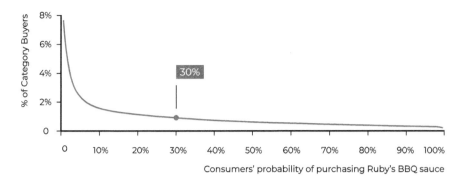

Figure A3.
Beta
Distribution
for Ruby's
BBQ Sauce
at 30 Percent
Market Share

The beta distribution has two parameters, alpha and beta, which have very natural interpretations for marketers. A brand's market share is the same as the mean (average) value of its beta distribution curve, which is a function of the ratio of alpha to beta (specifically by dividing alpha by the sum of alpha + beta). In our barbecue sauce example, we know that this ratio must be 30 percent to equal Ruby's market share. However, there are infinite possibilities for alpha and beta that would give the same ratio (e.g., .3/.7; 3/7; 6/14). How can we choose? That is where the consecutive repeat rate comes in.

In statistics, there are two things we always want to know about the shape of a probability curve: its mean and its variance. We established that the beta distribution's mean is a function of the brand's market share. Similarly, the beta distribution's variance is a function of the brand's consecutive repeat rate. Here is how we know this. The variance of any probability distribution is $E(x^2)- [E(x)]^2$. When applying the beta probability density function to consumers' probabilities of buying a given brand, these terms take on intuitive meaning.

The expected share of buyers is $E(x)$, and the expected consecutive repeat rate is just as formulaic; it is $E(x^2)/E(x)$. So, if you know a brand's market share and its consecutive repeat rate, you can solve for alpha and beta and get the whole curve! That's how powerful knowing the consecutive repeat rate is!

Fortunately, you don't need to memorize these formulas to benefit from them. What you do need to know is that a brand's beta distribution curve (which quantifies the probabilities of consumers buying the brand) can be derived from the brand's market share and consecutive repeat rate. This is pretty remarkable when you think about it; knowing two statistics about a brand allows you to predict with 99 percent accuracy the percent of consumers who have a specific probability (e.g., 80 percent odds) of buying your brand![4] That's not because market share and consecutive repeat rate dictate the beta distribution, but because the probabilities of consumers buying a given brand drive all three. Put another way, a brand's market share cannot move independently from consumers' underlying purchase probabilities or their consecutive repeat rates.

> A brand's market share cannot move independently from consumers' underlying purchase probabilities or their consecutive repeat rates.

*Figure A4.*
Alpha and Beta Can Be Derived from Market Share and Consecutive Repeat Rate

| | OBSERVABLE MEASURES | | | DERIVABLE ATTRIBUTES | |
|---|---|---|---|---|---|
| | Market Share | Consecutive Repeat Rate | | alpha | beta |
| **Morty's** | 60% | 75% | | .99 | .66 |
| **Ruby's** | 30% | 56% | | .5 | 1.16 |
| **Reggie's** | 10% | 44% | | .17 | 1.49 |

4    The authors modeled the beta curve based upon actual Numerator consumer purchase data for forty-five brands, across laundry detergents, nutrition bars, toothpaste, and frozen pizza. The correlation of the beta curve predictions to the observed share of wallet across nine hundred observations was literally 99 percent (using 5-percentile bands for each prediction bucket; 0–5 percent probability of buying, 5–10 percent, etc.).

In fact, it's not just market share and consecutive repeat rate that emerge from this underlying distribution of consumers' purchase probabilities. Brand purchase cycles, any type of repeat rate measure, and household penetration are all emergent outcomes of consumers' purchase probabilities as demonstrated by the beta distribution.

## BREAKING OUT

What happens when market shares are not stable and a brand begins to grow? We have already seen that it implies a switching imbalance and that consecutive repeat rates must be growing for the winning brand and declining for any losing brands. Now let's apply our new-found knowledge to dive one level deeper. If a brand's market share and consecutive repeat rate are increasing, then the vector of purchase probabilities across all consumers of the category must have "shifted to the right"—a higher proportion of shoppers are now more likely to buy the brand.

As shown in Figure A5, for Ruby's to increase its market share from 30 percent to 50 percent, the beta curve representing consumers' probabilities of purchasing Ruby's must also shift. The most noticeable shifts occur at the tails of the curve. On the left side of the chart, the proportion of category buyers with low odds of buying Ruby's shows a drastic reduction. This will play itself out in terms of increased buyer penetration. On the right side of the chart, we see a large increase in the proportion of category buyers with a high probability of purchasing Ruby's. This equates to the brand having significantly more highly loyal consumers. This is the scientific explanation for why market share increases always come from having both greater penetration and greater loyalty.

When the beta distribution shifts (as we just saw in the case of Ruby's), the brand's consecutive repeat rate must simultaneously change correspondingly. While we cannot directly observe the distribution of consumer purchase probabilities, we *can* observe changes in a brand's market share and its consecutive repeat rate. When those measures change, the probability curve must have shifted because those are the only two inputs required to solve for the beta distribution's parameters.

*Figure A5.*
Ruby's Beta
Distribution
Curve Shifts as
It Gains Share
from 30 Percent
to 50 Percent

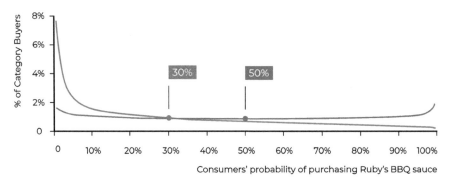

If a brand's curve is shifting, and all measures (including purchase cycles, household penetration, and loyalty) change as a result, why should we prefer one metric as a stronger indicator than any other? Which metric is the best indicator for separating a temporary perturbation or measurement failure from a trend?

Consecutive repeat rate offers additional benefits versus the other measures when it comes to distinguishing short-term fluctuations in a brand's share from longer-term trends. This is because traditional metrics such as market share and household penetration are measures that occur in "calendar time." This means that a market share gain in one month could reflect short-term marketing forces (such as advertising campaigns and temporary price reductions) that might vanish or reverse the next month. On the other hand, the consecutive repeat rate occurs in "event time," that is, it reflects a smoothing over weeks or months (or even years) of consumers' probability of buying the brand twice in a row. It is more likely to reflect fundamental, non-fleeting shifts in the underlying distribution of probabilities of consumers purchasing the brand.

## PENETRATION IS *NOT* PREDICTIVE

There is a widespread belief in our industry that the most predictive path to market share growth is to grow your brand's buyer base, or "household penetration" (i.e., the percent of consumer households buying your brand at least once in a year or some other specified time frame). The problem with penetration as a predictive measure is that it is not fundamental to the generating process; it is an emergent outcome of consumers' purchase probabilities. When it is hot and sunny, more people buy ice cream; a rise in ice cream sales is, therefore, an emergent outcome of the weather. Buying ice cream does not cause hot and sunny weather! However, hot and sunny weather does increase consumers' probability of buying ice cream, which in turn increases penetration rates for all ice cream brands. Consecutive repeat rates, however, are immune to the weather and other seasonal forces. Furthermore, if a brand's market share, consecutive repeat rate, and the overall category's purchase cycle are known, then the brand's penetration can be accurately estimated within 0.2 percent.[5]

Penetration is an emergent property of consumers' underlying purchase probabilities. Without a proper understanding of this generating process, it's too easy to mix up cause and effect.

## BETA DISTRIBUTION VERSUS THE DIRICHLET DISTRIBUTION

The Dirichlet distribution used by many marketing scientists is often characterized as a multivariate beta distribution. In other words, the beta distribution models one brand at a time while the Dirichlet models all brands within a category simultaneously. However, we find

5   Mobile Marketing Association, "Outcome-Based Marketing v2.0." This R&D effort, led by the Mobile Marketing Association, documented the accuracy of estimating penetration by knowing the underlying generating process.

that the Dirichlet is overly restrictive in its assumptions, which hinders marketplace understanding.

The Dirichlet model has a hardwired assumption that all brands in a category are in direct competition. In reality, that is rarely the case. Instead, most well-developed markets are characterized by subsets of brands being more directly competitive within the subset than across subsets—just as we saw in the switching data (e.g., Interaction Index) that measured how winning brands won more than their fair share from smaller, niche brands. For example, Sensodyne toothpaste competes more directly with other sensitive-gum toothpastes than with all other toothpastes. Secondly, the Dirichlet distribution forces us into modeling based on the assumption of market equilibrium. Since we are also interested in spotting departures from equilibrium, fitting individual beta distributions for each brand offers a more agile way of spotting when a brand is breaking out (or breaking bad).

## KEY TAKEAWAYS

- Know what equilibrium looks like. To identify when a brand is breaking out, we must first establish the baseline of what equilibrium looks like regarding market share and consecutive repeat rate.

- Market share gains can only be sustained by brands with corresponding increases in their consecutive repeat rate. Temporary increases in penetration will not sustain market share growth if repeat purchases do not follow. Increases in consecutive repeat rates can be used to predict new, sustainable market share levels.

- Consecutive repeat rate is the best early signal of brand growth. Of the three primary measures of brand performance, market share, household penetration, and consecutive repeat rate, the last one is the best leading indicator of a trend in brand growth. That is because market share reporting is a time-based metric that is retrospective and susceptible to noisy fluctuations caused by temporary marketing programs such as advertising campaigns and trade promotions. Penetration can change for reasons other than gaining or losing market share (e.g., category seasonality). Consecutive repeat rate is native to the generating process and is calculated whenever a consumer makes their next purchase of the category, making it a longer-term measure that reflects a blend of marketing conditions unbound by time.

CPSIA information can be obtained
at www.ICGtesting.com
Printed in the USA
BVHW011225300623
666625BV00001B/1

9 781544 535050